11/04
$55.00

D0163392

INDIA

A Global Studies Handbook

Other Titles in
ABC-CLIO's
GLOBAL STUDIES: ASIA
Series

China, Robert André LaFleur

Indonesia, Florence Lamoureux

Japan, Lucien Ellington

The Koreas, Mary E. Connor

Nepal and Bangladesh, Nanda R. Shrestha

Vietnam, L. Shelton Woods

INDIA

A Global Studies Handbook

Fritz Blackwell

A B C ❤ C L I O

Santa Barbara, California • Denver, Colorado • Oxford, England

Library of Congress Cataloging-in-Publication Data

Blackwell, Fritz.
    India : a global studies handbook / Fritz Blackwell.
        p. cm. — (Global studies, Asia)
    Includes bibliographical references and index.
    ISBN 1-57607-348-3 (hardcover : alk. paper)
    ISBN 1-85109-364-8 (e-Book)

    1. India — Handbooks, manuals, etc. I. Title. II. Series.
DS407.B63 2004
954—dc22   2004007013

08 07 06 05 04 10 9 8 7 6 5 4 3 2 1

This book is also available on the World Wide Web as an eBook.
Visit abc-clio.com for details.

ABC-CLIO, Inc.
130 Cremona Drive, P.O. Box 1911
Santa Barbara, California 93116-1911

This book is printed on acid-free paper.
Manufactured in the United States of America.

To Julian and Austin, grandsons—and to Tasha

Contents

Series Editor's Foreword

It is imperative that as many Americans as possible develop a basic understanding of Asia. In an increasingly interconnected world, the fact that Asia contains almost 60 percent of all the planet's population is argument enough for increased knowledge of the continent on our parts. In addition, there are at least four other reasons why it is critical that Americans become more familiar with Asia:

First, Americans of all ages, creeds, and colors are extensively involved economically with Asian countries. U.S.-Pacific two-way trade surpassed U.S. trade with Europe in the 1970s. American companies constitute the leading foreign investors in Japan. With the world's second-largest economy, Japan is also the second-largest foreign investor in the United States.

The recent Asian economic crisis notwithstanding, since World War II, East Asia has experienced the fastest rate of economic growth of all the world's regions. Recently, newly industrialized Southeast Asian countries such as Indonesia, Malaysia, and Thailand have joined the so-called Four Tigers—Hong Kong, the Republic of Korea, Singapore, and Taiwan—as leading areas for economic growth. In the past decade China has begun to realize its potential to be a world-influencing economic actor. Many Americans now depend upon Asians for their economic livelihoods, and all of us consume products made in or by Asian companies.

Second, it is impossible to be an informed American citizen without knowledge of Asia, a continent that directly impacts our national security. America's war on terrorism is, as this foreword is composed, being conducted in an Asian country—Afghanistan. (What many Americans think of as the "Mideast" is, in actuality, Southwest Asia.) Both India and Pakistan now have nuclear weapons. The eventual reunification of the Korean Peninsula is fraught with the possibility of great promise or equally great peril. The question of U.S.-China relations is considered one of the world's major global geopolitical issues. Americans everywhere are affected by Asian political and military developments.

Third, Asia and Asians have also become an important part of American culture. Asian restaurants dot the American urban landscape. Buddhism is rapidly growing in the United States, and Asian movies are becoming increasingly popular. Asian Americans, though still a small percentage of the overall U.S. population, are one of the fastest-growing ethnic groups in the United States. Many Asian Americans exert considerable economic and political influence in this country. Asian sports, pop music, and cinema stars are becoming household names in America. Even Chinese-language characters are becoming visible in the United States on everything from baseball caps to T-shirts to license plates. Followers of the ongoing debate on American educational reform will constantly encounter references to Asian student achievement.

Fourth, Asian civilizations are some of the world's oldest, and their arts and literature rank as some of humankind's most impressive achievements. Anyone who is considered an educated person needs a basic understanding of Asia. The continent has a long, complex, and rich history. Asia is the birthplace of all the world's major religions, including Christianity and Judaism.

Our objectives in developing the Global Studies: Asia series are to assist a wide variety of citizens in gaining a basic understanding of Asian countries and to enable readers to be better positioned for more in-depth work. We envision the series being appropriate for libraries, educators, high school, introductory college and university students, businesspeople, would-be tourists, and anyone who is curious about an Asian country or countries. Although there is some variation in the handbooks—the diversity of the countries requires slight variations in treatment—each volume includes narrative chapters on history and geography, economics, institutions, and society and contemporary issues. Readers should obtain a sound general understanding of the particular Asian country about which they read.

Each handbook also contains an extensive reference section. Because our guess is that many of the readers of this series will actually be traveling to Asia or interacting with Asians in the United States, introductions to language, food, and etiquette are included. The reference section of each handbook also contains extensive information—including Web sites when relevant—about business and economic, cultural, educational, exchange, government, and tourist organizations. The reference sections also include capsule descriptions of famous people, places, and events and a comprehensive annotated bibliography for further study.

—*Lucien Ellington*
Series Editor

Preface and Acknowledgments

This handbook is intended to provide basic information about India. It is not a substitute for a good travel guide (a number of which are listed in the annotated bibliography), nor for intensive study on Indian culture, history, literature, religion, politics, society, ecology, or economics. Some in-print books on those subjects are described in the bibliography.

As one whose career has for the most part been oriented toward the humanities, I regret the necessity of not including the arts—aural, visual, and written. Such coverage simply is not within the scope of a handbook of this design, which is that of providing basic information about India today, for students, businesspeople, potential tourists, and the merely curious. It is, hopefully, a starting point for further information about this magnificent culture and country.

I am obliged to Washington State University, the college of liberal arts, and the department of history for a semester's sabbatical in which to initiate this project.

Much of this handbook—not only the writing but the tearing apart of newspapers for articles—was done at my daughter-in-law's kitchen table. She also suggested including observations on fashion. I am grateful to her, Jean, and to my son, Raymond (her husband), for their patience and support under trying circumstances. I had lost my wife and was completely disconsolate.

My two editors—Lucien Ellington of the University of Tennessee at Chattanooga and the editor of *Education about Asia* and Alicia Merritt of ABC-CLIO—exercised superhuman patience with me and my delays after my wife's death—patience well beyond the call of duty. They will never know the degree of my gratitude, for I cannot express the depth of it.

xvi Preface and Acknowledgments

This handbook could not have been done without two magnificent newspapers as sources—*India Abroad* and the *New York Times*. I was especially fortunate that during the time I was putting the book together, the chief correspondent in Delhi for the *New York Times* was Amy Waldman. Her articles, in particular on Indian society, had a breadth of scope and depth of understanding, an objective sensitivity beyond that which I have ever observed elsewhere.

I want to thank Gina Zondorak, production editor, Michelle Asakawa, copy editor, and Giulia Rossi, media editor, for their talents in bringing order out of often near chaos. Their skills and suggestions improved the manuscript greatly.

Finally, I want to acknowledge those who made this possible: the students. There are way too many to recognize, and I know that after thirty-five years I have probably forgotten more than I'd remember. So I shall just say thank you, to them all.

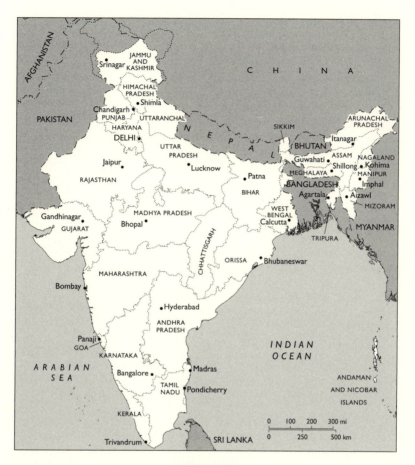

India Today

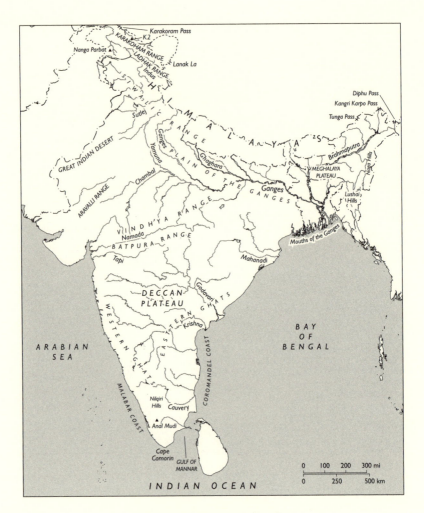

Physical Features of India

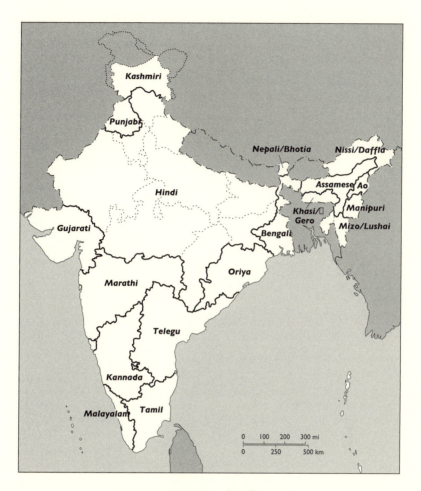

Languages of India

PART ONE
NARRATIVE SECTION

CHAPTER ONE
India's Geography and History

India is geographically and culturally part of an area known as
the Indian subcontinent, or more aptly, South Asia, represented by a loose confederation of nations known as the
South Asian Association for Regional Cooperation (SAARC).
This confederation is not political in design, but economic
and social, dealing with matters such as women's issues and
mutual trade benefits. All decisions are reached on a basis of
consensus; technically, the smallest nation, Maldives, has as
much say as the largest, India. The other nations are Pakistan,
Bangladesh, Nepal, Bhutan, and Sri Lanka. India has the hegemony in the region and is carefully watched by the other
members. A hidden advantage of SAARC is that it provides a

A tree-covered atoll in Maldives (Corel)

venue for leaders to discuss, unofficially, political issues in a private manner and without a summit atmosphere.

The distribution of population within SAARC ranges from about 200,000 for Maldives to more than a billion for India. Religious distribution is as diverse as well, with Maldives being by law entirely Sunni Muslim, whereas India, a constitutionally secular state, has representation from perhaps every religion of any significance. Geography is as diverse, Maldives being a collection of atolls, mostly uninhabited, so low that the president has observed that if the greenhouse effect is correct, before this century is out there may well be no more Maldives. India, in contrast, has every imaginable range of topography, from seaports to Himalayan peaks, desert to lush jungle. The much-used word *diversity* fits the area in general, and India in particular, in many different ways.

THE PHYSICAL AND HUMAN GEOGRAPHY OF INDIA

India's hegemony in the area is cultural as well as political. To that end, the word *India* has both a specific political denotation for a contemporary nation and a broader historical connotation indicating a cultural entity composed of subentities with regional variations within the larger, more inclusive, tradition. Before 1947 there was no Pakistan or Bangladesh; the culture, history, and geography of each are inextricably linked to north India; and the major cultural forces for most of South Asia, such as Hinduism and Buddhism, arose in India (Islam was an outside intervention; however, with major impact). The hegemony is due not only to a much larger population but to a much larger geographical area as well, about 1.3 million square miles. Roughly speaking, India is about the size of western Europe, and it has as much historic and cultural diversity as well in terms of languages, political divisions (the states often reflecting historical divisions like the kingdoms of medieval Europe), diet, manners of dress, ethnic and religious identities, and, in addition, caste identities. Far more so than most European countries, these divisions and identities are reflected within states as well as between them. That is, each state has its varied mix of communities and cultures, as well as being distinct from other states. To say that someone is Indian is like saying someone is European, and there is as much difference between, say, a Punjabi and a Tamil as there is between a Scot and a Rumanian; however, the religious identity in the Indian situation is not as predictable as in the European situation. The Scot is likely to be Protestant, the Rumanian Catholic; the Punjabi is equally as likely to be either Sikh, Muslim, or Hindu.

Were one to picture India, including Pakistan, Bangladesh, Nepal, and Bhutan, as a diamond-shaped mass jutted into the underside of Asia (which geologically it apparently is), there would be several very noticeable geographical characteristics. The subcontinent is sealed off from Asia proper by mountains on the north: the western ranges to the northwest, and the Himalayas (also a series of ranges) to the much wider northeast. Two great river systems that arise in the mountainous north, not far from each other in origin but flowing in almost opposite ways, dominate the northern area below the mountains. The Indus and its tributaries flow southwest, and the Ganges flows east-southeast. It is on the plains of these two mighty river systems that north Indian civilization developed. Whereas north Indian civilization had tremendous impact upon south Indian civilization, in many ways they are separate, for reasons historical, ethnic, linguistic, cultural, and geographic. The important facts are that it is on the Indus where the first civilization developed more than four millennia ago (prehistoric only because its writing has not been cracked), and it is on the Gangetic plain where the dominant strains of Indian political and cultural history developed. It could be argued that the Gangetic plain is not only historically the single most important area of India, but it is so politically as well.

A couple of smaller series of ranges separate the north from the Deccan, or, literally, "south." The Deccan is a plateau, easing down toward the sea by *ghats,* or "steps," which give way to slim coastal ranges, with a sultry climate in marked contrast to the milder weather of the 3,000-foot-high plateau. Four states comprise the Dravidian cultures, Dravidian being a linguistic term to mark four major languages (and a handful of minor ones) with nothing in common with any languages outside of South Asia. A language in the Indus area that is Dravidian has led to much speculation as to the origin of the Dravidian peoples in south India being from the Indus civilization. To sum: In the extreme north of India are mountain ranges, below which is the Indo-Gangetic plain, then the Deccan with slim coastal plains along the ocean front.

There is yet another general feature, the rivers of India. Except for the great Thar desert southeast of the Indus system, India is virtually crossed by rivers (by far the most of which flow west to east). India is dependent on these rivers, and rivers are venerated, most of all the Ganges, known as Mata Ganga, or Mother Ganges. Indeed, the Ganges has long been considered holy, spiritually pure, and physically pure (until nonbiodegradable pollutants began to be poured into it). She is a goddess in the eyes of most Hindus.

Although rivers can be considered the life system of India, their life is sustained by the monsoon cycles. The monsoon is vital to India; without it, crops cannot grow, people cannot live. The beneficent results of the Green Revolution may well be due as much to the luck of years of fortunate monsoons as to agricultural innovations. Even in the cities (perhaps especially in the cities) the monsoon is looked upon as the renewer of life, breaking drought and the torrid heat and reviving vegetation and people's nerves and attitudes. In the past few decades, India's rivers have become a source of controversy as well. The exploding population and rising material expectations have led to the development of dams, which have displaced rural people and alarmed environmentalists.

Hindu pilgrims cleanse themselves in the Ganges River during Ganga Mahotsava, an annual festival that honors the Ganges for providing for the farmers who grow rice on its neighboring plains. (Corel)

It needs to be reiterated that the Himalayas on the northeastern edge of the subcontinent effectively isolated India, with the exception of a few traders and Buddhist monks, until the twentieth century. The northwest area is bounded by lower ranges, with three passes through which invasions took place, including the waves of migrations of the Aryans from sometime after 1500 B.C.E., Alexander the Great in 327 B.C.E., and from about C.E. 1000 Muslim invaders and conquerors up to and including that of the first Mughal, Babar, in 1526.

India has twenty-nine states (most with their own distinctive language) and six union territories (areas administered by the central government in Delhi). The number is fluid, as territories can become states, and states have been divided, usually to accommodate ethnic groups who compose a majority in a certain area but are a minority within the state as a whole. The danger of accommodating such demands, in the view of the central government, is that it encourages others with less clear claims for division to become more strident. These demands have upon occasion developed into secession movements leading to violence and military reaction. In some instances areas have been closed to tourists. A principal concern for the nation is continued unity in spite of divisive forces and pressures.

It is difficult to overemphasize the cultural and historical differences between the "Dravidian" south and the "Aryan" north, differences that have distinct political and cultural repercussions today. Generally speaking, the south has gone its own way both historically and culturally. It must be stressed that *all* of India has never been united, even under the Mauryas, and even under the British (although the latter distinction might be argued to be mere formality); the point is, the history of India, culturally and politically, can be said to be analogous to that of Europe.

"Fissiparous tendencies," the Indian press calls them; that is, tendencies that pull toward fragmentation at the expense of unity. It is the age-old problem of centrifugal forces pulling at political centralization, a concern reinforced by the fall of the Soviet Union and collapse of Yugoslavia. Indeed, political leaders need to be concerned, for the history of India is not one of unity, and its diversities are so many and so deep as to be overwhelming to the outsider. The label used is "communalism."

Communalism implies a primary sense of identity—or more correctly, identities—stronger than that of the nation. It would be as an American identifying by state or region, religion, or ethnicity primarily and clearly over that of being an American. It is difficult for Americans to conceive; our history is too short, too unified in a political sense (the one great fissure—the Civil War—supposedly decided the question). The Indian concept of political union, of "Indianness," is one developed by leaders strongly influenced by the ideals of Western liberal democracy, of British parliamentary ideals. In fact, M. K. Gandhi and Jawaharlal Nehru were London-trained lawyers. The independence movement is also called the nationalist movement: a sense of nationhood needed to be developed before the nation could become independent. For that to happen, an identity needed to be forged as something above that and inclusive of all the communal—community—identities. These community identities reinforce one another and by their very nature contribute to divisiveness by emphasizing differences on a number of levels. One's "community" can be described in one or more (usually more) categories: family, ethnic group, caste and subcaste, religion, language, village and region, state, educational status, and socioeconomic class. To further complicate the matter, there is considerable overlapping among categories. In itself that is not so different than many similar ethnic and religious identities in the United States, except that in India the pulls are much stronger in a historical sense, and the encompassing national identity much weaker.

The major factor is simply that India has a very short and shallow history of nationhood. Caste, the institutional compartmentalization of society, is often blamed, and in some ways it does play a factor; but in a social sense caste has been a unifier in that it has assimilated groups into a system of coalescing relationships. The caste system provides the rules for social interaction and is the basic social pattern. It is far more adaptable than it has been given credit for. At the time of independence, skeptics said democracy could not work in a society based on caste. It has worked remarkably well. Indian democracy has had its problems, including some very serious ones, but Indians are very serious about their democracy. It has worked very well in the rural areas, with illiterate peasants being much more knowledgeable about the system than had been anticipated, and castes learning how to play power politics, especially at the state and regional levels.

Recently communalism has had an adverse affect on democracy, however, and that is in regard to religious identity. Throughout its history Hinduism has been a fairly toler-

The Indus River in Pakistan (John Noble/Corbis)

ant religion; indeed, the word *Hindu* is not Indian in origin, nor is the related term, *India*. They are words that were used by Greeks and Persians to refer to the people who lived across the Indus River. Hindus did not think of themselves as Hindus, but as participants in a particular sect or followers of a particular god. These sects and followers were not absolutist, but tolerant of one another; religion was a matter of choice, not of right or wrong. For various reasons that has somewhat changed, and a strain of intolerant political Hinduism has developed. It is far from new; such a group was responsible for the assassination of Mahatma Gandhi; what is new is the apparent legitimacy it has achieved in mainstream politics. For instance, the idea of *hindutva* has been advanced as a measure of citizenship: one must be Hindu to be Indian. This would be an anathema to the founders of free India; the constitution declares India to be a secular democracy. Unfortunately, the practitioners of hindutva have gained power at various local levels.

The city of Calcutta grew immensely in the eighteenth century. The Battle of Plassey in 1757 put British rule into effect, and Calcutta became the capital of British India in 1772. (Hulton Archive)

One would think that hindutva might be a rural phenomenon; but it has been quite noticeable in certain urban locations, especially Bombay (now Mumbai; the recent renaming of Bombay and Madras, or Chennai, and Calcutta, or Kolkata, may well be a milder form of the same characteristic). The nearly catastrophic increase in population has been most evident in the cities, with Bombay, Calcutta, and even Delhi reaching near-exploding points. In just a few decades these cities have increased multifold. Living space for the poor is almost nonexistent; slums are of such magnitude as to be unbelievable. Pollution of all sorts is overwhelming. Although nongovernmental groups, especially in Bombay, are doing much, they cannot resolve the problems; the local governments are either impoverished (as in Calcutta, where storm sewers are almost nonfunctional during the monsoon) or apathetic. Urban blight is a manifestation of two interrelated problems: environment and population explosion.

In some ways India is an ecological catastrophe in progress, and the source for it is the catastrophic increase in population. At the time of independence in 1947 the population was less than 350 million; in 1999 it reached one billion. The problems develop and increase in a geometric fashion. Although agricultural developments have increased food production substantially, the result has been like running on a treadmill: the energy has been expended on just keeping up with the increase of mouths to feed. Crowding has increased communal tensions. More space has been taken up and more trees cut down, with erosion ruining mountainous soil, which slips into the riverbeds, raising their levels and increasing flood damage. Population growth has declined in recent years but not halted.

The outlook, of course, depends upon to whom you talk. In the twenty-first century India's problems are unlikely to be unaffected by, or not to affect, situations of a more global nature. But they are still primarily India's ecological problems, and they need to be addressed in long-run terms. One of the shortcomings of democracy is that politicians are reluctant to act in terms of the long run.

Nevertheless, India remains the world's largest democracy, with a fascinating culture. For the visitor, it is a cross between a metropolitan museum and a fair: it is extremely interesting, and a great time. People are genuinely friendly and helpful, and very interested in outsiders. Indeed, the questions asked strangers can seem a bit personal. Family matters will be inquired about, as well as salary and other subjects generally not discussed in public or with others in Western societies. But the sense of inquiry is meant to be friendly, not probing.

The visitor is seldom affected by the social problems described above, although if astute, he or she will notice them easily enough. In spite of the multitude of languages, English usually is adequate to get one around in any city (and not just the largest ones). Furthermore, economically the country is a good bargain for the tourist, and it is increasingly becoming attractive for business investments.

A word needs to be said about color. Over the last few decades, Western movie producers have discovered the photogenic atmosphere of India. For the traveler, India is a myriad of colors, from women's bright dresses and saris to the countryside itself. The entire culture, including daily events, seems to be infused with color. And the contemporary culture is the pinnacle of a very colorful history.

PREHISTORY

Table 1.1   History of India prior to 1600

3000 B.C.E.	"Start" of Indus, or Harappan, civilization (c. 2300–1750 B.C.E.)
1500 B.C.E.	First of invading waves of Aryans (Indo-European speakers)
500 B.C.E.	Buddha; historical recordings; philosophical challenges to Brahminism
326 B.C.E.	Alexander at the Beas, tributary of the Sutlej, hence, Indus
321 B.C.E.	Chandragupta Maurya founds Maurya dynasty (321–185 B.C.E.)
260 B.C.E.	Asoka defeats the Kalingas; promulgates "dhamma"
320 C.E.	Chandragupta I founds Gupta dynasty (C.E. 320–480 or 490)
400 C.E.	Gupta (and Indian) Golden Age; Chandragupta II (C.E. 380–415)
606 C.E.	Harsa's (d. C.E. 647) accession ("Camelot")
711 C.E.	Muhammad ibn Qasim in Sind
1000 C.E.	Mahmud of Ghazni commences series of invasions/raids
1185 C.E.	Muhammad Ghuri conquers Lahore
1206 C.E.	Commencement of Delhi Sultanate (i.e., "medieval India")
1526 C.E.	Commencement of Mughal empire

Indus Civilization

For about a millennium or so (c. 3000–1500 B.C.E.; 2300–1750 its prime period) a complex civilization existed, largely at peace, spread over a great deal of what is now Pakistan and northwest India, well into the Gangetic plain eastward and into the modern state of Gujarat southward. It seems to have been the largest of ancient civilizations, estimated as covering about 500,000 square miles. Although there were two major centers (today known as Harappa and Mohenjo-daro) on the Indus, there were numerous secondary cities as well, all highly sophisticated and well-planned, complete with covered drains, carefully laid-out streets, and public buildings. This impressive civilization was indigenous to the region.

There is evidence of extensive trade, including with Mesopotamia and possibly eastwards as well. Technology included the use of metals. The surviving writing has yet to be deciphered (what has survived are amulets and seals with strange markings and pictographs). Archaeological evidence suggests the presence of some features that were later to be incorporated into Hinduism—particularly Dravidian or south Indian Hinduism (e.g., yoga, fertility symbols, the mother goddess). The society seems to have been socially and economically stratified and was perhaps a type of theocracy.

Gradually, the civilization declined, perhaps due to internal disturbances, or maybe the soil became saline, or perhaps the Indus shifted course, or after 1,500 years, it may have simply exhausted itself. One theory is that as the buildings were all built of baked brick, which required extensive use of wood for firing the clay, the end came as a result of deforestation and the resulting ecological consequences. Regardless, the declining civilization was superseded by incoming Indo-European peoples, who referred to themselves as "Aryans"—nobles—and possessed awesome horse-drawn war chariots. These waves of invaders, probably only distantly related to one another, were part of the great migrations of

Indo-European–speaking peoples who exploded out of central Asia into Europe as far as Ireland or Eire (cognate with the word Aryan) and into Iran (also cognate with Aryan) and India. The tensions generated in India, racial in origin, survive to this day in political, linguistic, and even ethnic manifestations between the Dravidian south and the Aryan north. (The terms *Dravidian* and *Aryan,* or Indo-Aryan, apply to language families, but certain ethnic contrasts exist as well.) Lately there has been some speculation, even insistence, that the Aryans came not from outside what is now India, but were indigenous. It has been suggested that this issue may have become ideological in a postcolonial sense, and that emphasis perhaps should be put on the word *migrations* rather than *invasions.*

The Aryans

The Aryans contrast markedly with the people of the Indus civilization, as they were nomadic, martial, and highly patriarchal. They brought with them the core of sacred texts—albeit memorized rather than written—known as the Vedas (from the root *vid,* "to know, understand, perceive, learn"), which, in addition to its religious importance, contains information of historical, sociological, and anthropological significance. The Vedic hymns also provided the catalytic germ for what was to become Hinduism—a synthesis of the Aryan and pre- or non-Aryan elements. With no specific founder, no pope or ecclesiastical council, Hinduism is not so much a religion as a perspective, can be said still to be developing, and has been referred to as "a federation of cults and sects."

The Vedic hymns represent the oldest documents of the many Indo-European languages, and the later epics (*Mahabharata* and *Ramayana*) show features strangely similar to Greek and other Indo-European epics and mythology; similarly, the language in which they are written, Sanskrit, has been demonstrated to be related to Greek, Latin, and English (among others). Classical Sanskrit is largely an artificial language developed (for religious and literary purposes) from Vedic Sanskrit. The Aryan impact, though modified and assimilated into Indian culture, remains as the primary cultural connector for India with European culture.

One development of the cultural (and racial) clash between Aryan and non-Aryan was the four-tiered caste system (or five-tiered, counting outcastes or those excluded from the other four categories), which was perhaps an extension of the three-tiered class system found elsewhere in Indo-European culture. Here, however, the priestly group became superior to the political or martial aristocracy (at least nominally), probably because of the importance given priestly power over ritual and sacrificial magic. Today the caste system (perhaps it would be more apt to say "systems") is far more complicated in actuality than its theoretical roots would lead one to suppose.

The Upanishads, later additions to the Vedas (hence, their philosophy is termed *Vedanta,* or "end of the Veda"), also represent cultural synthesis, the movement of ritualistic religion toward philosophical inquiry. Typical of Hinduism, the new introspective interrogation did not replace the older sacrificial approach but supplemented it—and to this day the two aspects exist side by side, both of which are exercised by practitioners, without apparent conflict. Essentially, the Upanishads seem to imply that Vedic ritual is fine in its place, but just doesn't go far enough into questions as to the nature and purpose of existence. It should be reiterated that the Upanishads are interrogative, not dogmatic; dogma in Hinduism seems to be a very contemporary, very political, and very unfortunate development of a decidedly nonspiritual nature. Behavior (or orthopraxy) rather than belief (or orthodoxy) has been the cement traditionally holding Hinduism together.

Finally, the development of the gods themselves (or, from another point of view, manifestations of the Divine) represents a curious amalgamation, in part developments from the

Vedic gods, in part from Indus (or Dravidian) and tribal features. Thus, for example, Siva, represented by fertility indica-
tors (*lingam* and *yoni*, phallic and vaginal symbols, respectively), seems to have evolved from a so-called proto-Siva, an
artifact of a figure with an erect phallus yet in a yogic posture,
found in archaeological digs from the Indus civilization; yet
the god is also considered a development from the Vedic god
Rudra (and one of his most important manifestations,
Sivanataraja, or Siva Lord of the [Cosmic] Dance, is a much
later development, from around C.E. 1000). Though prominent in south India (where Dravidian influence is strongest),
Siva is pan-Indic; indeed, the ancient holy city of Banaras is
in the north, yet is considered to be his city.

ANCIENT HISTORY

History, as such, begins to emerge in north India during the
sixth century B.C.E., partly because of socioeconomic and
political changes—the abandonment of tribal structure in
favor of the establishment of cities and kingdoms in the
Ganges plains—but also because of the rise of Buddhism. This
new faith was born of Upanishadic or Vedantic Hinduism but
went further in clearly denying the efficacy and validity of ritualistic brahminism (the brahmins, or priestly caste, had the
monopoly on ritual, hence on religion).

The center of action and power, as it has remained to the
present day, was the so-called Aryan heartland (Aryavarta),
the Gangetic plain. The battle for preeminence was reduced
from many small states to four, with Magadha, under Bimbisara (540–493) and his patricidal son, Ajatasatru (493–461),
becoming dominant.

By 321, perhaps in part inspired by the example of Alexan-
der of Macedon, who had arrived in northwestern India,
Chandragupta Maurya made Magadha the first empire in
India, with its capital at Pataliputra (modern Patna), east of
Banaras on the Ganges.

Yet Chandragupta did not establish his empire from nothing, for he built upon the work of his predecessors. Bimbisara had expanded his rule through marriage and conquest and had established an administrative system and built roads. His successors had continued expansion through military conquest and built a strong army and an efficient land-tax system. Chandragupta took control by skillfully stepping into a power-vacuum left by the decay of the Magadha kingdom and the abrupt departure from northwest India of Alexander. He can certainly be given credit for starting the imperial dream and founding a strong government, albeit somewhat totalitarian and under the firm guidance of his mentor and capable minister, Kautilya (also known as Chanakya), author of a rather Machiavellian treatise on running government (the *Arthasastra*). The empire was expanded by his son, Bindusara (297–273), and consolidated by his grandson, Asoka (273–232), described by the nineteenth-century British historian and novelist H. G. Wells as the greatest emperor the world has ever seen.

Asoka inherited a system that was essentially a police state. He also extended the empire until it covered a greater area than in any other time in Indian history. But after the last bloody battle, he experienced remorse and, also strongly influenced by Buddhism, renounced force (though not implied force) as an instrument of state policy. Concurrently, he developed the idea that the monarch had an obligation to his subjects. He exercised a policy known as *dhamma* (the vernacular for the Sanskrit term *dharma,* moral duty), described by the eminent historian Romila Thapar as a policy of paternal despotism and social responsibility.

Dhamma was a secular policy, not a religious doctrine, stressing social responsibility on the part of the subjects of the empire. It stressed mutual respect and moral behavior, based on human dignity, as the means for the smooth running of society, the basis for law and order. It was, in turn, the responsibility of the ruler to provide structure and policies geared toward the well-being of the people. The policy was expounded in a series of rock edicts and on pillars, and it espoused dhamma as replacing force for the means of conquest.

It should be pointed out that the empire had been conquered, so war was really no longer necessary, though it remained as a potential—but only to be used as a last resort (e.g., against unruly tribes). Asoka's empire was united administratively and, equally as important, economically. Indeed, the administrative and economic unity was paramount; Asoka resisted militarily campaigning in the south, allowing the four separate kingdoms there to go their own ways. After all, he had the hegemony on the subcontinent; the added territory would do him no economic good and would just be an administrative burden. Such wisdom is in marked contrast to the southern campaign of the last great Mughal, Aurangzeb, almost two millennia later.

Though dhamma was an ethical concept, its purpose was clearly practical: to make a better society, and one easier to govern. Often and somewhat superficially labeled Buddhist, it owed considerably to the Hindu concept of dharma, for the key was not nonviolence so much as it was responsible social behavior. Almost foreshadowing Gandhi, it was the application of philosophical thought to society and politics; it certainly did not come out of a vacuum but was a culmination of a rising social and intellectual consciousness.

Unfortunately, dhamma disappeared with Asoka. There is not a historical connection to Gandhi (although Gandhi was very favorably impressed with Asoka). Indeed, with the death of Asoka, political and economic decline set in and the structure soon collapsed. Politically, loyalty was geared to the king rather than to the system, which retained much of the inherent tension of a highly centralized administration. Just the logistics of running such a vast extent of territory (said to have been larger than that of Rome at its height) must have been technologically insurmountable. Further, there was no concept of nation or state: primary group identity was focused on village and caste (as it generally is today). Without the leadership—in terms of charisma as well as ability—of an Asoka, the structure may well have collapsed in on itself.

Within a century or so of Asoka's death, northern India had entered a period of invasion, with the development of peripheral regional kingdoms (e.g., the Indian territory of the Kushans, part of a central Asian empire, first century C.E.). Nonetheless, considerable cultural development occurred, especially in terms of Buddhist thought and art, both indigenously and from outside influences.

Pataliputra did not arise again as a center of power until C.E. 320, although it should be remarked that much of the classical or so-called Golden Age of the Gupta dynasty had antecedents in the Kushan period.

The Gupta dynasty marks the heyday of cultural achievements in ancient northern India, intellectually and artistically (this observation is not meant to denigrate the remarkable cultural achievements in south India). The period is perhaps exemplified by the great poet and dramatist Kalidasa, especially by his masterpiece *Sakuntala.* This golden era reached its height during the reign of the grandson of the founder (just as was the case in the Maurya dynasty centuries earlier and was to be in the Mughal dynasty over a millennium later), Chandra Gupta II (380–415). The empire was neither as extensive nor as stable as the Maurya empire.

Legend holds that Chandra Gupta II came to the throne through heroic overcoming of an invading Saka (Hun) king, who had demanded his beautiful sister-in-law as tribute. Chandra Gupta prevailed, then seized the throne, and the sister-in-law, from his weak brother. After his reign the threat of invaders from central Asia increased, until about C.E. 500 it brought on a dark era of feudal fragmentation. A brief Camelot-like period of revival occurred under Harsa (605–647), who presided over a large kingdom loosely connected by feudal ties. It did not outlive him. Still, it marked a slight pause in a period of decline (including of the Roman trade).

After Harsa, the history of northern India is one of disunity and distrust among backward regional kingdoms, until the start of the Delhi Sultanate, under invading Muslims from central Asia; even then, the unity of the Delhi Sultanate was more apparent than real.

Geography and cultural adaptation were major factors in the development of south Indian history. During frequent political upheavals and the rise and fall of dynasties (many of which were, however, stable for remarkable lengths of time), constant tension existed between the plateau kingdoms and the coastal kingdoms for control of the waterways.

There was also constant tension between the Dravidian society and the Aryan features brought into south India by brahmins, the highest or priestly caste. Thus, caste was adopted in a modified form, with the high-caste brahmins from the north (who were to become viewed much as the carpetbaggers of the nineteenth-century United States were) imposed at the top. The vast majority, sudras and pariahs (the south Indian term for outcastes or untouchables), were at the bottom of the caste scale. This in itself is emblematic of the dichotomy and tension that so characterizes north-south (or, in a sense, Aryan-Dravidian) relations in India even today.

It was in the south where anti-caste, anti-brahminical, anti-ritual devotional cults (influenced by the heterodox Jainism and Buddhism) first developed and were to have such important influence on later poetry and music throughout the north as well as the south. From about the fall of the Gupta empire, initiative in cultural progress lay with the south—an initiative, however, that had antecedents in pre-Mauryan times and that included architecture, literature, trade, and administration. The languages of the south are of the Dravidian family—decidedly non–Indo-European, although with some absorption of Sanskritic terms for philosophical and religious purposes, and the southern Tamil language and culture are likely older than Sanskrit and Aryan culture.

EVENTS LEADING TO THE SULTANATE

There had been early Muslim contact in Sind (C.E. 711), the area of the lower Indus, and it was largely of a peaceful nature. The Caliph of Baghdad had dispatched a brilliant young general, Muhammad ibn Qasim, to handle some pirates and unruly Hindu rulers. He seems to have been well-received by the general populace (probably sick of their local rulers, Hindu or not), and the issue of religion, later of such importance, apparently did not arise. Baghdadi politics resulted in his recall and execution, and the contact was not permanent.

Further, Arab traders had, well before the advent of Islam, been present along the western coast of central and southern India. Steady contact, commercial and cultural, between India and the West has not received the attention it deserves (e.g., the disciple Thomas brought Christianity to the southwest coast of India, and many of Aesop's fables can be traced to Buddhist jataka tales). But in the year 1000 matters were to change significantly, with a series of invasions, or, more properly, raids.

In C.E. 1000 Mahmud of Ghazni conquered the Hindu prince Jayapal, making the Punjab a frontier province of his central Asian empire. His interests were focused on central Asia, not India. He wanted to make the kingdom established by his father a central Asian power. He was interested in northwest India as a source of wealth to finance his central Asian adventures, and his systematic plunder ruined the economy of the Hindu states, making possible the later subjugation of north India and the establishment of the Delhi Sultanate (1206). His motive of plunder was reinforced by religious motivation—to destroy the temples and icons of the unbelievers. These frenzied raids continued almost to his death in 1030, but the Hindu princes failed to see the significance and failed to unite.

After Mahmud's death his empire, built and held together by force and terror, disintegrated. A new kingdom arose near

Ghazni (south of modern-day Kabul, near the Afghan-Pakistani border), called Ghur, in the next century. In 1185 Muhammad Ghuri conquered Lahore. In 1191 the Rajputs (a martial ethnic group) defeated him, but the following year he came back and defeated the Rajputs, which gave him northern India right to the gates of Delhi. Soon his generals had conquered the Gangetic plain, clear through Bengal. Muhammad's purpose was conquest, not merely raids. By the time of his assassination in 1206 the north of India was under Muslim control. Muhammad was succeeded by his general, a manumitted slave, Qutb-ud-din Aibak, who founded a dynasty (the first of the Delhi Sultanate) thus known as the "Slave" dynasty.

The year 1206 is therefore a landmark date. The Hindu era of governance was over, for the Delhi Sultanate was succeeded by the Mughals (1526), who were in turn succeeded by the British.

How did this happen? On the eve of Mahmud's raids, northern India was characterized by a proliferation of regional states marked by mutual distrust. Any unity was only cultural ("Hindu"), and even then cultural diversities (e.g., languages and literatures) were developing along strictly regional lines. Even when the depth of the Muslim threat became obvious, the Hindus of northern India were unable to unite.

It was a new era, with a startlingly new ingredient. These outsiders were not about to be assimilated in the manner of previous invaders (e.g., the Rajputs) and most certainly not so into Hinduism. They were Muslims and were to retain a distinctly separate identity, even from those Hindus whom they managed to convert to Islam. Conquerors, and the ruling class for the next three centuries, they were not to identify themselves as Indian. They were Turkic chieftains from Afghanistan and neighboring areas of central Asia, with Afghan armies that included Persians among their number.

They were successful for three broad reasons: first, the condition of the Hindu kingdoms of north India—stagnant and disunited; second, Muhammad's armies were far superior professionally than those of the Hindus. Finally, the Muslims were more committed not only militarily, but religiously—they were, in the literal sense of the word, zealots.

A particular event can stand as a symbol of the Hindu situation: In 1008 one king, Anandpal, was able to unite a number of other kings against Mahmud. During the battle Anandpal's elephant became frightened and bolted. The allied army, thinking that Anandpal's flight was intentional, broke ranks and fled, literally snatching defeat from the jaws of victory. The defeat of this confederacy was the last gasp of an era.

THE DELHI SULTANATE AND THE GREAT MUGHALS

The term *Delhi Sultanate* can be misleading, if it is taken as applying to a unified kingdom or empire comprising north India. It was the dominant political power of north India, but it was more feudal than imperial in structure. The problem was in the position of the sultan vis-à-vis the nobles. Typical of Indian political history from earliest times to the present day, there were pronounced centrifugal tendencies, with regional leaders attempting to establish their own bases of power, challenging the "center" (i.e., the central authority in Delhi). Frequent changes of dynasty, as well as of sultans within dynasties, and the inability of most sultans to exercise power over the nobles, who were able to maintain and make hereditary regional power bases, prevented the development of empire. The continuation of local rulers and the basically unchanged land and tax system allowed for underlying stability despite the relatively frequent changes at Delhi. Upon occasion, a sultan or two did exercise supreme power, but it was based on military force and did not last after his death. Administrative infrastructure was never developed to the extent that Akbar, the greatest of the Mughals, developed it, making it possible for his son and grandson to rule without having to pay attention to day-to-day events.

An interesting footnote in history occurred in the first dynasty of the Sultanate. When Iltutmish (who had succeeded his father-in-law, the founder of the Sultanate) died, he was succeeded by his daughter, Raziya (after she had dispatched a brother or two), in 1236. There are legends galore about her, even though (or perhaps because) little of a factual nature is known of her short reign. But she was glamorous—and single. Nobles clamored after her, for con-

Table 1.2   The Delhi Sultanate and the Great Mughals

Sultanate Dynasties

1206–1290	Slave
1290–1320	Khilji
1320–1413	Tughluq
1414–1450	Sayyid period
1450–1526	Lodi

Mughals

1526–1530	Babur
1530–1556	Humayun
(in exile 1540–1555)	
1556–1605	Akbar
1605–1627	Jahangir
1627–1658	Shah Jahan
1658–1707	Aurangzeb
1707–1857	various

quest of her represented not only the acquisition of the lovely lady but of the throne as well. She stalled, and when she finally did choose it was too late, and the wrong (politically) choice. She and her husband were killed in 1240, less than four years after her reign had begun. Muslim historians tend to lay the blame on Hindus, and vice versa. She certainly must have been one of the first women to reign over a Muslim kingdom (or, for that matter, to reign in India). Nevertheless, because she was a woman, her overthrow was almost a foregone conclusion. There is an eerie twentieth-century parallel—or at least similarity—with the first administration of Benazir Bhutto of Pakistan.

When the last sultan of the last dynasty, Ibrahim, pushed the matter of central power too far, two of his governors (one of whom was his uncle) invited another central Asian, Babur, to intervene. He did, defeating a far larger but slovenly army and slaying Ibrahim at Panipat (north of Delhi). Babur stayed to found a new dynasty, which under his grandson Akbar developed into a true empire.

Meanwhile, a significant portent occurred on May 27, 1498: the Portuguese explorer Vasco da Gama appeared off the southwest coast of India. The Portuguese were to be the first Europeans into India and last out, Prime Minister Jawaharlal Nehru having to send troops into Goa to dislodge them in December 1961.

A look at the list of the reigns of the six great Mughals might lead one to infer that successions were smooth; the last three, and those following Aurangzeb, were violent and bloody, with blinding and murder as the sons of one father but several mothers fought it out in a system without clear rules of accession. Aurangzeb, for instance, usurped the throne, slaying his brothers (one of his older brothers, and his father's favorite son, was executed only after extreme public humiliation), and kept his father under house arrest in a fort across the river from the Taj Mahal for the last eight years of his life. The old man spent his time, with a devoted daughter, gazing upon the magnificent view of the beautiful tomb of his beloved wife Mumtaz.

Babur's heart was in central Asia. It was almost as though the Indian adventure were a divertissement for him, and not a very happy one at that, for he found the heat and atmosphere of the plains oppressive, as mountain people often do in the plains of India. He loved poetry and wine and hard work. His condition weakened, he succumbed allegedly in asking God to take his life rather than that of his very ill son, Humayun. One suspects he wore himself out. Humayun spent most of his reign in exile, having been chased out by a relative of the Lodis, Sher Khan (known also as Sher Shah), who, belatedly for the sultanate, structured an administrative system. But he was too close to a cannon when it was fired, and was mortally wounded. His accidental death may well have prevented the Mughals from being merely a footnote to Indian history. Humayun returned just in time to die, falling (or perhaps being pushed) down steep stone stairs of his "library," a tall brick structure from the top of which his tomb, the precursor to the Taj and majestic in its own right, can today be seen in the distance; the government has sealed off the stairs, and the top is no longer accessible. Humayun was succeeded by his illiterate thirteen-year-old son, Akbar, who as a ruler of India is matched only by Asoka.

Akbar's intelligence, character—and, above all, policies—ensured success. He was curious and tolerant, humane yet firm. He wed a Hindu princess, of the martial Rajputs, who were located in the sensitive northwest and had been a thorn for his predecessors. He thus made allies of erstwhile foes. This policy was followed by his son and grandson. He lifted the hated *jiziyah,* or tax on non-Muslims, and established works projects designed for the well-being of his subjects, with whom he was very popular. He strengthened and improved the splendid administrative system of his father's rival, Sher Shah, and appointed people on the basis of ability and loyalty. He seemed aware that the major problem with the Sultanate had been its failure to achieve centralization of power. Regional nobles had played off from the center, expanding their own power as they could and developing hereditary fiefs. Akbar was determined that such was not to happen in his rule, and he frequently transferred regional rulers, reducing them from rulers to servants in his administrative structure, and making sure regional power bases were removed. He thus established empire and a system strong enough to carry on after his death. His son and grandson, Jahangir and Shah Jahan, are noted for their cultural interests and achievements, specifically art and architecture, respectively, which they were able to pursue thanks to the self-sustaining nature of the imperial administration developed by Akbar. India had experienced nothing like it since the golden age of the Gupta empire a millennium earlier. Akbar may

Emperor Jahangir and his father, Akbar (Francis G. Mayer/Corbis)

have been illiterate, but he was perhaps the most intelligent ruler India had until Nehru in the twentieth century, holding his own quite well in learned discussions with adepts from the world's leading religions.

Unfortunately, the last great Mughal pursued a different policy. Well-meaning and sincere, initially popular, he overextended the empire militarily and financially in his foolish and unnecessary quest to subdue the south, including spending the last two decades away from the capital in army field camps the size of a large city. Historians are not in agreement in their assessment of Aurangzeb, and certainly historical factors not within his control contributed to the disintegration of the empire, which occurred in the decades following his death; nevertheless, certain of his policies seriously weakened the foundations. In addition to his extensive and expensive campaigns, he allowed the Rajput alliance to lapse and alienated Hindus by reinstituting the hated jiziyah, exhibiting contempt for Hindu customs, and tearing down shrines and temples. He also exhibited a self-righteous intolerance toward Sikhs and even Shi'a Muslims (being a Sunni himself).

At the time of the death of Aurangzeb, Muslim rule had been exercised from Delhi over varying parts of India for five centuries. During all that time, Hindus had constituted the vast majority (80 percent is a conservative figure) of the subjects of the Sultanate, then empire. The basic level of society was the village. The villager's identity and loyalty were to family and caste, his identity regional at best, if even extending beyond the village. There was no identity with or even concept of state. He was not interested in who governed, but rather in how he was governed. He was relatively content as long as he was not overtaxed or interfered with in regard to religion and custom. All successful rulers, regional or central, realized this fact. Aurangzeb's policies alienated the villagers. Yet in actuality, it was probably Akbar who was the exception in attitude toward his subjects, not Aurangzeb. Although Aurangzeb's negative excesses were not the norm, seldom did a ruler identify with his subjects, and in general the sultans and the Mughals in general neither identified with nor even conceived of India as a culture.

The factors involved in the disintegration of the Mughal empire are extremely important, for they explain as well how the British were able to rise to a position of supremacy. In the power vacuum that resulted from the breakdown of central authority and the failure of any other Indian group to establish dominance in its place, British dominance developed—not by design but from necessity, at least at first. The idea of a British empire was to come, but that was a nineteenth-century development.

First and foremost is the problem of chaotic successions and shrinkage of empire. Aurangzeb's immediate successors were puppets of various factions within the nobility. His son Bahadur Shah I succeeded only after (in the time-honored Mughal fashion) defeating and destroying his brothers. By then he was already an old man, and he died in 1712. His son Jahandar was a fop who fought with his brothers over succession, had a brief reign of violence and debauchery, was deposed, and then strangled in 1713. There followed a succession of puppets and phantom emperors, with degraded and dissolute nobles squabbling behind the scenes. By 1803 the empire was roughly coextensive with the city of Delhi, and the emperor, Shah Alam II, facetiously referred to as the "king of Delhi," threw himself on the protection of the English—protection from fellow Indians, tribally organized groups of marauders who were dispossessed of Delhi by Lord Gerard Lake, an English general. The fox was in the henhouse; the Mughals thus became dependents of the British, and the last pitiful emperor was deposed in 1858, after the so-called Sepoy Mutiny, and died an imprisoned exile in Rangoon in 1862.

Coupled with this deterioration were four other factors: foreign invasions from Persia, including two sacks of Delhi; the rise of new independent Muslim states in the north as well as in the south; the political and military revival of Hindu groups (Rajputs, Jats, Marathas) and the Sikhs (in the Punjab); and the arrival of the Europeans and subsequent ascendancy of the British.

THE RAJ (BRITISH EMPIRE IN INDIA)

The motivation for the European contact with the East was trade: Asian countries had items Europeans wanted (e.g., silk and spices) but had little to offer, other than gold, in exchange. Further, at the time of initial contact, Europe was technologically inferior to much of Asia.

Although the Portuguese were the first Europeans into India by way of the sea, their power soon waned, and their attention turned largely to Brazil. (They did maintain three small enclaves in India until late in 1961.) The Dutch interest was in the Spice Islands, or Dutch East Indies, now Indonesia. By the late seventeenth century the chief competitors for commercial and territorial leverage within India were the British and the French. Within the next century, chiefly because of political and military events in Europe, Britain was

Table 1.3   Rise and Fall of British Influence in India

1600	East India Company chartered
1612	First company "factory" (post) at Surat (moved to Bombay in 1674)
1640	Company post established in Madras
1690	Company post established in Calcutta
1773	First of several parliamentary acts seeking to regulate the company
1858	Transfer of government following the Sepoy Mutiny
1877	Queen Victoria declared empress of India
1919	Amritsar massacre
1947	Partition and independence

Robert Clive receives from Shah Alam, the Mughal emperor, a decree conferring upon the East India Company the administration of the revenues of Bengal, Bihar, and Orissa, c. 1765. (Hulton Archive)

to gain the advantage over all other Europeans, with the French maintaining an enclave at Pondicherry in southeast India. Because of the political disintegration and chaos in India with the decline of the Mughals, Britain was on its way to becoming the paramount power in India.

How could this be? It was simply that the Indians were not united and did not view themselves as Indians but as members of groups such as the Rajputs or Marathas. To them, the British were just another group. Further, the British did not arrive with the idea of conquest, but of trade. Indians, or more accurately, various groups in India, saw no reason for alarm.

Indeed, it was not the British as such—that is, not the British government—but a private company that eventually accomplished hegemony. The East India Company, founded in 1600, was designed for profit purely as a trading company. Administrators and soldiers later became necessary to secure the trade. Unlike its French counterpart, Le Compagnie des Indes Orientales, the East India Company was not tied directly to the government, although Parliament increasingly sought to curb the independent power of the company from 1773 on.

The early advances of the company were somewhat haphazard. Factories (trading posts with warehouses) were established at Surat in 1612 (moved to Bombay, now Mumbai, in 1674), at Fort St. George (Madras, now Chennai) in 1640, and Fort William (Calcutta, or Kolkata) in 1690. Thus, three of India's most important contemporary cities, Madras, Bombay, and Calcutta, developed from what were essentially British trading centers. These centers had to be protected against the chaotic conditions of the period. They were at first fortified, then expanded, until eventually they became regional powers in their own right. Relations were entered into with native regional states, leading to alliances. Each of the three cities became the center of the area surrounding it, called a presidency (so-called because the governor sat as president of the governing board). In 1774 these were brought under the unified control of a governor-general in Calcutta. Although territory may well have at first been acquired for defensive reasons, the nineteenth century saw conscious design and rationale develop, both in India and in England, especially in Parliament. Indians came to be viewed as inferior in culture, religion, and race. The sources were a mixed bag of seeming opposites: Utilitarianism and Evangelicalism, or disdain in regard to the culture and concern about its non-Christian souls. In retrospect it is apparent that an empire was developing early on, although few then likely had conscious conception of such.

From the beginning there was cultural clash between the British and the Indians. The British lifestyle did not fit well with the Indian climate (the clichéd "heat and dust"), nor did the European-Christian intolerance toward other cultures and religions: it was a clash between an absolutist society and a relativistic one, reinforced by patterns of seclusion present in both (e.g., Indians thought European women immoral because they danced in public). After the 1857 uprising (to be discussed presently), neither side felt it could trust the other ever again. Fear reinforced racism, developing into a strong intolerance. It is necessary to emphasize that the initial and continuing purpose of the company was profit. Reinforced by belief in cultural, religious, and racial superiority, the drive for profit became self-righteous exploitation.

The Sepoy Mutiny of 1857 was more than a mutiny and less than a war of independence (as some Indians have dubbed it). It was a rebellion, confined to north-central India, by conservative Hindu and Muslim rulers alarmed by encroachment by the British upon their dwindling hereditary and territorial rights. Passions were inflamed by the introduction of technological innovations, railroad and telegraph, English-style education, and missionary activity. Christianity and Westernization were viewed as being forced upon the society. The introduction of a new rifle in the army led to *sepoys,* Indian soldiers, mutinying, because the ammunition cartridges were coated with animal fat that had to be bitten off before loading.

Atrocities occurred repeatedly on both sides. The result, once the British had reestablished order, was the demise of the company and the assumption of control by the Crown. The perceived moral superiority of the British was now viewed as a sham, and the separation between governed and governors was irreparable. It also brought a violent end to the pitiful remnant of the Mughal empire.

Well before the mutiny, pressures in both England and India had led to government interference in Indian social customs, such as the abolition of suttee (*sati*), the practice of burning the widow alive on her husband's funeral pyre. Such atrocities were very visible, but not visible to the British were the arts and sophisticated philosophies. This outlook developed into a "white man's burden" type of guardianship in governmental approach. The British believed they were doing the Indians a favor by ruling them. They referred to themselves as "ma-bap," mother-father, and considered the Indians as children in their care. They also developed an English-style education for the upper classes, whom they hoped would work as an intermediary, a buffer, between themselves and the masses. To a degree it worked, but it also sowed the seeds of the independence movement.

The period from the end of the mutiny to the departure of Lord George Curzon as viceroy, 1858–1905, was the heyday of imperialism, and of British superiority. But it was a superiority that became increasingly resented by the new Westernized class, and that came increasingly to rest upon suppression and racism. The breach became totally insurmountable in a political sense on April 13, 1919, when General Reginald Dyer directed his Gurkha and Baluchi troops to fire, without warning, on an assembly of unarmed people in Jallianawala Bagh, a walled enclosure at Amritsar in the Punjab. The people were gathered on a holiday on the outskirts of the city, unaware of the curfew pronounced by Dyer. He later stated he was fearful of another 1857 and wanted to teach them a lesson. By official British estimate, 1,600 rounds were fired, 379 people killed, and about 1,200 wounded (who, because of the curfew, were compelled to lie unattended throughout the night). Indian nationalists put the figures considerably higher. At the token hearing following the incident, Dyer gloated and later boasted.

By ironic coincidence, Jawaharlal Nehru, a young lawyer, found himself in an overnight train compartment with Dyer and a couple of his aides and overheard Dyer's boasting (likely done for young Nehru's benefit). It infuriated him. The unofficial reception Dyer received as hero in England infuriated other Indians, who reacted with revulsion, typified by the Nobel laureate Rabindranath Tagore, who relinquished his knighthood.

There was no turning back after 1919; the question was now when, not if, full independence was to be achieved. A series of intended reforms initiating Indian participation, on a very limited basis, in the government was simply a matter of too little, too late. Indians became increasingly aware that their economy was straight-jacketed to benefit the British economy. Winston Churchill once estimated that 25 percent of the national income of Britain was derived from India. Industrial development was stifled so as not to become competitive with British goods in the vast Indian market. Foodstuffs were exported for purposes of profit during periods of famine. There was development—railroads, port, irrigation— but the system was designed to serve British interests, not Indian. Nothing was done for the poor of the villages.

The British idea of empire was by no means clear, or even agreed upon among the British. Raghavan Iyer, an astute student of the British Raj, has suggested that the imperial approach was a mix of four concepts: trusteeship, utilitarianism, the platonic idea of being guardians, and evangelicalism. Individually or together, these concepts represented the belief that outsiders were qualified to govern others, to be masters, because of cultural and racial superiority.

INDEPENDENCE/
NATIONALIST MOVEMENT

Even before 1919, Indian leaders had demanded more rights and participation in government. British rule was approached two opposite ways: through parliamentary procedures and through violence. There was an awareness, often ambivalent, of certain advantages the British had brought, such as civil service and the English language, the latter which was to become the vehicle of communication among leaders with different mother tongues. British legal education introduced law students in London, such as Gandhi and the young Nehru (son of the eminently successful lawyer Motilal Nehru), to English constitutional history and resulted in a cadre of Western-education freedom fighters.

The origins can be said to have been in Bengal, the most potently intellectual culture in northern India. Calcutta, founded by a Briton named Job Charnock, became an amalgam of British and Indian culture. It was here where synthesis and reform developed, with Bengalis such as Dwarkanath Tagore taking advantage of the new economic opportunities by working with British partners. His wealth was to be the foundation for a family of cultural geniuses. Reformers such as Ram Mohan Roy, influenced by Western education but remaining Hindu in culture and religion (albeit a reformed Hinduism), worked for social and cultural reform. Encouraged by such examples, Thomas Babington Macaulay, an adviser to the viceroy, presented a "Minute on Education" (1835), which specified English-style education for the upper-class elite, who Macaulay believed would become British in outlook. He wanted to bring the advantages of Western thought to India, which he took to be bereft of culture; he stated that all the literature of India and Arabia could not match one shelf of English literature. It was from this elite that the leaders of the freedom movement came.

Among these was the Gujarati lawyer M. K. Gandhi, who had practiced for a number of years in South Africa, where he developed his concept of *satyagraha,* the means of affecting and effecting social change through direct nonviolent action. As leader of the Indian National Congress (later the Congress Party), he had not only the British to deal with, but those Indians who believed in pursuing independence through violence. Gandhi's advocacy of nonviolence was not merely idealistic. He believed it to be the only method that could succeed not only in vanquishing the British, but in forging a nation. The Nehrus were in agreement with the use of satyagraha as a tactic.

Through a number of satyagrahas, such as the Salt Satyagraha, or Salt March, Gandhi brought a sense of unity to the movement. He also selected targets that would have great symbolic value, like the tax on salt. This approach had great

impact on the American civil rights movement, especially on
Martin Luther King Jr. The irony of the symbol of salt was that
when Gandhi scooped some from the sea, it was inedible. But
the law had been broken, and after some initial hesitation the
British reacted with violence. This only served to further
unite the Indians. No matter what caste, what region, what
language, whether urban or rural, they had a unifier, a common enemy in the oppressive government. A concept of
nation, of one India, was emerging and was fostered by the
leaders of the movement. The approach of the British had
consistently been one of divide and rule, emphasizing the differences among Indians. Their behavior made shambles of
their philosophy, however.

In a sense Gandhi and the Nehrus seem almost opposites;
perhaps, rather, they were complementary. Motilal Nehru
(long active in attempting to get British reform in government) owned the first motor car in Allahabad, had a wine cel-
lar, and wore fine English suits. His daughter, Krishna Nehru
Hutheesing, relates in her autobiography how in his last ill-
ness he called for a drink, much to the concern of Gandhi,
who was sitting by his bed and chided him for thinking of
earthly rather than spiritual matters. Motilal replied that he
would leave such matters to Gandhi, and to his own wife (a
traditional Hindu), and that while still on earth, "I will be
earthly."

Jawaharlal was early on more radical than his father, influenced by Fabian socialism while at school in England. But he
was very pragmatic and one of the great political leaders of
the twentieth century. He became India's first prime minister, and in retrospect it is difficult to imagine how anyone
else could have succeeded as he did. He welded the many
diverse communities and various states into one nation. He
was definitely, as has often been said, a mix of East and West.
He had more to do with shaping modern India than Gandhi
did. Through his policies of "benevolent socialism and controlled capitalism," nonalignment (with either Western or

Jawaharlal Nehru conferring with M. K. Gandhi in 1946 (Library of Congress)

Communist powers), and his faith in democracy and his close relationship with the people, he ensured an independent India of its place in the world—its *independent* place in the world.

SINCE INDEPENDENCE

When the British decided it was time to leave, after World War II, Prime Minister Clement Atlee persuaded a member of the royal family, Lord Louis Mountbatten, to become the last viceroy of India and to develop with the disparate Indian leaders plans for independence. Mountbatten not only accepted the challenge but also worked out a calendar that resulted in independence a year earlier than had been anticipated. But with independence came partition, with the Pun-

---

Table 1.4   Notable Events in India since Independence

August 15, 1947	Establishment of the Republic of India
January 30, 1948	M. K. Gandhi assassinated
May 27, 1964	Jawaharlal Nehru dies
October 31, 1984	Indira Gandhi assassinated
May 21, 1991	Rajiv Gandhi assassinated

---

jab in the west (and areas to its west) and Bengal in the east split in two, India retaining East Punjab and West Bengal, and the remaining territory becoming the new nation of Pakistan. The result was chaotic violence, just what the partition was supposed to prevent.

An English geographer, Sir Cyril Radcliffe—who knew little about India—was brought to Delhi, sequestered, and told to draw the lines of partition on maps. Muhammad Ali Jinnah, the leader of the Pakistan movement, had insisted upon a division of the subcontinent along religious lines, India to be Hindu, and Pakistan Muslim. Interestingly, this had little effect on Muslims living in south India, but did result in huge migrations in the north of Hindus and Sikhs to India and Muslims to Pakistan. Many Muslims chose to remain in India. The loss of life, through slaughter, was in the hundreds of thousands. Jinnah was unhappy with what he considered a moth-eaten Pakistan; he had wanted more territory than Radcliffe had allotted. Gandhi was so devastated over the split of his beloved India that he refused to take part in the independence celebrations. To his credit, Gandhi worked in Bengal to alleviate tensions. The largest number of atrocities were in the Punjab area. Mountbatten, so popular with the Indian leaders that he had been asked to stay on as the first governor-general of independent India, observed that whereas a host of troops could not pacify the Punjab, one frail old man had brought quiet to Bengal.

A major bone of contention was Kashmir, a Muslim populace with a Hindu ruler who, when Pakistani-backed guerril-
las invaded, acceded to India. Since then, part of Kashmir has
been occupied by Pakistan, and constant turmoil occurs in
the other part. India and Pakistan have gone to war three
times—twice, 1948 and 1965, over Kashmir—and each has
spent billions of rupees on armaments that might have been
better spent on development. The third of these wars, in
1971, occurred when East Pakistan (East Bengal) broke what
it considered a colonial relationship with West Pakistan and
became Bangladesh.

On May 27, 1964, Nehru died. Upon the death of Nehru's
successor about a year and a half later, Nehru's daughter,
Indira Nehru Gandhi, became prime minister. Her husband
was not related to M. K. Gandhi; indeed, he was not even
Hindu, but Parsi. (Parsis are descendants of Zoroastrians who
fled Iran when it was conquered by Muslims.) Indira had been
very close to her father, her mother having died of tuberculosis when Indira was young. She was so close that the relationship may have contributed to her divorce. She had two
sons, one of whom was to succeed her as prime minister.
Indira was an astute politician, but she was a woman, and an
old-boys clique in the Congress Party thought they could control her. She split the party and turned her adversaries out.

But divisive troubles continued, especially over her economic policies. She was so concerned about extralegal
maneuvering by her opponents that she decided to beat them
to the punch and had the president of the nation declare a
national emergency on June 26, 1975. This move, which was
constitutional, was an unfortunate relic left over from the
British Raj. The irony is that she herself, as well as her parents and grandparents, had been placed in jail by this procedure during the freedom struggle.

The problem was that the declaration was taken by numerous regional and local officials as a carte blanche to settle old
scores. There were atrocities. The playwright and actress

*Indian prime minister Indira Gandhi with her younger son Sanjay,
just before his death in a plane crash in Delhi on June 23, 1980.
(Hulton Archive)*

Snehlata Reddy, for example, expired while in jail because her
keepers would not let her have her asthma medicine. Such
instances were most often perpetrated by police. The army, as
always and in marked contrast to the situations in Pakistan
and Bangladesh, kept out of politics.

When the emergency was lifted, Indira lost her power, and
in March 1977, Morarji Desai became prime minister. A former comrade of Nehru and Gandhi in the freedom movement,
Desai was somewhat of an eccentric, and his political views
were considered strange. He was a fruitatarian (eating no
meat or vegetables) and once remarked to the wife of the Australian ambassador that she should drink her own urine for
purificatory reasons. Her response is unknown. He was
absurdly accused by a writer for *The New Yorker* of being a
CIA agent. After a caretaker successor to Desai, Indira Gandhi

was again elected prime minister and took office in January 1980, when the economy was bad.

One of the most festering problems faced by the Indian government since independence was that of separatist movements. A militant branch of the Sikh religion was an especially troublesome terrorist group. The more radical among them holed up in the Golden Temple in Amritsar, sacred to all Sikhs. Prime Minister Gandhi had the army storm the temple in June 1984. It cost her not only her moderate Sikh support but also her life: she was assassinated by two Sikh bodyguards on the morning of October 31, 1984, on her way to her office for a television interview. In response, a number of innocent Sikhs were slaughtered by mobs in Delhi. (The Sikhs are a religious group, largely Punjabis, who arose during the Mughal era, but with earlier antecedents, as an attempt to synthesize Hindu principles with Muslim principles, and took on their own religious and communal identity.)

Mrs. Gandhi (a designation she preferred; she abhorred "Ms.") was succeeded by her son Rajiv, an airline pilot with no political experience (it was her younger son, Sanjay, who had been groomed for the succession; he was killed in an air accident). The leaders of the Congress Party felt that he was best suited, by inheritance, to hold the country together in this crisis. Further, with no political liabilities, he would be failsafe in regard to the corruption becoming increasingly rampant in Indian party politics. It worked, for a while. Rajiv was able, sensitive, and committed to bringing his country into the modern technological world. But some crucial issues, such as ecology, were ignored, and he found himself spending more time on party politics than he had wanted. Scandals appeared, one in particular with a Swedish armaments firm, which as head of government he had to answer for. In the 1989 election he was defeated by one of his former cabinet members, V. P. Singh, who had bolted the party. Singh himself was out the next year, victim of a vote of no confidence in the Lok Sabha (Parliament's lower house), arising in large part in reaction to his stringent affirmative action policies. The Congress Party, then headed by Rajiv Gandhi, did not have a majority and decided against forming a government. It was an astute move, and Chandra Shekar, also without a majority, became prime minister. Predictably, his government fell in a few months, and elections were called. It appeared Rajiv Gandhi would return as prime minister.

While he had been prime minister, Rajiv deployed troops to Sri Lanka to help the government in its struggle—almost a civil war—with separatists known as the Tamil Tigers, a guerrilla group descended from coolies brought from Tamil Nadu by the British. He had almost been assassinated on a visit there while reviewing troops. There had been another attempt in Delhi, as well. On May 21, 1991, while campaigning in Tamil Nadu, Rajiv Gandhi was killed by a suicide bomber, a young woman with a bomb strapped to her stomach. When she bent to touch his feet, a traditional gesture of respect, the bomb detonated, killing several bystanders as well as herself and Rajiv. There is a chilling picture of her before the incident, taken by a news photographer. She is chatting, calmly waiting for Rajiv, who was a few minutes late because he was finishing an interview with a *New York Times* reporter in his limousine. She was a Tamil Tiger.

So ended, apparently, the Nehru political dynasty. Rajiv's widow, Sonia, was asked to take the reins but declined. After a few years she did agree to accept leadership of the party, and finished second in a later election to Atal Bihari Vajpayee of the Bharatiya Janata Party. She has a handicap: although an Indian citizen, she is native Italian. She and Rajiv met while in school in England. She remains the leader of the opposition, but her Congress Party has fallen on hard times. For years neither of her children showed any interest in political involvement, but on March 23, 2004, the *New York Times* reported that Rajiv and Sonia Gandhi's son, Rahul, age thirty-three, would run for parliament in the April elections. The seat he would be contesting is in Uttar Pradesh and had been held by his father and currently held by his mother. Presumably, she would be seeking a seat elsewhere, as in India one need not reside in the district to represent it, and "safe" seats are often contested by prominent politicians (that is, the voters in the constituency would be overwhelmingly of the contestant's party).

After Rajiv's death, P. V. Narasimha Rao became prime minister. He appeared to be effective, serving from 1991 to 1996, when he was succeeded by four prime ministers over about a year's time. Years later he was indicted on charges of bribery. The prime minister in 2004 is Atal Bihari Vajpayee (who had previously served very briefly), a former Congress Party member. His party is chauvinistically pro-Hindu and has injected religion as a major issue in politics. India has a parliamentary system, so leaders can and have changed quickly with a vote of no confidence in the Lok Sabha, but Vajpayee has fairly successfully distanced himself from the exclusionary religious rhetoric of his party.

While all this has been happening, India has been at war with Pakistan three times, had border tensions with the Chinese (including a brief war), and experienced poor relations with the United States except for a few warm moments, those coming only recently. The Kashmir dispute is unresolved, environmental decay is extremely serious, and the population has increased two and a half times since independence.

Yet there have been a dozen national elections, and an abiding sense of democracy exists at local, state, and national levels. American politicians of both parties are increasingly aware that India deserves to be, needs to be, and must be dealt with on a very serious basis, by the United States and by the United Nations, wherein India is pressing for a seat on the Security Council. President George W. Bush has expressed an awareness of India's importance in the world community, and the visit to India by his predecessor, President Bill Clinton, and the resulting return visit by Prime Minister Vajpayee to the United States were huge successes in terms of increasing goodwill by both countries.

The nuclear threat between India and Pakistan, especially with the emotional issue of Kashmir, is, or at least should be, of global concern. A nuclear war could start in the subcontinent, but in the long run the greater danger may lie in the population explosion, which could well result in a situation of desperation, not only in regard to Indo-Pakistan tensions but ecological collapse as well. Indeed, the failure of the government of India to come to face with the population-ecological problem could well lead to catastrophe far more serious than the tragic earthquake of January 26, 2001.

The geography of India, its history, and its ethnicity have made India what it is: culturally divided; yet, a handful of men and women forged it into a nation. The heritage from the British has been both denounced and embraced by India: beyond the imperial excesses have come a strong civil service system; the ideals of Western nationalism; the English language as both a common means for communication within India and a window on the world outside of India; and, perhaps most important, the structure of parliamentary democracy.

This observation is not meant to excuse imperialism: no country, culture, or race has a right to impose rule over another; but it happened, and the Indian leaders of the independence movement made the best of it, preserving those features that could further India's entry into the world as a free nation.

References

Baron, Archie. *An Indian Affair: From Riches to Raj.* London: Macmillan, 2001.

Copland, Ian. *India 1885–1947: The Unmaking of an Empire.* London: Longman, 2001.

Embree, Ainslee. "10 Top Things to Know about India in the Twenty-First Century." *Education about Asia* (winter 2003): 7–11.

Internet History Sourcebook. http://www.fordham.edu/edu/halsall/india/indiasbook.html

Itihaas. http://www.itihaas.com

James, Lawrence. *Raj: The Making and Unmaking of British India.* New York: St. Martin's, 1998.

Johnson, Gordon. *Cultural Atlas of India.* New York: Facts on File, 1996.

Keay, John. *India: A History.* New York: Atlantic Monthly Press, 2000.

Khilnani, Sunil. *The Idea of India.* New York: Farrar, Strauss, Giroux, 1999.

Majumdar, R. C., et al. *An Advanced History of India.* New York: St. Martin's, 1958.

Mallory, J. P. *In Search of the Indo-Europeans: Language, Archaeology, and Myth.* London: Thames & Hudson, 1987.

McIntosh, Jane R. *A Peaceful Realm: The Rise and Fall of the Indus Civilization.* Boulder, CO: Westview, 2002.

Moorhouse, Geoffrey. *India Britannica: A Vivid Introduction to the History of British India.* Chicago: Academy Chicago, 2000.

Renfrew, Colin. *Archaeology and Language: The Puzzle of Indo-European Origins.* Cambridge: Cambridge University Press, 1988.

Thapar, Romila. *Asoka and the Decline of the Mauryas,* 2nd ed. Delhi: Oxford University Press, 1973.

———. *Early India: From Origins to A.D. 1300.* Berkeley: University of California Press, 2002.

Tharoor, Shashi. *India: From Midnight to the Millennium.* New York: HarperCollins, 1997.

CHAPTER TWO
India's Economy

HISTORY

As early as the third millennium B.C.E., trade occurred between Mesopotamia and the Indus civilization, as is demonstrated by artifacts present in both areas. Thus, on a piece of art from the Indus, a hero or god grasps two tigers by their throats. This scene is matched by a piece from the Fertile Crescent, except that the beasts are lions. Furthermore, Indus artifacts have been found in Mesopotamia, and Mesopotamian objects found in archaeological digs of Indus cities.

A Greek merchant's account from the first century C.E., the *Periplus Maris Erythraei*, includes information about routes across the Arabian Sea to central coastal India, around Cape Comorin, and up the east coast to the mouths of the Ganges. Prior to the first millennium B.C.E. the Arabian Peninsula served as a point of transmission for Mediterranean goods bound for India and Indian goods bound for the eastern Mediterranean. Greek (or Roman) discovery, about the first century C.E., of how to use the monsoon for sailing purposes changed that, at least until Arab dominance after the establishment of Islam. That Arabs were to be the intermediaries between India and the West is attested to by the label of "Arabic numerals" for what were originally Sanskrit numerals. The Hindu decimal system and concept of zero arrived in Europe from India, by way of Arabia.

Maps of ancient trade routes from Rome to coastal Chinese cities show connections from the central Asian (Silk) routes, to northern Indian cities, and thence to southern ports. Sea routes from Indian ports on the Arabian Sea connected with

49

ports on the Gulf of Aden and the Red Sea, thence to cities on the Nile. Eastern routes were even more complex, extending from several Indian ports on the Bay of Bengal to the Andaman and Nicobar Islands, Arakan (in present-day Myanmar, or Burma) to Sumatra and Java (in modern Indonesia), and upwards to Chinese coastal cities. Centrally located in this web of routes, India played an important role in, to use a modern term, international trade. Eastwards, India's impact can be noted in the names "Indochina" and "Indonesia." Political and religious influence was strong in the area until the arrival of Islam, and cultural impact, especially that of the Sanskrit epics the *Mahabharata* and the *Ramayana,* is still prevalent throughout Southeast Asia.

The European desire for spices from South and Southeast Asia is almost legendary. An ancient Tamil (Tamilnadu, southeast India) poem describes merchants as "arriving with gold and departing with pepper." The very word *pepper* is of south Indian origin (as is *ginger*). This desire for goods from India and beyond remained strong throughout the Middle Ages, with Arabs as middlemen. It had much to do with the development of the European Age of Exploration. The spiciness of South Indian and Southeast Asian food developed as a means of preservation before the advent of refrigeration. Europeans, from ancient times until they were able to develop sea routes to get around the Arab monopoly in East-West trade, were anxious to avoid putrid meat and other food spoilage, hence their interest in trading for spices. Perfumes and cotton were other commodities Europeans wanted. In turn, they had little to offer that interested Asians, other than gold.

Commercial agents from a number of Near Eastern cultures had been stationed in various South Asian ports. About 710 C.E. a king in what is now Sri Lanka contacted the caliph of Baghdad in regard to returning a number of widows and children of such agents to their Arab homelands. Off Sindh, in present-day Pakistan, their ship was attacked by pirates. The caliph demanded that local Hindu rulers rescue the passen-

*A buyer from Kishore Spices ("Spices for Export") in Cochin
purchasing from a wholesaler (Vo Trung Dung/Corbis Sygma)*

gers and punish the pirates. They refused, whereupon the
caliph dispatched an army under an eighteen-year-old general
to punish the Hindu princes. This was the first military and
political contact between Muslim invaders and Hindu populace, and it went without religious rancor. A change of governments in Baghdad led to recall of the army.

Hindu India was politically divided—as India has been
throughout most, if not all, of its existence. But some regional
economies were apparently doing quite well, and they caught
the attention of a ruler near Kabul, who commenced yearly
raids in about 1000 C.E. that continued until his death thirty
years later. His primary purpose was loot: grain and golden
idols (which he melted down) from rich Hindu temples. He
also took artisans back to his capital, but for the most part he
viewed India as a source of revenue. The Hindu princes were
not inclined to unite against him (with a single failed exception). A century and a half later, another Muslim adventurer
from the same area invaded with the intention of establishing

an empire. The Delhi Sultanate resulted, but it never really developed an imperial infrastructure, politically or economically. The people were Hindu, the rulers Turkic-Persian-Afghan Muslims. With the exception of some sporadic building of irrigation canals, the economy remained so undeveloped and primitive that when a fourteenth-century sultan tried currency reform, it failed miserably; every home was said to be a potential counterfeiting mint. The fact is that the gulf between ruled and rulers was never bridged, and economic development seemed not to be a priority, if even a thought, of the Sultans.

When the Mughals dislodged the Sultans in 1526, it took until the third reign, that of the great Akbar (r. 1556–1605) for political dominance and stability to be extended over northern and central India. Akbar had foresight and was keen on administration. He recognized his Hindu subjects as his responsibility, and he viewed himself as their governor rather than merely an exploiter. The administrative structure that he developed, building on innovations of Sher Shah, a successful competitor of his father, was so strong that it virtually ran itself through the reigns of his son, grandson, and into that of his great-grandson, making possible the culture that developed magnificent works of art and architecture, epitomized by the Taj Mahal. Akbar's own popularity was marked by his removal of the hated *jiziyah,* or tax on non-Muslims. Perhaps more of symbolic value than economic, it nonetheless must have done much to unify his subjects and make possible the development of an economic infrastructure.

Akbar's wise policy of religious tolerance was reversed by his great-grandson, Aurangzeb (r. 1658–1707), who persecuted not only Hindus but Shi'a Muslims as well. He discouraged the arts to the point that the dispersion of painters from the capital contributed to the development of regional schools in miniature painting, like the various *pahari* ("mountain") studios in the foothills of the northern mountain chains. He lacked the foresight to imagine economic development, instead concentrating on destroying major Hindu temples and religious centers. Most of all, he bankrupted the empire by spending the last two decades of his life traveling around south India with a huge army complete with camp-followers, trying to conquer the small, harmless Muslim kingdoms. His attitudes created a political and economic vacuum that made possible the rise and eventual supremacy, economic and political, of the British.

PERIOD OF EUROPEAN DOMINANCE

A number of European nations were to become involved, to varying degrees, in India. Of these, the Portuguese were the first to engage in trade and acquire territory in India at Goa, three smaller enclaves to the north, and Bombay until 1668. As their power in the east waned, their attention and energy switched to Brazil. They remained in Goa until December 1961, when Prime Minister Jawaharlal Nehru had the army chase them out. They were never a major factor in the colonial struggle for dominance in India. The Dutch had minimal interest in India, their prize was Indonesia. The final competition was between the French and British, with the British winning out, in part because their presence was that of a private company, not, as with the French, a company owned by the government and thus susceptible to the vicissitudes of government failures in early eighteenth-century wars with the British in Europe, America, and India. The British private company, the East India Company, had one goal in mind: profit. Its conquest of territory grew from the necessity of protecting commercial centers—"factories"—at Surat (later moved to Bombay), Madras, and Calcutta. The power vacuum left by the Mughal decay after the death of Aurangzeb necessitated fortification of these centers that have become, today, along with New Delhi (also built by the British) the major cities of India. In short, the Raj (the British empire in India) was not planned, it happened.

The company, certainly at first, neither thought of responsibility toward Indians nor desired it. It was one of a number of players, Indian as well as European; and commerce was always foremost. Even in the twentieth century, foodstuffs were exported from India during periods of famine; this legacy continued under the British, who refused to make concessions on the salt tax during famines. (The tax on salt became a cause célèbre during the independence movement.) Indeed, the major feature of the British imperial economy in India was that the home society, government, and economy were to become hopelessly dependent upon India. India itself became a captive market, with cotton raised in India and processed in England (with a few token Indian mills, such as at Ahmedabad, allowed to develop), and then returned to India for sale. Virtually all manufactured cloth or clothing was made in England. Competitors, such as the United States, were not allowed into the Indian market. (The idea behind the spinning wheel during the independence movement was to crush the British textile industry through "cottage industries," or homemade clothing.)

The East India Company did find itself in a position of having to take responsibility for law and order, and starting in 1773 an alarmed Parliament passed a number of regulatory acts designed to put restraints on the company's activities— and those of its officers, who often set themselves up in business outside company structures. The bottom line remained profit, even after the crown took over direct control of the government of India in 1858, dissolving the company. India existed as a source of income for Britain, although to varying degrees Parliament and individual Britons began to feel and exercise a sense of responsibility, albeit largely paternalistic. India missed the Industrial Revolution, and this was to play a dominant role in the development of postindependence economic policies. Whether India would have had industrialization had the British not been there is another matter, one quite touchy to many Indians. The novelist M. M. Kaye, herself a descendant of an official in British India, once remarked to an Indian reporter that "you" were lucky to have got the British rather than someone like the Belgians in the Congo. The reporter was understandably incensed, musing in her article about what made the British think Indians needed anyone else ruling them.

Although the British, even given the so-called quasi-independent "princely states," imposed a governmental unity of sorts, it was up to the leaders of the independence movement—English-trained lawyers like Gandhi and Nehru—to forge the idea of a national Indian identity. It was also necessary to jump-start the economy, and that is exactly what the Republic of India's first prime minister, Jawaharlal Nehru, tried to do.

POSTINDEPENDENCE DEVELOPMENTS AND CONDITIONS

A deep divide existed between the Gandhians and the Nehruvians as to what the course of economic development should be after independence. Gandhi felt very strongly that economic focus must be on the village—on rural agricultural development. This economic ideology was tied to his political ideology; he distrusted strong centralization and felt India should become an interconnected series of cooperatives and *panchayats* (village councils), a federation of politically and economically autonomous village republics, with caste and economic disparities being balanced in a sense of natural order and goodwill, a spiritual (in the widest, nonsectarian sense) harmony permeating all aspects of existence. It seems to have been an idealistic view of the central Hindu concept of dharma, or duty. And it is not as far-fetched as it may seem, for it inspired, in large part, Eric Schumacher's concept of "Small Is Beautiful." Gandhi was worried about the dehumanization of economic centralization—whether it be socialist or capitalist. At the time, however, his notions appeared romantic.

Nehru was determined to build India economically, to make up for the skipped industrial revolution. He had a model: the Soviet Union and its five-year plans. He also had a competitor in the eyes of the world: China. India and China were (and to a degree still are) natural competitors: the two largest populations in the world, the two most ancient continuous civilizations, with two radically opposed political structures and philosophies. The question was, which system was better; that is, which could develop the economic system that could deliver the goods. It may seem quaint to put it that way today, but it was not so at the time.

The Soviet Union's economic plans, designed to catch up with the West, seemed to Nehru a probable model, although he abhorred the political brutality of Stalinist Russia. He adapted—not adopted—the Soviet economic plan. Labeled as socialist by detractors, and although containing Fabian socialist ideals, India's economy was really a mixed one. Large industrial powers such as the Tata Group and the Birla family continued to exist and to develop. Where there were marked deficiencies, such as steel, the state took the lead. Even today there are remnants of this mixed economy: in January 2002 when an Indian component of Houston-based Enron was put up for bids, the bidders were two private Indian energy companies and a state-owned entity. The major problem with government involvement was that it became too entrenched, an end in itself rather than a means, dominating the economy and leading to stifling bureaucratic overregulation.

The government's program to privatize state commercial holdings hit a snag in September 2002 in regard to Hindustan Petroleum, India's largest oil refinery, and Bharat Petroleum, the largest retailer. Companies that had expressed an interest in purchase included Exxon Mobil, Chevron Texaco, BP, and Shell. This alarmed George Fernandes, defense minister in the coalition government, a socialist and head of the Samata Party (a member of the ruling coalition), who was worried about the degree of foreign influence in the economy and possible compromise of energy security. He was joined in his objection by Petroleum Minister Ram Naik. This concern was backed up by workers fearing job cuts if private companies, particularly foreign ones, were to take over. When bids were tendered on or before March 17, 2003, by twelve foreign companies (for percentages as strategic partner, not complete control), thousands of workers struck, in spite of a court injunction (*New York Times,* March 26, 2003).

The minister for disinvestment (i.e., privatization), Arun Shourie, an economist formerly with the World Bank, and former editor of the prestigious newspaper *Indian Express,* was likewise concerned—but his concern was with the "glacial" nature of progress in disinvestment of government involvement in economic enterprises, which include, in addition to petroleum, economic enterprises such as hotels, glass, and even condoms. He felt the divestment program had to go ahead in order "to contain fiscal deficit, attain high growth rate and reduce poverty" (*India Abroad,* September 20, 2002).

He appears to be on the right track. As examples, the *New York Times* "World Business" section reported several recent improvements in the Indian economy: On June 13, 2003, it noted that India's industrial output was up 4.9 percent in April and up 4.3 percent for the fiscal year April 2002–March 2003 (compared with 5.6 percent for the previous fiscal year). A month later it reported that Bharti Tele-ventures, India's largest cellular provider, doubled the number of subscribers (cellular and fixed line) in 2003, going from a yearly loss of $14.6 million to a gain of $6.7 million (*New York Times,* July 24, 2003). Perhaps most important, privatization is advancing, with Arun Shourie announcing that the government would sell its remaining share in five already privatized companies, including Indian Petrochemicals (*New York Times,* July 12, 2003). Also, exports rose by more than 11 percent in the April–June quarter, with merchandise exports rising from $3.86 billion in June 2002 to $4.28 billion in June 2003 (*New*

York Times, August 2, 2003). Industrial output has risen further (6.2 percent in December 2003) with projection of more than 8 percent for the fiscal year ending March 2004 (*New York Times,* February 13, 2004). The farm and manufacturing sectors are significantly up as well (*New York Times,* February 10, 2004). The United States and the European Union receive over half of Indian's exports.

In September 2002, Prime Minister Atal Bihari Vajpayee put a three-month freeze on privatization sales because of the ministers' dispute. Subsequent to the lifting of the ban, Shourie's powers were expanded to include the communications and technologies ministries. According to the *New York Times* (January 31, 2003), "Telecommunications stocks surged on the outlook for the sale of government shares in the leading companies."

Meanwhile, India's industrial output expanded, and private conglomerates such as the largest, Reliance Industries (oil and petrochemicals), experienced impressive increases in earnings. Hindustan Lever, the largest consumer products company, showed a 7 percent profit increase the last quarter of 2002. The *New York Times* (January 20, 2003) stated that "the performance of the company, 51 percent owned by Unilever, is seen as a bellwether of consumer activity in the Indian economy." Foreign exchange reserves rose from $19 billion in April 2002 to more than $73 billion by the following February, resulting in Moody's Investment Service upgrading the foreign currency rating. "The upgrade by Moody's," reported the *New York Times* (February 4, 2003), "is likely to help Indian companies borrow from foreign markets at cheaper rates, because the perceived risk of investing in India has declined."

Nevertheless, some multinational corporations have pulled out of India, complaining about excise taxes and the slow market of "fast moving consumer goods." However, in a poll of 118 American companies, 93 percent "found the business climate excellent" (*India Abroad,* November 8, 2002). Other

Anil Ambani, vice chairman and managing director of Reliance
Industries, Ltd., addresses a news conference in Bombay on January
29, 2004. (Punit Paranjpe/Stringer/Reuters/Corbis)

positives and optimistic signs include a November 2002 trip
to India by Bill Gates, founder of Microsoft (one of the richest
men in the world), who visited with 250 Indian CEOs and
leading state and national politicians. He dispensed millions
of dollars worth of software and other aid, including a ten-year
$100 million pledge to fight AIDS. Almost simultaneously
with Gates's visit, high-level U.S. government delegations
traveled to seek stronger trade relations. At about the same
time, the government of the United States created the position Assistant U.S. Trade Representative for South Asia. General Motors, world leader in car production, is developing a
$21 million auto research laboratory in Bangalore (GM's first
outside the United States), to focus on vehicle design, manufacturing technology, and electronics (*New York Times,*
November 12, 2003). GM, with less than 3 percent of the vehi-

cle market in India, announced it would double its output in
2005, as it planned on buying the Indian facilities of Daewoo,
a South Korean car manufacturer. America Online has set up
a call center in Bangalore, citing lower costs than in the
United States. Within the next three years, a $280 million
international airport for Bangalore is to open, eliminating the
need for international travelers to transfer from other major
airports. Passenger traffic, at 2.2 million from Bangalore in
2002, is estimated to be 4 million by 2005 (*India Abroad,*
February 13, 2004). An entirely new socioeconomic class has
developed: young college graduates working for U.S. companies who are a manifestation of economic globalization.
Columnist Thomas Friedman, however, has posited that the
equipment used in these jobs—including air conditioners, as
well as computers and software—are all from the United
States and that "total exports from U.S. companies to India
have grown from $2.5 billion in 1990 to $4.1 billion in 2002"
(*New York Times,* February 26, 2004).

Bangalore (in Karnataka, southwest India) has developed
into "the Silicon Plain" of India, with more than one thousand software companies. In 2001 Infosys Technologies was
visited by a delegation from the Chinese Ministry of Higher
Education. This company is visited by dozens of groups
weekly. Its physical size is reputedly second only to that of
Microsoft, and it plans to develop a center in the nearby state
of Kerala. India has several advantages in information technology: (1) after independence, educational emphasis shifted
considerably from traditional-style universities to technology
institutes; (2) there is a strong historical tradition in mathe-
matical genius; and (3) English is the lingua franca in a
nation of eighteen official languages, with virtually all educated people fluent in English.

A major result of the Indian success in intelligence technology has been the outsourcing of American jobs to India. Of
course, the matter is more complicated than the phrase "outsourcing of American jobs" suggests, but emotion has run

Urban traffic and pollution (Kapoor Baldev/Corbis Sygma)

high in the United States; it is a major political concern, accompanied by the usual emotional reactions such issues raise. For example, in a response to a March 11, 2004, column by Thomas Friedman in the *New York Times*, the writer of a letter to the editor stated, "I lost my job because someone in India will work for one-sixth of what I was paid," (March 14). Friedman's argument (as well as in an earlier and a later column, March 4 and 14) was that it is a very intricate matter, involving more than just outsourcing, which in itself does not exist in a vacuum, but is part of economic globalization. Despite the painful immediate hurts, in the long run, he states, the process will be of benefit for all. He carries the argument further in his March 14 column in which he contrasts India to the closed societies that spawned Al Qaeda: free market, democracy, education, science and rationality, and empowerment of women, in stark contrast to the oppressive atmosphere that produces frustrated terrorists. The implication is clear: We're better off with some temporary economic disruptions such as outsourcing than with terrorism.

There are other facets to the problem, which are developed in a feature article by Amy Waldman, also in the *New York Times* (March 7, 2004). She quotes a popular English language magazine, *Outlook,* as determining that U.S. internet debates on outsourcing as revealing a "barely concealed racism." Like the United States, India is having national elections in 2004, and some business leaders are concerned that the anger expressed in the U.S. electoral atmosphere will not only affect U.S.-India relations, but will result in a backlash in Indian politics—both toward the United States and in regard to the still-controversial opening of the economy and disinvestment of government-owned enterprises. That there are more than twenty states and some national politicians targeting India with punitive legislation also acerbates the situation.

There is a certain puzzlement. Indians say that what they are doing is what the United States wanted, that is, developing private enterprise, and the United States itself "is propagating capitalism" (in the words of a member of the gigantic Tata industrial complex) and competition. Arun Shourie, the minister overseeing government disinvestment, has put it: "Those who lecture about free trade should practice it" (ibid.).

Nevertheless, the chairman of a major outsourcing firm advised government leaders that India needed to face the U.S. backlash as potentially explosive. Azim Premji, chair of Wipro, "one of the largest offshore outsourcing companies in the world" (*New York Times,* March 21, 2004), told the prime minister that the issue needed to be faced as a national priority.

According to company figures, the number of employees rose from slightly less than 10,000 in 2002 to more than 30,000 in 2004. The firm, located in Bangalore, counts among its many clients Boeing, General Motors, and Home Depot. But an increasing number of U.S. clients are requesting that they not be identified as such. Tasks include staffing telephone desks for airline programs, designing a navigation system for cars, and interpreting X rays for a hospital—all in the United States.

Premji told the *New York Times* that while 800,000 people are employed in the technology industry in India, 10.2 million are employed in the United States. Thirty thousand work in Indian call centers, while there are 6 million in the United States. Yet, this business leader of world stature felt compelled to warn his government—and had the ear of the prime minister in doing so—of possible dire consequences in bilateral relations with the United States because of outsourcing.

The colonial experience resulted in a protective psychology, at times bordering on paranoia, regarding foreign investors and businesses. For instance, Coca-Cola found itself in and out and in again. In the late 1960s and early 1970s, rumors abounded that Coke was addictive and was leading the youth of India astray; in August 2003, Coke and its competitor, Pepsi, got into legal trouble for reported pesticides in the soft drinks.

Similarly, Shell Oil is to return to India after three decades; its subsidiary Burmah Shell was nationalized thirty years ago (and became the Bharat Petroleum Corporation). Shell will set up two thousand gas stations, including some in rural areas. Other private oil companies are also being allowed to enter a market hitherto confined to the three public-sector firms (which have 19,800 gas stations). Reliance, for example, plans 5,849 stations, and three other companies plan 2,810 among themselves. (Reliance is an industrial conglomerate that on July 31, 2003, announced a 28.5 percent increase in quarterly profit, $255 million compared to $199 million the previous year. Referred to as "India's most valuable private enterprise," Reliance has "a market capitalization exceeding $10 billion" with "businesses spanning petrochemicals, energy, textiles and communications"; *New York Times,* August 1, 2003.) Shell hopes to bid on the government-owned Hindustan Petroleum, which has 4,860 retail outlets. A successful bid would give Shell a head start on infrastructure in a retail market that is diffused both in terms of geography and consumption.

In the past couple of decades, deregulation has resulted in a more flexible economy. There are a number of reasons for this, including a clear decision by the government in 1991 for radical, drastic reform of the economic policies—a decision encouraged if not dictated by the World Bank and International Monetary Fund. There were problems that developed, but a drive toward flexibility in economy had some abstract causes behind it, including a generation less xenophobic about Western businesses and capitalism; changing attitudes toward Westernization; the collapse of the Soviet Union; and, most certainly, the information and technology explosion. But as well, what some economists have called "a change in mind-set" has occurred, with decentralization and less interference from the central government—including "licensing" of firms for virtual monopolies, thus preventing the development of open markets. If India's economy continues to grow at 5 to 6 percent a year, there is reason for optimism.

Indeed, the New York Times reported (April 1, 2004) that the Indian economy soared 10.4 percent in the last quarter of 2003. However, much of it was due to outstanding agricultural production resulting from exceptional monsoon rains.

Liberalization, globalization, and privatization have all been key in economic reform, but they have attendant problems: reforms demanded by the World Bank and the International Monetary Fund have been deleterious to the poor, especially the agriculturally poor, and there is still a hangover from the colonial period. Many politicians and bureaucrats have a mental legacy of socialist and civil service regulations. An increasing middle class has benefited from reform, but there has been little for the poor. New jobs are not being created at a rapid enough pace, even with an expanding economy. Reforms have barely touched agriculture, have not affected small industry, and have not made a difference in the lives of the vast majority of the Indian people. The widening of markets has opened choices in consumer goods like automobiles, airline tickets, computers, televisions, and Scotch whisky. Meanwhile, the poor, including even farmers, often do not have money to buy food.

According to CNN's ongoing program "Country Watch," agriculture accounts for 25 percent of the gross national product and 65 percent of labor. Once, India was dependent on the United States to make up shortages in food; now there is a surplus, but still millions go hungry. Nobel Laureate Amartya Sen has observed that "a major failure of the Indian economy" is "a massive level of endemic hunger across the country," in spite of elimination of famines and "the presence of exceptionally large stocks of food grain" (*India Abroad*, August 15, 2003). Storage and distribution are the problems, and the government has been told by the World Bank and the International Monetary Fund that it must cut the deficit and subsidies to small farmers. It seems as though reform is working against the well-being of the very people it should be helping. In 1970 Prime Minister Indira Gandhi nationalized the banks, partly in hopes of making cheap credit available to farmers. Yet farmers are still borrowing at exorbitant rates from village money-lenders, who offer less bureaucracy and fewer regulations than the banks.

In balance, it must be said that villagers themselves often resist change, especially if it seems challenging to tradition (e.g., "my father and his father did it this way") and is viewed as imposed from outside. An example is Jagdish Shukla, an Indian American who for more than thirty years has returned annually to the village where he was raised and where he still has family. He has dedicated a great deal of money as well as time toward bringing change to the village. Some efforts have been successful, such as his establishment of a small college of 500 students, of whom 70 percent are women. Nevertheless, even though he is, in the words of one villager, "very well-respected," he "provides . . . suspicions," as another put it, because he is viewed perhaps more of an outsider than an insider (*New York Times,* August 17, 2003).

Perhaps foremost among the problems that have hindered economic development in India is the persistency in the program developed at independence. It had clearly ceased providing any benefit by the late 1960s, yet with a seeming existence of its own, it bureaucratically trudged on. Attempts at reform after Prime Minister Indira Gandhi's assassination in 1984 were at best an extension of exceptions to the stiff regulations and overprotective tariffs. When India's foreign reserves all but disappeared during the Gulf War in 1991, the country faced a 14 percent rate of inflation; internal debt payments took 20 percent of the budget. Only Brazil and Mexico had larger national debts. Black market rates for the rupee were 25 percent below the official rate of exchange.

When Mohan Singh, a professional economist rather than a politician, became India's finance minister (1991–1996), he instituted liberalizing reforms that allowed for an increase in foreign investments, a decrease in restrictions on the private sector, moves toward globalization, and abandonment of the myth of self-sufficiency. Yet, all too often political necessities overrode economic policies. The hold on power can be tenuous in a democracy, and the Congress Party was a federation of interest groups with often differing views, practically rather than ideologically oriented. All too easily, entrenched interests opposed true reform—especially in the agricultural sector—and found easy fall-guys to target: the World Bank, the International Monetary Fund (IMF), the General Agreement on Tariffs and Trade (GATT), and the old bugaboo of "Western decadence." (For example, MTV was seen as a threat to traditional values because it is a form of entertainment not easily monitored). Further, short-range painful cuts were difficult to rationalize as being necessary for long-range benefits. Loaning agencies such as the World Bank and IMF demanded constraints, such as the aforementioned cutting of farming subsidies, which seemed harmful to the poor.

Priorities were sometimes confused—about half the population was illiterate (compared to less than a quarter of China's), a factor of considerable hindrance in the emerging high-tech era. India's infrastructure needed a great deal of attention: roads were in disrepair, and even the Grand Trunk Road was in places dangerous at night because of bandits. Urban power blackouts were common. The telephone system was worse than archaic. Such problems were often met with indifference, with failure to realize that an adequate telephone system was essential for business. The railway system was excellent, efficient, and inexpensive (though crowded), yet although a great amount of freight was hauled by small trucks, the road system was largely ignored. There was a general ignorance of the fact that other developing economies were helped by a recognition that the education of women helped the economic situation of individual families and of society in general. Nongovernmental organizations (NGOs) did fill gaps, such as the Self-Employed Women's Association (SEWA), which had been established in 1972 in Ahmedabad, a city of textile mills where the labor movement was started in 1918 under the guidance of M. K. Gandhi. SEWA soon extended beyond Ahmedabad into rural areas, and it expanded to include social services and a cooperative bank. Villagers, especially women, have developed and profited from this and other self-help movements.

Still, problems persist. Some, such as the federal rather than centralized nature of political power (national, state, regional, local, caste), may have to be circumvented rather than surmounted. The Indian people generally identify at levels lower than the national. The fundamental problems—illiteracy, poverty, inequalities, health, and corruption—have not gone away. And new problems inevitably develop. For example, India is the world's leading producer of tea. Globalization has brought cheaper producers into the market, and a glut of Indian tea has developed. Tea lately has been auctioned at a loss. Low prices have resulted in plantation shut-downs. Younger potential drinkers of tea are developing preferences for other beverages. The social aspect of tea-drinking is disappearing in the cities. Overseas markets, such as Russia, have fallen off. Producers have noted cyclical downturns in the past, but this one is longer and deeper and has them concerned.

Fortunately, the emergency food distribution system makes it unlikely that a monsoon would create disaster as occurred under the British. Nevertheless, a balance has not been found between the needs of restraint and the subsidy needs of small farmers. One source has speculated that whereas the overwhelming majority of all workers are in agriculture, not much investment has been directed toward them. This was a complaint a couple of decades ago in regard to the Green Revolution: it did nothing for the landless laborers.

Change has been overwhelmingly urban, fueling the economies of those states with significant investments in new technologies, such as Andhra Pradesh (in southeast India). The capital, Hyderabad, a city of almost 7 million people and

Tea pickers wait in line for their harvest to be weighed in order to collect their wages for the day. (Lindsay Hebberd/Corbis)

with a rich historical and cultural legacy, "has become a green, prosperous hub for computer programming, telephone call centers and drug manufacturing," as described in the *New York Times* (December 17, 2002). The newspaper went on to observe that "most of the state's 76 million people still live in rural villages where change has been slow, and where a two-year drought has brought considerable suffering." In a visit to Hyderabad (November 14, 2002), Bill Gates stated that the Microsoft programming center there would be expanded from 150 to 500 people. A leading official with the company observed that there were fifty "serious applicants" for each programming position.

Famine may not have occurred in India since independence, but hunger and starvation have. It has been estimated that a third of the population is constantly hungry and half of the children are malnourished. Amartya Sen has stated that in sub-Saharan Africa 20 to 40 percent of children are malnourished ("in terms of weight for age"), whereas in India the percentage is 40 to 60 (*India Abroad,* August 15, 2003). Indeed, starvation has been termed as "widespread" even with the surplus of grain, hoarded by the government for economic and political reasons because of pressure from agricultural lobbies that want price increases (*New York Times,* December 2, 2002, and March 1, 2003).

The proposed budget for fiscal year 2003–2004 presented by the current finance minister, Jaswant Singh, includes some tax breaks, deficit reduction, and economic growth incentives, all of which may well benefit both the economy and the middle class. It does address the poor by proposing health and food programs. Critics have pointed out that elections are on the horizon in several states, and a national election is scheduled to be held in four phases: April 20, April 26, May 5, and May 10, 2004. Results are to be announced May 13 (*New York Times,* March 1, 2004). Deputy election commissioner A. N. Jha explained that the four phases were necessary because of "the various festivals that fall during the next few months, the harvesting season in some northern states, school examination, the weather conditions, and other related factors" (*India Abroad,* February 27, 2004).

Many observers are concerned that without social reform, such as for women and the poor, and a reining-in of the bureaucracy, the economy will not become "self-generating" and will remain sluggish. Millions of jobs need to be created yearly. Short-term shock needs to be minimized for popular confidence in the long-term program, and corruption needs to be eliminated for the same reason (indeed, corruption seems to be endemic to the system). A clear agenda needs to be developed, announced to the public, debated, and then instituted so that politically inspired shenanigans can be averted. Although foreign trade must be increased, it must be controlled in a manner so that the Nehruvian ideal of social justice is not subverted, and so that India does not become so globalized that its distinct character is lost (a complaint one sometimes hears from Canadians about the impact of American business and popular culture on their country). In short, economics must be the means to social and cultural ends.

It needs to be noted as well that the Indian union contains a diversity comparable to that of the European Union, in terms of multiple languages, religious and ethnic distinctions, cultures (or subcultures), and regional identities. For the economy to succeed, somehow a national cohesion must be achieved. Unlike the situation in the European Union, Indian economic cohesion likely will have to come from above. The problem is how that can be done in a democracy with strong sectional identities and forces that pull at the central core.

Yet, were all the above concerns met and resolved, India might still be unable to provide economic well-being to either the society as a whole, or the poor in particular, for one major reason: population explosion, with the resulting ecological catastrophe in the making. The population of India has risen from around 325 million at independence in 1947 to well over a billion today. Much of the nation's economic gain has been expended just treading water: a trebling of the population when the economy was underdeveloped does not bode well for future development. Village women have to walk farther and farther to find wood for fuel. (Although cow dung provides a basic fuel, it does not do so everywhere or in entirety.) Wood in many regions, such as the Himalayan foothills, is a diminishing resource losing to an ever-increasing population. The cutting of trees (and grazing of branches by livestock) has taken its toll not only on the forests, but on the soil as well. Erosion has destroyed roads, washed away topsoil, and caused river bottoms to rise, resulting in more frequent and serious flooding. Ecology is a concern Indian governments have not readily faced.

The population crisis has brought about crises in the cities. Delhi, for example, is now home to some 16 million people (it was about 1 million at independence); of course, its geographical size has increased, consuming what were once sub-

Hindu woman harvesting crops in Himalayan foothills (Corel)

urban villages, but the existence of an out-of-control growth is shown by the quality of its air—among the worst in the world. In 1900, Calcutta's population was less than a million; in the late 1930s, about 12 million; in 1997, 132 million; projected for 2025, an astounding 300 million. During the annual monsoon, the city's sewers are not fully functional—to state the situation gently. The quantity of slums in the earlier-mentioned British-founded cities is incomprehensible to a Westerner—and to many Indians. It is difficult to assess how much of an economic drain the slums are for the cities; they have become institutionalized as neighborhoods, with local politicians courting them as constituencies. Many of the women in the Bombay (Mumbai) slums are domestic servants in condos of the well-to-do in nearby wealthy neighborhoods. Families have actually made homes in the slums—but they are still in dire poverty.

The crowding in the slums can exacerbate preexisting communal tensions. India has been described as "a land of minorities," and diversity does exist in dimensions unimagined in the United States: religious, ethnic, regional, linguistic, and caste. Most often, the primary identity of an individual or group is in terms of community, with national identification being an overlay in regard to dealing with the outside world, such as in confrontations with Pakistan. The crowded slums sometimes rip open from the tensions. There are regional tensions even more potentially explosive: a particular group demanding greater autonomy from the central government in Delhi, and sometimes even separation. These are most often highly distinct groups, such as in the northeast (of Tibeto-Burman heritage), without the major characteristics shared by the dominant groups, caste-wise, linguistically, and ethnically. The centrifugal forces (or tendencies toward separation) have not resulted in a breaking of the union, as was feared just after independence (and which some still fear in regard to Kashmir). There was a call in the south for an independent Dravidistan, the four southern states speaking separate but similar Dravidian languages. Distrust of the strongest of these states by the other three was a factor in the collapse of such a movement, but also important was a realization of the overwhelming economic advantages of staying in the union. The differences in economic policies among the various states is mitigated by a national government—just as in the United States.

Perhaps of as great concern is the enormous socioeconomic gap between the cities and the villages, increased by the globalization policies geared toward the middle class. The future may well depend upon how the interaction between urban India and rural India plays out. To some degree, the huge slums represent a failure of that interaction (and as twentieth-century fiction in virtually every Indian language shows, such has been the case for decades). Population pressures increase the disparity and decrease opportunities of earning a living in rural areas. Communal differences can be kept somewhat isolated; economic disadvantage affecting the huge majority of Indians is a nationwide, and nation-deep, problem. As technology increases—including advertisements on television—wants increase; former luxuries such as shampoo become seen as needs. This phenomenon struck the evolving lower middle class in the cities in the 1970s and 1980s as lesser-income wannabes started demanding televisions and VCRs, refrigerators and cameras, from prospective in-laws as dowry for their sons. Something called "bride-burning" resulted. Although dowries are illegal, the goods were referred to as gifts. The village custom of the bride living with her husband in his family continued among these groups in the cities. If her parents did not deliver, the kerosene cooking stove could explode, killing her. Even if the goods were delivered, the bride might meet a fatal accident. The son could always remarry and gain another dowry. These situations were not easy to prove, at first; the numbers of these events have decreased in recent years.

Almost a symbol of the socioeconomic gap is the automobile,

the market for which is highly competitive, with U.S., European, Korean, Japanese, and Indian products. The edge is held by the Indian company Maruti, with dealerships in 118 cities and towns (*New York Times,* June 13, 2003). Since 2000, sales have held steady—600,000 sold in 2003, 85 percent of which were minis and compacts. The government is selling one-quarter of its 45.8 percent ownership in Maruti, and when the stocks went public there were more buyers than shares.

Finally, another historical heritage has adversely affected India's economy: the partition of the subcontinent into two separate countries. The resulting arms race, involving wars in 1948, 1965, and 1971—with one that was looming in 2002 and beyond—have drained much of the "butter" part of the budgets of both countries for "guns." It has hurt stability, which always affects economics; Pakistan is constitutionally an Islamic nation; India is secular, but many from among the majority Hindus sometimes distrust the loyalty of the minority Muslims, and the Muslims can be fearful as a result. Politically organized destruction of mosques and even programs has resulted.

India is the world's largest producer of feature films—primarily in Hindi, but in other languages as well. The movies are getting better; they are no longer merely escape films (although some are—especially with the spate of "patriotic" films after a terrorist attack on the parliament buildings on December 13, 2001). Perhaps this is an assessment for the economy: getting better but with a long way to go. Another bright spot is the apparent connection, economic as well as cultural, between Indian Americans (NRIs—nonresident Indians) and their motherland; they are maintaining contact and are investing in India. Further, the report on industrial output for the fiscal year ending in March 2003 showed a growth in manufacturing of 6 percent, with a rise in overall industrial output of 5.8 percent, which is up from 2.7 percent for the previous year (Central Statistical Organization, as reported by *New York Times,* May 13, 2003).

Perhaps most important is the strong sense of optimism, which was not present so very long ago. A recent economic supplement in *India Abroad* (August 15, 2003) displayed two front-page banner headlines: "India a Magical Transformation" and "Indian Economy: Dramatic Turnaround." U.S. political and business leaders sometimes have expressed concern that U.S. investment in exports to India is still considerably lower than it ought to be. According to Deputy Secretary of Commerce Samuel W. Bodman, investment is less than "in Chile, Colombia, Malaysia, and Peru" (*India Abroad,* June 20, 2003). Yet, interest by both India and the United States is in strengthening—at an increasing rate—economic ties. Furthermore, Amartya Sen has expressed professional optimism that in the long run, the economy will become solid and strong, by the very nature of democracy: the power of people to put pressure on government.

Nevertheless, the specter of ecological catastrophe resulting from uncontrolled population growth—with no apparent need seen by the government to regulate it—may make reform no more than whistling in the dark. Oddly, where regulation is most needed in an overregulated economy, it is absent.

References

Coll, Steve. *On the Grand Trunk Road: A Journey into South Asia.* New York: Random House, 1994.

Country Profile: India, Nepal 1999–2000. London: Economist Intelligence Unit.

Das, Gurcharan. *India Unbound.* New York: Knopf, 2001.

Desai, Rajiv. *Indian Business Culture.* Oxford: Butterworth-Heinemann, 1999.

Doing Business with India: Resource Directory and Reference Guide. Silver Springs, MD: U.S.-India Enterprises, 1997.

Far Eastern Economic Review: Asia 2002 Yearbook. Hong Kong: Far Eastern Economic Review, 2002.

Heitzman, James, and Robert L. Worden, eds. *India: A Country Study,* 5th ed. Washington, DC: Federal Research Division, Library of Congress, 1996.

India 2000: A Reference Annual. Government of India: Publications Division, 2001.

James, Lawrence. *Raj: The Making and Unmaking of British India.* New York: St. Martin's, 1998.

Keay, John. *India: A History.* New York: Atlantic Monthly Press, 2000.

Khilnani, Sunil. *The Idea of India.* New York: Farrar, Straus, Giroux, 1998.

Kohli, Jitendra, ed. *The Business Guide to India.* Singapore: Butterworth-Heinemann, 1996.

Moxham, Roy. *The Great Hedge of India.* New York: Carroll & Graf, 2001.

Salatore, R. N. *Early Indian Economic History.* London: Curzon, 1975.

Schumacher, E. R. *Small Is Beautiful: Economics as if People Mattered.* 25th anniv. ed. Berkshire Hills, MA: E. F. Schumacher Society, 1999.

Tharoor, Shashi. *India: From Midnight to the Millennium.* New York: Harper Perennial, 1998.

Weller, Anthony. *Days and Nights on the Grand Trunk Road.* New York: Marlowe, 1991.

CHAPTER THREE

Indian Institutions

GOVERNMENT AND POLITICS

In some ways, speaking of a united India is akin to the concept of a united Europe. The twenty-nine states and six union territories to a considerable extent represent separate subcultures, just as Scotland and Poland, for instance, can be thought of as European subcultures. Indeed, eighteen languages are recognized by the constitution, and since independence in 1947, new states have been carved out of old, and boundaries have been adjusted for linguistic and ethnic reasons.

India has seldom, if ever, been fully united—not under the Mauryas or the Mughals. Although the British certainly had hegemony, there was still the matter of semiautonomous princely states. Further, primary identity in India has historically been social (family and caste) rather than political. The caste system does provide a social ordering that even with its many regional variations allows for a social structure on an all-India basis, even affecting religions besides Hinduism.

There were empires in precolonial India, some large, many merely regional. The idea of a nation-state, however, was developed—perhaps even imported—by the group of leaders who led India to independence. The independence movement is also known as the nationalist movement, for the English-educated Indian lawyers had to develop a sense of nationhood among the diverse peoples while they pushed the demand for independence. As James Madison and his colleagues recognized in the United States, a union has to be forged in order to have national independence. The goal for India was a secular state with a parliamentary system of government. Despite the built-in inequalities of caste, the new nation was to be one person, one vote. In fact, some of the more populous lower castes soon recognized the advantage in numbers and in alliances among ethnic blocs of voters, just as in some urban areas of the United States.

The Indian National Congress (later the Congress Party), was the political instrument that led India to independence. Its most famous leaders were M. K. Gandhi and Jawaharlal Nehru, the latter also being India's first prime minister (1947–1964). His strong and lengthy leadership provided a firm democratic foundation. Although Gandhi favored political decentralization—an almost romantic notion of loosely federated village republics—and the disbanding of the Congress as a political party, his younger associate, Nehru, wanted political centralization with a focus on urban-industrial development.

For two and a half years (1947–1950) a constituent assembly met to develop a constitution. It also acted as a parliamentary body. The constitution contained borrowings from Western democracies and provisions from the Government of India Act of 1935. The result was a federal form of government with the strongest powers concentrated at the "center" (the capital, New Delhi) and regional powers relegated to the states. The constitution has been criticized for being too long—395 articles (about 250 of which are from the 1935 Government of India Act) and too easily amended by Parliament. Strong powers are vested at the center in an effort to combat the centrifugal forces inherent in Indian history and society and to provide a mechanism for instituting social change, particularly in regard to disadvantaged segments of the society such as the lower castes. The result has been not only a centralized state but an interventionist one in which "reservations" (a form of affirmative action) are promised to "backward" castes. The "forward" or upper castes have often felt threatened and at times have responded with violence.

Furthermore, promises made by political candidates cannot always be met in an era of conflicting group—or "communal"—demands. The term *communal* includes ethnic, religious, regional, and linguistic groups as well as castes (in some instances the groups overlap).

Nevertheless, the basic British pattern should not be ignored. Various British parliamentary acts from 1773 on were largely intended to curb the power of the East India Company (which, until its dissolution in 1858, was responsible for the political administration of British India); later actions were often viewed as "too little, too late" by Indian leaders. As it happened, the British were sometimes restrained by the international situation, such as the 1935 demand for dominion status with neutrality (Europe was on the verge of World War II). Ironically, just a hundred years prior to the Government of India Act of 1935, an event occurred that to a large extent made it possible for Indians to make political demands. A member of the British Indian government, Thomas Babington Macaulay, issued the Minute on Education, which set official policy on education in India. The intention was to produce a class of people "Indian in colour and blood but English in tastes, in opinions, in morals and in intellect." English, rather than Indian languages, was to be the medium of instruction. What this did produce was a cadre of leaders educated in English law and constitutional history, such as Gandhi and Nehru.

Of course the attitude of English superiority did not exist in a vacuum. Various factions in the British parliament wanted to extend the benefits of Western—particularly British—civilization to India as well as the benefits of Christianity—Protestant, of course. Hinduism was especially reviled, both as a culture and a religion. Also early in the nineteenth century, a number of reformers within Hinduism called upon the government to help purge the religion of decadent practices such as *thugi* (so-called ritual killing of travelers for their money) and *sati* (ritual burning of widows on

Members of the Indian National Congress on the dais at Haripura.
From left to right: Seth Jamnalal Bajaj, Darbar Gopaldas Desai,
M. K. Gandhi, and Subhas Chandra Bose. (Hulton Archive)

their husbands' funeral pyres). Calcutta was the capital of British India as well as of Bengal. Understandably, the primary impact of British influence was there, resulting in what has been termed the "Bengal Renaissance."

Fifty years after Macaulay's Minute, the Indian National Congress was formed (1885). Originally, it was a tame group of Indian professionals and some interested Britons who met annually to politely discuss various political issues. In the meantime, however, the rebellion (or "mutiny") of 1857 had occurred (see chapter 1), with savage reprisals on both sides. Perhaps always "birds of a different plumage," the gap in trust between the British and the Indians had become irreparable. In just a short few decades the Indian National Congress became the party that led India to independence, using British ideals of democratic self-government as its motivation.

The format of the government is also British in design. The president is head of state, but not head of government, although he does have the power to dismiss Parliament following a vote of no confidence or to seek someone to form a new government. He is chosen by Parliament for a five-year term. So far, all the presidents have been male, although not all have been Hindu.

The head of government is the prime minister, who represents the majority party in the lower house, or a coalition that forms a majority. He—or she (Indira Gandhi, Nehru's daughter, was twice prime minister)—loses power on a vote of no confidence (or in resigning in anticipation of a vote of no-confidence).

Like the British Parliament, the Indian Parliament is composed of two houses, with real power resting in the lower house, the Lok Sabha (Assembly of the People). Terms are for five years unless an election is called before (by the prime minister or the president). There are 545 seats in the Lok Sabha.

The Rajya Sabha (Assembly of States) is composed of 250 or fewer members. Terms are for two years, with one-third of the house being elected. To provide a semblance of continuity, the Rajya Sabha is never dissolved. Members are selected in a complicated manner involving the various states, the president, the prime minister, and various minorities. If the Rajya Sabha votes down a bill, the lower house can override with a simple majority.

The prime minister selects members of the Council of Ministers. They must be members of either house of Parliament, or become one within six months. Although not specified by the constitution, an inner cabinet from among the principal ministers is selected by the prime minister for purposes of efficiency and advising on major issues.

From necessity, the British developed an outstanding bureaucracy, particularly the elite Indian Civil Service (now the Indian Administrative Service, or IAS). The IAS is the

Government House, Calcutta (Hulton Archive)

cream of a much larger bureaucracy, both at the national and state levels. Today there is concern about morale and low pay in the civil service, including in the prestigious IAS. Efficiency is also a problem, in part stemming from interference by politicians at all levels, dilution of responsibility, delay, and protection of vested interests. Policy implementation, even at the center, has suffered.

India's judicial system is centralized, and overburdened, sometimes involving delays of years even at the Supreme Court level. Besides the years-long backlog in cases, the system has been accused of having become politicized at both the state and the national levels. The insulation protecting judicial independence is not as strong as in the United States.

In comparison, India's military has remained nonpolitical even though it has been called upon increasingly to quell disturbances of communal and political nature—in large part because of local inability or unwillingness to do so; further,

the military is neutral in regard to local communal disturbances, simply interested in enforcing the law and restoring
peace. The all-volunteer army is the fourth largest in the
world and has maintained the British tradition of pride and of
noninvolvement in political and governmental matters.

Each of the twenty-nine states is organized in a manner
similar to the center. A governor is appointed by the prime
minister (through the president), but the power rests with
the chief minister, leader of the dominant political party in the
state. There are a number of powerful regional parties, so the
governor and the chief minister are not necessarily of the same
party. The current parties of national prominence are the Congress Party (currently the leading party of the opposition) and
the Bharatiya Janata Party (leaders of the ruling coalition).
The six union territories are run by governors appointed from
the center. In addition, states are composed of districts, the
chief administrative officers of which are civil servants
appointed by the chief ministers of the states. City governments are usually run on a council basis, with state intervention possible in the case of an ineffective government.

Intervention in state government by the federal government is also possible, with state government being replaced
by direct rule from the center. There is concern that this
process, known as President's Rule and inherited from the
British, has upon occasion been abused for purely political
reasons; thus, in the first twenty years of independence it was
invoked only ten times, but in the next twenty it was invoked
seventy times.

Another potentially dangerous power is that of a Declaration of Emergency, providing for the president (upon advice
from the prime minister) to suspend certain constitutional
rights if (in the words of the constitution) "a grave emergency
exists whereby the security of India or any part of the territory
therein is threatened, whether by war or external aggression
or internal disturbance." This provision was imposed in 1962
(during Chinese military incursion in the Himalayas), 1971

(the war with Pakistan involving Bangladesh), and 1975–1977 (for what Prime Minister Indira Gandhi perceived to be "internal disturbance"). During the latter state of emergency, over 100,000 people, including key opposition political leaders, were arrested, without being advised of charges or provided trial. This "preventive detention" is also a holdover from the British Raj. The 1975 instance involved police abuses at the local level and censorship at the national level. The result was what has been termed a "constitutional dictatorship."

Yet another source of tension has been affirmative action programs, including that of "reservations," wherein a quantity of government positions and entrances into universities are reserved for disadvantaged groups. This has resulted in antipathy sometimes turning to violence on the part of groups not so classified; political manipulation, particularly at the local level; and reinforcement of the already strong group-identity, or communalism, which in turn feeds the atmosphere of conflict.

Because of the social and historical depth of multiculturalism in India, there is a natural tension between group identity and nationalism. The question is, does one deal with the nation as an individual citizen or as a member of a group? Does the government deal with individuals or with groups? This very matter perplexed the leaders of the independence and nationalist movement and was used effectively by the British in their "divide and rule" policy of governing. The Congress Party had insisted before independence upon common laws for all citizens. A seemingly trivial example illustrates the nature and extent of the problem: In 1978 a Muslim divorced his wife of forty-four years. Muslim custom does not require alimony, but the question arose in regard to the maintenance of the wife. The case reached the Supreme Court, which in 1985 granted alimony. Conservative Muslim clerics vigorously protested interference in Muslim law by what they viewed as a Hindu-dominated court and government. The administration of Prime Minister Rajiv Gandhi, with the support of moderate Muslims in Parliament, backed the decision,

only to reverse itself (resulting in the resignation of a number
of embarrassed Muslim moderates) when it realized that Muslims were significant in key parliamentary elections. A bill
was passed affirming the demands of the community over the
rights of the individual. For their part, conservative Hindus
were furious, claiming that the bill weakened unity and
encouraged separatism.

This instance reflects the increasing demands made by
communal groups upon the government and the catering of
politicians to such groups. The government has had to face a
number of separatist demands—tribal, ethnic, religious,
regional, linguistic—that have been difficult to resolve. The
instance also reflects the degeneration of the focus of democratic politics from developing programs to finding ways of
sustaining power. It has been observed that elections have
changed from means to ends to ends in themselves. Politicians at all levels have at times shown more concern with personal power than with democratic institutions. It seems
almost inevitable under such circumstances that police and
the civil service would become politicized. Governing has
become increasingly difficult and less effective. Energy is
directed toward staying in power over the development of
programs designed to solve problems. Cynicism has increased
in and with the political process.

Nevertheless, India is still a democracy, and it is important
to note a number of problems that have not arisen:

- Prospect of a military coup. This is in part due to the British
  heritage—but then Pakistan and Bangladesh also share that
  military heritage, and each has been subject to military
  coups. Here perhaps the size of India, its diversity, and the
  foundation established by Nehru's lengthy rule are the principal factors.

- Secession. Almost from the beginning, secession existed as
  a threat, with a call for a "Dravidistan" composed of the four
  southern states. The most powerful, Tamil Nadu, was viewed

warily by the other three, however. Further, each of the four states exhibited what is common in most areas of India and has been termed "heterogeneity within heterogeneities"; that is, there are differences within each state, minorities of such dimensions that a clear homogeneous majority may be more apparent than real. Further, the economic advantages of staying within the union are usually very clear.

- Revolution. Economically and socially depressed classes or groups are too disparate; that is, there is no sense of unity among them, no vision of a common cause. Undoubtedly, the Hindu concepts of karma and rebirth are relevant as well—one's position or situation has a religious rather than socioeconomic rationale. Furthermore, the adaptability of caste to electoral politics provides an avenue for seeking change within the system.

- Famine. Although people do starve in a country of over one billion, and hunger and poverty are too common, widespread famine has not been the problem it often was in British India. This was in part because of the British policy of exporting foodstuffs even during periods of famine and the failure to develop adequate means of transport from areas of surplus to areas of famine. Much of the current success has to do with the amazing improvements in agricultural technology in recent decades. Then there has been great luck with the monsoons, the importance of which for India—including in ways beyond the raising of crops—cannot be overemphasized.

When the governmental structure and political system of India are looked at in relation to other former colonies, the picture looks bright; it is unlikely India would succumb to dictatorship any more than would the older parliamentary democracies based upon the English system, such as Australia or Canada. The problems of governability must not be neglected—and most likely will not be. When the Bharatiya Janata Party became the governing party, there were dire predictions of conservative Hinduization resulting; so far this has not happened, and given the diversity within the country, it is unlikely that it will.

EDUCATION

Traditional Learning

Traditional education in India was, and is, closely tied to religion. Well into the Common Era, Buddhist universities in northern India at Nalanda and Taxila attracted students from China and central Asia, as well as from India. At the basic levels, learning was in the vernaculars. The medium for higher learning in the Hindu tradition was Sanskrit, whereas in the Muslim, Persian and Arabic were used. Likewise, the literary foundations and heritage for Muslim learning were within the Islamic Persian and Arabic traditions.

The importance of Islamic scholarship in preserving ancient Western culture, as well as for advancing scientific learning, is well known; it had a similar role in medieval India. However, such an eminent Islamic scholar as Alberuni (who

View of the ruins of the Great Stupa and smaller stupas. Nalanda was one of the world's first universities and an important Buddhist center until it was sacked by the Afghans in the twelfth century. (Lindsay Hebberd/Corbis)

was in the party of an eleventh-century central Asian invader) had high praise for Hindu mathematicians and scientists, and he learned Sanskrit in order to study their works.

The Vedas are the oldest documents in any Indo-European language—sort of. That is, as oral texts they are, but they were not written down for centuries, if not millennia, after their development. They were passed on through memorization, which is a hallmark of Indian education even today. The Vedas and their attachments dealt also with subjects that would today be considered secular rather than religious, such as medicine. Especially impressive branches of Sanskrit learning were mathematics (including the concept of zero and the decimal system), poetics (including dramaturgy), and, surprising to many Westerners, linguistics. There is also a fourth-century-B.C.E. political treatise considerably anticipatory to Machiavelli's *The Prince*.

In ancient Hindu tradition, the boys of the brahmin caste studied under their fathers to become priests. A competing tradition developed among the kshatriyas—nobility, or aristocratic caste—wherein many of the young men studied in ashrams (forest retreats) under gurus (spiritual preceptors). The students would sit around the guru as he propounded nondualistic philosophical discourses, which were collected in what have become known as Upanishads (literally, sitting-down-near). These teachings were largely considered as supplemental to brahminical ritual; that is, they did not directly challenge ritual. Rather, the Upanishads asked essential questions about the meaning of existence; ritual was fine, as far as it went. Two exceptions (there were others) in regard to the outlook toward ritual were Mahavira, the major propagator of Jain belief, and the Buddha; both dismissed ritual and brahminism, and as a result their faiths are considered—to use a Western term—heterodox.

Something also should be said about scientific thought in traditional India. The most important—as well as fascinating—is the concept of zero, its philosophical correlatives, and accompanying order of numbers into the decimal system. Although some other ancient cultures were aware of zero, the ancient Indians used it as a symbol—employed in its numerical, decimal system—and as a concept, "zero-ness." The greatest impact of zero (other than allowing for the decimal system of numbers—which were of Indian invention, not Arabic) was in early Buddhist thought as *sunyata* (pronounced *shoon-ya-taah*)—"emptiness" or "nothingness" (although "no-thing-ness" would be a better designation), which in spite of the connotations in the English translations is not intended to imply nihilism or even negativity, but is meant as a descriptive term for the lack of permanence—or, the ever-changing nature—in existence, and, as one scholar, D. P. Singhal, has put it, "simultaneously the All and the None." It is a descriptive term, connoting a "process" philosophy in distinction to a "thing" philosophy; thus, the universe, for instance, is an interrelated series of events rather than some thing.

It should also be noted that science and religion, and the arts as well, for that matter, are not opposed to one another, but complementary, each representing not different truths but different approaches or emphases. In that regard, as life was thought to be cyclical (i.e., birth, death, rebirth), so was the cosmos itself (creation, destruction, re-creation): this axiom of Hinduism, Jainism, and Buddhism was expressed in terms of mythology, philosophy, and science. Further, although there were thoughts of heliocentrism, it was also conceived that there were many suns, many worlds. The fifth-century C.E. astronomer Aryabhatta commented on the position and relation to the planets, declared the earth to be spherical in shape, and estimated the length of the year as 365 days, 6 hours, 12 minutes, 30 seconds (it is 365 days, 6 hours). His treatise (Aryabhatiya) was translated into Latin in the thirteenth century.

Perhaps most interesting is that before Lucretius (first century B.C.E.) and perhaps even Democritus (fifth–fourth century B.C.E.), several Indian philosophies were positing and examining, in different but complementary manners, theories of atoms: the unmanifest become manifest (Samkhya); atoms form aggregates (Vaiseshika); atoms are the cause of matter and effect (Jainism); an atom is transitory (Vaibheshika); the "foundation" of existence is nothingness (no-thing-ness; Madhyamika).

British Period

Understandably, the traditional approaches to education in India were conservative, so much so that they became static and stale. Some Indians, such as those of the Bengal Renaissance, were ready to embrace aspects of Western thought. British-style education was introduced and developed in India in the nineteenth century. In the 1820s, missionary schools were established. In 1833 a governmental committee in Calcutta was charged with establishing an educational policy. The result was a Minute on Education in 1835, which stated a procedure of Western education with English as the medium rather than Indian vernaculars or classical languages.

The intent of the minute and its author, Thomas Babington Macaulay, seems to have been mixed. There was a desire to create a class of Westernized Indians to act as intermediaries between the government and the masses. In the process, the members of this new class would, it was assumed, become Christians as well, eagerly abandoning their native religions once they were educated in Western culture. Altruistic reasons also appear to have been considered. Macaulay, for one, believed it would be of inestimable benefit for India and Indians to be able to deal with the world in English. Indeed, it did have benefits he could not have imagined, producing a cadre of leaders trained in British law. In a sense, the Minute of 1835 was a major early step toward independence over a century later; and for that matter, information technology almost two centuries later.

With the establishment of five universities in major cities in the middle of the century and the increase in primary and secondary schools, political consciousness also increased. The curriculum was Western, and the response was impressive; for example, Calcutta in 1900 was reportedly the largest university in the world, with more than eight thousand students. Further, a number of Indians, including as Gandhi and Nehru, attended university in England.

Yet the Muslim community, for the most part, held back, keeping to the traditional nonsecular education and becoming insulated from change. There were admirable exceptions, but they remained exactly that, and for the most part communal identity became strengthened, most Muslims remaining isolated from an emerging national identity. It should also be noted that the new education was urban-oriented and seldom affected village India.

Independent India

In the days since India's independence, its constitution and subsequent parliamentary acts have developed a national policy and an evolving national system of education with a number of emphases: primary, secondary, higher education; science, technology, vocational; women, depressed groups and castes; rural and adult education; and egalitarian opportunities. The policies have been shaped, reviewed, and reshaped for decades. An ongoing concern has been the "deleterious consequences" of neglect of education. Because of the great concern about education providing uniformity of curriculum and being an instrument of social change, major responsibility was transferred from the states to the central government.

Primary

The central problem at the primary level is not only getting children to go to school but keeping them there as well. Too often, especially in villages—yet among the poor in cities as well—children are viewed as necessary field hands or wage earners; their schooling costs labor rather than bringing in immediate funds needed by the family. Long-range advantages of an education are not viewed as relevant to the day-by-day struggle for survival. Presently in India there is a concerted effort to retain children in school through the age of fourteen. Although children are prohibited by law from working in factories, they can work in cottage industries (handicrafts), agriculture, and restaurants. Admittedly, the laws concerning child labor are often difficult to enforce, and the poor need income from all members of a family (as child beggars in the capital, and other cities, evince). There are problems of school facilities and of staffing. A 1999 report (*PROBE: Public Report on Basic Education for India*) supported by the Center for Development Economics and published by Oxford University Press, relying on a survey done in 1996, estimated that if all the children in the survey had been in school there would have been "113 pupils per *pacca* [baked brick or other finished material, rather than temporary shelter] classroom [and] 68 pupils per appointed teacher." Further, it reported the following percentages:

Blackboard in every classroom	26 percent
Playground	52 percent
Drinking water	59 percent
Toilet	89 percent
Maps and charts	59 percent
Teaching kit	67 percent
Toys	75 percent
Library	77 percent
Musical instrument	85 percent

That last percentage may be an interesting cultural observation.

Secondary

Concerns at this level include "emphasis" on enrolling girls and children from oppressed castes, "particularly in science, commerce, and vocational streams"; and, vocational skills, computer skills, work ethics, and Indian culture. Private and public employers are called upon for support of vocational training and experience. Of course, secondary schools are concerned with preparing students for higher education, but the official emphasis is most definitely on practical fields—for benefit of the student and of the nation.

Higher Education

A major focus, if not *the* major focus, is on "producing teachers for the education system." For academicians, the importance of research is recognized, including in "Indology, the humanities and social sciences." It is interesting that Indology has been pulled out to be separate from humanities and social sciences. Indology is important, as is the study of any ancient civilization; but there is a directive that such study should "relate it to contemporary reality," which is fraught with danger: Indology can be highjacked for narrow chauvinistic religious purposes, and the constitutional secular base of education could be seriously eroded—particularly when the curriculum has been centralized and nationalized at the lower levels. Thus, the *Christian Science Monitor* on April 25, 2001, reported that a standard history text written by one of India's most respected historians had after many years been replaced in high schools with one promoting "patriotism" and "values education." A column in the *New York Times* (December 30, 2002) headlined the procedure of revamping school textbooks to reflect politically and religiously dominated government policy as "Hijacking Indian History"; that is, subordinating academics to politics. A professor at Delhi University saw the move as "a conflict between those who want to define India as a Hindu society and those who think it must be a secular society," which reflects the electoral turmoil present today in Indian politics.

Nevertheless, higher education is more concerned with emphasizing technology than Indology at the approximately 150 universities and 5,000 colleges in India; the latter include a large number of technological institutes. In addition, "open university and distance learning" are fostered as alternatives for place-bound and other students (e.g., fully employed) restricted from attending classes on campuses. The concept of "rural university," based upon the innovative educational concepts of M. K. Gandhi, is under consideration for development.

The Indian Institute of Technology (IIT)

The CBS News magazine *60 Minutes* in an episode telecast March 2, 2003, characterized the Indian Institute of Technology as "maybe the most important university you've never heard of." Bill Gates of Microsoft has termed it "an incredible institution" and "a world-class institute" (*India Abroad,* January 21, 2003).

IIT is a system of seven campuses, the first of which was established some fifty years ago, with the goal, as enunciated by Prime Minister Jawaharlal Nehru, "to provide scientists and technologists of the highest caliber who would engage in research, design, and development to help building the nation toward self-reliance in her technology needs."

IIT has more than fulfilled its directive. It has turned out graduates who have become successful not only in the technologies, but in education, business, and service careers. They have given back to their alma maters as well, in terms of millions and millions of dollars. Many of these graduates are in the United States but have kept professional contact with technological centers in India, some helping to establish Indian subsidiaries for their U.S. companies. As one graduate put it, "This has resulted in millions of dollars of new foreign direct investment in India, which has created thousands of technical and non-technical jobs" (Ram Kelkar in *India Abroad,* January 17, 2003). The professional and personal contributions of IIT graduates has been of advantage to both the Indian and U.S. economies. Indeed, such is the appreciation for IIT importance and success that a two-day celebration of its fiftieth anniversary was held in Cupertino, California, with Bill Gates and the U.S. ambassador to India, Robert Blackwill, among the guest speakers.

Something needs to be said about the pluses and the minuses in regard to technology and technological education in India. As stated previously, technology can be seen as deepening the socioeconomic wedge between city and village. In 2001, however, the government's technology ministry in collaboration with the Massachusetts Institute of Technology developed a research center, Media Lab Asia (MLA), to address the matter of extending technology into rural areas, including wireless handheld computers designed for those without formal education; for use by nurses to monitor basic medical needs; to teach literacy; and to collect rural economic data, among other purposes. The government has advanced $13 million into MLA, and private companies have made investments into the project. The prime minister has included it as "one of the government's top 15 priorities" (*Christian Science Monitor,* May 1, 2003).

Then there is a matter that is a decades-old problem: the brain drain, or how to keep scientists and others educated in the technology industry at home—or to bring them home—especially when the lure of better pay, comforts of Western living, and more highly sophisticated equipment and working conditions are so tempting. The situation has had a severely adverse effect on India's economy. Anthony P. D'Costa in the *News Tribune* (Tacoma, Washington, June 1, 2003) has cautioned that "rapid information-technology growth might bypass India's poor," that globalization is largely responsible for brain drain, and that "knee-jerk responses by the United States and Western Europe" could severely set back India's achievement in software exports—from less than $100 million in 1987–1988 to almost $10 billion in 2003, with the possibility of $50 billion by 2008. By "knee-jerk responses" he means in large part state governments in the United States attempting "to limit outsourcing of government information technology contracts to India" in order to protect their local companies. Similarly, columnist Thomas Friedman quoted an Indian business executive: "It's that you want all your products marketed globally . . . but you don't want any jobs to go." Friedman notes further, "what's going around is also coming around"; that is, outsourcing to India "isn't just taking American jobs, it's also making them." (*New York Times,* February 26, 2004). In short, the urban-rural economic contrast may be creating an elite, but much of that elite goes abroad after Indian rupees have paid for their education, and globalization can beget a protectionist reaction at local levels.

In considerable contrast—although certainly more so symbolically than quantitatively—is the example of Naresh Trehan, a heart surgeon who left India in 1969 "and by the mid-1980s was earning over $1.5 million a year as a Manhattan heart surgeon." He returned to New Delhi and, with funding from an industrialist, established the Escorts Heart Institute and Research Center in 1988, a large (325 beds, nine operating theaters) and complex (satellite operating rooms in five cities) institution (*New York Times,* May 18, 2003).

This story contains a poignant observation: When Dr. Trehan returned to India with his family, "he found that ethics and family values that shaped his youth had been corroded"—corruption was rampant, eminent families were squabbling over money; what he had failed to find in America he found disappearing in India.

Women and Oppressed Groups

An avowed purpose of the current national education plan is improvement of the situation of women, through calculated intervention and "a well-conceived edge in favour of women," including "social engineering." "Incentives" for oppressed caste families are designed to keep their children in school, and teachers are recruited from such groups. Tribals, minorities, and the handicapped are also focused upon for special programs. Finally, adult education is stressed to promote literacy—including beyond that of the mere level of reading—through a variety of means: employers, unions, libraries, media, learners' groups, and programs of distance learning. The traditional barriers in regard to women do exist—albeit probably not as much as in other even more traditional societies (e.g., Saudi Arabia). It is not yet possible to measure the degree of success of the national education plan in achieving its goals, in part because of the political implications involved.

Some Statistics

The available statistics in regard to education in India can be confusing and incomplete. Tables and charts will have blanks or the initials NA (for "not available"), sometimes at places that make comparisons and conclusions as to progress difficult if not impossible. This situation, which is reflective of the complexities of Indian society and political geography, is bound to improve with India's remarkable advances in technology. Nevertheless, some figures provided by the government are of interest.

Table 3.1   Percentages for Years of Schooling

	15+ Years	12–14 Years	7–11 Years	3–6 Years	Less than 3 Years
1971	0.6%	2.7%	6.0%	20.0%	70.5%
1991	1.8%	4.2%	11.0%	23.7%	56.7%

Source: Educational statistics compiled by Government of India Department of Education.

What is encouraging is that the percentages are down for the last category, whereas for all others they are up. Figures for women only are considerably less (except in the last category), by a third to a half. For the types of educational institutions available in India, see Table 3.1.

Table 3.2 Types and Number of Educational Institutions in India, 1961 and 1998

	1961	1998
1. Pre-Primary Schools	1,909	41,788
2. Primary/Junior Basic Schools	330,399	610,763
3. Middle/Senior Basic Schools	49,663	185,506
4. High/Higher Secondary Schools	17,257	102,721
5. Universities/Institutions Deemed to Be Universities/Institutions of National Importance	45	229
6. Degree Standard and above General Educational Institutions	967	7,199
7. Degree Standard and above Professional and Technical Institutions for:		
(a) Agriculture and Forestry	35	90[1]
(b) Engineering, Technology, and Architecture	111	607[2]
(c) Medicine (includes Allopathy, Homeopathy, Ayurveda, and Unani)	133	437[1]
(d) Veterinary Science	17	46[1]
(e) Teacher Training	147	848
8. Below Degree-Level Professional/ Vocational and Technical Institutions	4,145	6,561

[1] 1996 (latest available)
[2] 1997 (latest available)

Source: Educational statistics compiled by Government of India Department of Education.

As Table 3.2 shows, the most significant increase has been in categories 1 through 4; however, it should be noted that the population went from 439 million in the 1961 census to just over a billion in the 2001 census.

The strong emphasis on teacher education is reflected in category 6 of the table. Corresponding figures for the number of teachers in several categories from 1991 on are unfortunately not available; in categories 2 through 4 they are:

	1961	1998
Category 2:	741,515	1,871,542
Category 3:	345,228	1,218,803
Category 4:	296,305	1,521,186

Gender distribution for teachers in these three categories is almost two males to one female. One can assume that the unavailability of figures for the pre-primary schools is due to a considerably less formal structure than for the other three categories.

The 2001 census counted 1,027,015,247 people as of March 1. Literacy figures were:

General population: 566,714,995 (65.38 percent)
Male: 339,969,048 (75.85 percent)
Female: 226,745,947 (54.16 percent)

For comparison, the 1991 percentages are 52.21 percent in the general population, 64.13 percent among males, and 39.39 percent among females. Results vary by states; for example, Kerala has about 90 percent literacy, Bihar less than half that.

Summation

In sum, like most traditional societies, India has moved education from a reserve for the elite to egalitarianism; that is, stressing the intrinsic worth of each citizen in spite of social inequalities resulting from caste and the modern economic system. Whatever the ideals, the system has central planning and curricula. Further, the Indian government is by intent and design interventionist. Although intervention on behalf of uplift for women and oppressed groups is possible, so is intervention to direct curricula toward nonacademic purposes. For that matter, this sort of problem exists elsewhere too, as with U.S. school boards.

RELIGION

Hinduism is not merely the largest religion in India; it is the pervasive culture. It is a way of life that underlies and permeates the social fabric, rural and urban, traditional and modern. It has had tremendous influence outside of India as well, including on figures such as Arthur Schopenhauer (1788–1860), Ralph Waldo Emerson (1803–1882), and Aldous Huxley (1894–1963).

Four major religions originated in India, and four others (which have had impact in India far beyond their numbers) came from outside. A percentage breakdown is as follows: For the Indian religions, Hinduism, 82 percent; Sikhism, 2 percent; and Jainism and Buddhism, less than 1 percent each. For those religions that came into India from elsewhere, Islam, 12 percent; Christianity, 2.5 percent; Zoroastrianism and Judaism, less than 1 percent each. A number of "new religions," usually offshoots of Hinduism, have surfaced, primarily for import to the West, and generally are of little concern in India. Those religions that were brought into India from outside—Christianity, Judaism, Zoroastrianism, and Islam—will be dealt with first, and will be so only in terms of their Indian context. Hinduism, as the major cultural influence, will be treated in some depth; Jainism, Buddhism, and Sikhism less so.

Religions Entering from Outside

Christianity

Christianity came into India almost in layers. In the first century the apostle Thomas reached the southeast coast of India, made conversions, and was allegedly martyred and buried in the area of present-day Madras (Chennai). There is evidence of Syrian or Nestorian Christianity in the area from the sixth century on. Roman Catholicism arrived in Goa with the Portuguese, particularly the Jesuit Francis Xavier (1506–1552).

Tribal activists shout slogans while holding placards during a sit-in protest against Pope John Paul II's visit to New Delhi November 5, 1999. The activists were protesting against what they said were forcible religious conversions by Christian missionaries. (Reuters/Corbis)

Conversion was directed toward lower castes (as it was also by later missionaries), and intermarriage between Portuguese sailors and native women was encouraged (a practice not continued by subsequent European missionaries). As a result, there are prominent Indians with Portuguese names, such as the labor leader and minister of defense, George Fernandes.

Protestant denominations have made strides among tribals and low castes. At first the East India Company, which had control over British India until 1858, discouraged missionary activity, fearing it would disrupt its commercial pursuits. At times the government of independent India also has discouraged missionaries and prohibited some missionary activities. Although missionaries have provided quality education and medical care, many have also been culturally insensitive, referring to non-Christian religions in derogatory terms. There is a basic religious dichotomy involved, which Muslims faced before Christians: Hinduism is a relativistic religion, whereas Islam and Christianity are absolutist; that is, Hinduism is generally tolerant toward other religions, not considering them to be false (in spite of some recent politicalization). Further, missionaries are often viewed as remnants of the colonial era and mentality.

In many ways Christians have been assimilated into Indian culture, but there also has been violence directed toward missionaries. Some politicized fundamentalist Hindus have called for reconversion of Christians and Muslims whom they view as the descendants of Hindus. Because many if not most Christians are tribal or low caste, particularly in rural areas, reconversion has not been taken seriously by society at large. Christianity has become part of the diverse cultural milieu: Goa is a prime example of cultural fusion, Indian with a strong Portuguese flavor. Wealthy urban Hindus often send their children to prestigious Christian schools, apparently without concern about conversion.

Judaism

The number of Jewish Indians is estimated today at 0.0005 percent of the total population, which is a decline historically, perhaps primarily for reasons of emigration. Although the numbers are few, their history is long. Some sources put the arrival of Jews in India before that of Christians. Their presence is strongest in Kerala, a state of remarkable diversity in southwest India, and upward to Bombay (Mumbai). The preponderance on the west coast is likely due to ancient trading ties with the eastern Mediterranean. There also had been Jewish merchants visiting Calcutta not long after its founding. A small community, established in 1798, grew from fifteen people to almost two thousand by 1900. Businesses and schools were established, and the community became an active part of the larger community. Today there are only about a hundred Jews left in Calcutta, with the largest depletion coming after independence and the founding of Israel.

Zoroastrianism

Little is known about Zoroaster (Zarathustra), whose life has been dated as early as 1500 B.C.E. and as late as 600 B.C.E. He is considered to be a descendant of the Aryans who migrated into Iran and India. Nor is much known about the spread of the prophet's religion, although the doctrine of the cosmic battle between Good and Evil is well-known, as is the sacredness of the primal elements (hence, dead bodies are neither buried nor burned, but exposed for vultures on the famed Towers of Silence).

In the seventh century C.E. and following, large numbers of Zoroastrians fled Iran after the Islamic conquest. Today they are located largely in the central western states of Maharashtra and Gujarat, principally in Bombay (Mumbai). Although only 0.01 percent of the population of India (with estimates ranging as low as 75,000), and with numbers decreasing, they have been extremely influential in commerce and the arts. They are a tightly knit community, and most are very wealthy. They are known as Parsis (from Persia), and have a substantial role in Indian industry, as evinced by the giant Tata corporation.

They may well be an endangered community. The *New York Times* (April 23, 2003) has reported that whereas 1,000 Parsis die annually, only 300 to 400 are born each year. Further, one of three (in Bombay) marries outside the faith; children of mixed marriages are not accepted as Parsis. As to be expected, some are challenging that more orthodox interpretation, but so far without success.

Islam

People from the eastern Mediterranean had trading relations with the west coast of India seemingly since time immemorial. Among these merchants were Arabs, including from pre-

Islamic times. That contact continued after the Islamic conquest of the Arab world.

In the northern part of India, contact consisted of raids from central Asia in the early eleventh century and conquest in the late twelfth century. The advent of the Delhi Sultanate in 1206 marked the end of Hindu political domination, which was replaced by Muslims of a different ethnicity. These invaders were not about to become absorbed as had been previous groups. The new rulers were determined to keep their faith free from contamination by contact with the beliefs of their subjects, who vastly outnumbered them. They even kept themselves aloof from those Indians who converted to Islam. Through the centuries adjustments were made, of course (most notably under the great Mughal Akbar, r. 1556–1605), and some very important cultural developments resulted from the Muslim-Hindu contact, notably in the arts and even in religion.

Nevertheless, the two communities remained distinct and apart. Indeed, in some ways the only factor uniting Muslims in the subcontinent (other than their religion) was and is their concern about the intentions of the Hindu majority; conversely, the uniting factor among the diverse communities within Hinduism is often their antipathy in regard to the long Muslim rule and their distrust of Muslim loyalties. The violence between Hindus and Muslims that erupts all too frequently within India, and the acrimonious relations between India and Pakistan, are to a great degree the result of the political domination of Muslims over Hindus in north India from the early thirteenth century to the early nineteenth. While the majority of Muslims in India have been and are Sunni (as in Islam itself), Sunni-Shia antipathy generally did not reach the level that it has in the twentieth and twenty-first centuries worldwide. However, the last great Mughal, Aurangzeb (r. 1658–1707), is noted for attacking the Shia sect (as well as for his attacks on Hindu temples).

Differences within the Islamic world were reflected in

India, having impact on Muslim life in regard to education, lifestyle, politics, and relationships with the majority Hindu community. Such differences in outlook exist today, and perhaps can most clearly be seen in the election of A. P. J. Abdul Kalam in July 2002 to become the twelfth president of India. A seventy-year-old nuclear scientist, with somewhat of the aura of a folk hero, he is the third Muslim selected as president (a largely, but not entirely, ceremonial role). His selection by the ruling Hindu nationalist party (the election was almost a rubber-stamping by parliament and state legislatures) has been criticized as a ploy for securing some secular and Muslim support. He is also an ethnic Tamil (from south rather than north India), which removes him considerably from the machinations and communal politics of the capital, as does his immersion in scientific studies and his breadth of cultural interests beyond Islam (such as in the Hindu text the Bhagavad Gita). In short, he is viewed suspiciously and disapprovingly by militant and fundamentalist Muslims.

Although historically there was little interaction between the conservative cultures of Islam and Hinduism, there was often significant contact at the fringes, particularly through mystical devotees of each religion. By its nonrational approach, mysticism tends to transcend orthodox creed and sectarian differences. So, Muslim *sufis* and Hindu *bhaktas* were drawn to one another, resulting in cultural synthesis in certain poets and religious figures, such as Kabir (born about 1400), who decried orthodoxy and is claimed by both Hindus and Muslims. (Thus, legend has it that when he died his Muslim disciples wanted his body buried and Hindu disciples wanted it cremated. When they came for the body, in its place was a pile of flowers; the Hindus took half to burn, the Muslims half to bury.) Guru Nanak (1469–1539), the founder of Sikhism (itself an attempt at fusion), also came from this tradition.

Another point at which fringe elements of the cultures met was that of language. It was necessary for the troops of the con-

Precursor to the more famous Taj Majal, Humayun's tomb in Delhi is an example of Indo-Islamic architecture. (Corel)

querors to communicate with the populace, especially in the Delhi area. The result was Urdu, a word that means "camp" (and is cognate with "horde"). It was indeed a camp-language, with Hindi grammatical structure but a largely Persian and Arabic vocabulary. Through the centuries a rich literature was developed with an Indian base but strong Islamic influence.

There were also central cultural areas showing strong mutual influence: painting, music, dance, and architecture. Pre-Islamic India had a tradition of painting going back at least to the Buddhist cave paintings at Ajanta (fourth to seventh centuries C.E.), a series of fresco-like wall paintings of Buddhist themes that yet focused on the everyday life of the nobility. Interestingly, one of these is a picture of a picture on a wall. There also were parchment paintings in the Jain religious tradition. Through the early Mughals, Persian miniatures entered the Indian tradition, and several schools of Hindu and courtly miniatures developed. Northern Indian music and dance were also influenced by Islamic

The Taj Mahal was built in the seventeenth century by Shah Jahan to honor his wife, who died in childbirth in 1632. The construction lasted twenty-two years, and the Taj Mahal remains one of the most beautiful buildings in the world and an outstanding example of Mughal architecture. (Corel)

tradition, developing into styles separate from south Indian music and dance.

The most famous example of Indo-Islamic architecture is the Taj Mahal. The Taj could not have developed in Hindu India, for it is a tomb. There are many such structures throughout northern India and Pakistan. There are in addition forts, palaces, and mosques; the famed and beautiful Red Fort in Delhi is a combination of all three architectural types. The essential character of such architecture is Islamic, but with interesting features that make it distinctly *Indo*-Islamic, such as the *chata,* an umbrella-like protuberance, one or more of which crown a structure.

Near Agra is Fathepur Sikri, an assortment of buildings designed as a court by the great Mughal Akbar, which had to be abandoned for lack of water. Also needing mention is the

Jama Masjid, near the Red Fort of Delhi, which is the largest mosque in South Asia. The builder of the Taj, the Red Fort, the Jama Masjid, and other marvels was Akbar's grandson, Shah Jahan (r. 1627–1658).

Indigenous Religions

Hinduism

Hinduism is at the heart of Indian culture and history. It has been described as a complex mix of sects and cults. The word *Hindu* was used by Greeks and Persians to refer to the people who lived beyond the Indus river and related to the name of the country, India, which in centuries past was often referred to as Hindustan (or at least the northern part was).

Hinduism lacks many characteristics Westerners usually think of as pertaining to religion and contains features that would seem alien in any religious sense. It has no founder or date of origin, such as can be discerned in Buddhism, Christianity, and Islam. It has no revealed scripture (the Vedas are foundational to Hinduism but are considered as "heard" rather than "revealed"; that is, humans discovered them—much in the way that Newton discovered gravity—rather than God revealing them). It has no central church or council to determine what is proper belief and what is not. It has been described as orthopraxy rather than orthodoxy, meaning that correct behavior is emphasized rather than correct belief; and in that way it is social and is expressed through the caste system (which is described in the next chapter). It is thus extremely tolerant as to belief and generally intolerant in regard to wrong behavior.

To make matters more difficult, Hinduism has historically been inclusive rather than exclusive—it has incorporated much and excluded little. It has no Homer or Hesiod to put the gods in order, and it has accepted layer upon layer of gods without dismissing earlier layers. It would be as though Christianity had kept the Greek, Roman, and Norse gods. It is relativistic rather than absolutist: one's chosen deity does not invalidate other deities. Hinduism is polytheistic—containing many gods—yet also monistic; that is, there is one ultimate Absolute—or God—which underlies the varied manifestations. As human beings are but finite, we cannot "know" the infinite. Thus, no one has a monopoly on religious truth, and so followers must be directed toward finite manifestations; that is, particular gods and goddesses.

There are two fundamental principles common to Hindus. The first is rebirth. Just as surely as one is destined to die, so one is destined to be reborn. What people are reborn into is the relative world, the world of opposites, of multiplicity, of change, of uncertainty. The second principle is that there is an Absolute, which underlies the relative world, a Oneness beyond the multiplicity, the world of rebirth. Because that Absolute or Oneness is foundational to the world of relativity in which we live, it also permeates it: God is here and now. The word for the relative world is *maya*—a term that means "measurement"; and, of course, that would be space and time. One of the many terms used to indicate the Absolute (it can only be indicated, for the infinite can never be "defined") is *rta*, a word related to English "right" and "straight." Rta implies a harmony, a moral purpose to the universe (and hence, to existence).

So one is reborn into maya. The process of rebirth—actually the cycle of birth, death, rebirth, and so on—is *samsara* (literally, "going around"). What fuels samsara is *karma*—action and its results (or, behavior); karma also determines one's status in the reborn life—as you sow, so shall you reap. It is a law of cause and effect, not only for this existence but for the next one as well. The determiner—or litmus paper, as it were—is *dharma,* which perhaps is best rendered in English as duty, or moral duty. In a sense, it is derived from rta. It is how one follows and does one's dharma that determines one's karma; rta is the cosmic nature, dharma the individual's response in regard to it—a moral response of correct behavior.

In addition to the karmic character or personality, the *atman* is reborn into maya; or, put another way, undergoes the process of samsara. Sometimes atman is translated as "soul" or "self"; both terms are misleading. Whereas one's soul or self is considered in Western faiths to be one's own, such is not the case with atman. Atman is that spark of the Divine, of the Absolute, which is within the karmic character that constitutes an individual. The atman is uncreated and is actually one with the Absolute; that is, it is only in the relative world (maya) that the atman seems to be separate from other atmans and from the Absolute. There may seem to be billions of atmans, but actually there is only one, uncreated, and when stripped of the karmic stuff that encases it, it is pure and co-essential with the One Absolute.

The point is to break the chain of samsara so that the union of the atman with the Absolute is realized. That event is called *moksha,* release or liberation from the cycle of rebirth. The atman does not go any "where" when moksha occurs, for it transcends space-time (hence, there is no "where" to go to) and is free from maya and samsara. An analogy might be release from jail, wherein it is not where one goes that is important—it is the getting out of jail. But one must not conclude that samsara and maya are bad; they are means to the greater end. Most important, they are not self-substantial, their reality is only relative. A mirage, for example, has its own (relative) reality and must be seen as such; it is not real water in the desert, but as a mirage it is real; that is, it is a real mirage. Similarly, maya's reality is relative; all is not what it appears to be.

Modifications of these tenets exist in various philosophical schools. The principles provide the structure for Hindu thought, and although not of direct concern to the average Hindu, they permeate the culture just as surely as complex Christian concepts permeate the religious atmosphere of a

Greek or Mexican village. This approach to enlightenment or release is the path of wisdom. There is also a path of ritual— living one's life in a ritual manner, similar to "good works." But as in most religions, the most popular approach or path is that of devotion, wherein one forges a relationship with a god. That god is both separate from and one with God—that is, it (or he, or she) is a manifestation of the Absolute. There are different types of such relationships, depending upon the individual devotee and the particular god to be worshiped.

The Hindu gods and goddesses are difficult to deal with in an organized way. There are too many of them to note here, and regional variations often confuse the specific personality. Sometimes one can have multiple personalities; Krishna, for instance, is worshiped as divine babe, lover, hero, and sage. Furthermore, a god like Siva can show up in different ways and with different functions, sometimes in a contradictory manner; he is ascetic and yet is a fertility god. None of this should bother or even concern devotees, although they would be well aware that their own particular chosen deity is but one of many possible choices.

At risk of considerable simplification, a sort of ordering can be made. There are the ancient Indo-European gods brought in by the Aryans. At the same time there seem to have been antecedents in the Indus civilization of other gods, particularly Siva. There are folk and regional gods, some with particular functions such as Sitala, a goddess who protects children from smallpox. And then there are the major deities who have a pan-India basis, and lesser gods who are attached to them. The monkey god Hanuman is attached to Rama, an incarnation of Vishnu. The elephant-headed Ganesh, or Ganapati, is mythologically associated with Siva. Yet both can and do stand alone (e.g., Ganesh is the remover of obstacles, consulted before journeys and examinations).

The major groupings are around Vishnu and Siva. Vishnu has several incarnations, most important of which are Krishna and Rama. Vishnu and his avatars are blue-skinned.

Siva temple in Tamil Nadu (Corel)

Siva, who is gray-skinned, has relationships with numerous goddesses who can and do stand independently as well (yet are considered essential to Siva's mythology and being) and are each considered as Mahadevi, or the Great Goddess. These include Parvati, Durga, Kali, and Annapurna. The mythology of these deities can become confused (and confusing), as can the art and poetry devoted to them.

Not surprisingly, pilgrimage is important in Hindu devotion. Millennia old, pilgrimage may have started from observances at river fords. Pilgrimages can be periodic, a *mela* or "festival" held every few years, or once a year. It can simply be a holy place one visits at no particular time (e.g., Varanasi, or Banaras, on the Ganges). The benefits gained (e.g., a bathing in the Ganges at Varanasi "can wash away the accumulated sins of a lifetime") often seem contradictory to the theory of karma, but such can be rationalized by the commitment and intent of the devotee.

The history of Hinduism is almost as complex as the religion itself. There is not a precise starting point. It developed from the contact of two different cultures, the Dravidian and the Aryan. The Aryans brought with them and continued to develop in India the Vedas, four collections of hymns and texts preserved through memorization. Two major epics, the *Mahabharata* and the *Ramayana,* have features similar to other Indo-European epics but have been extensively worked over for religious purposes. The lengthy *Mahabharata* includes an eighteen-chapter poem, the Bhagavad Gita, a very popular treatise on duty (dharma) and devotion delivered by the god Krishna to Arjuna, a warrior and sort of Hindu "everyman." Both epics are sources for folk and classical literature, and the *Ramayana* has been adapted into every major vernacular, sometimes with endings different than in the original version. In the recent past both have been made into lengthy and extremely popular television series. The cultural impact of these epics cannot be overstated. Philosophical and devotional texts proliferated during the development of Hinduism;

The Golden Temple in Amritsar, the Sikh holy place (Library of Congress)

poetry, art, and music expressed religious themes, and the mythology are tied to the religion in the way that myths were tied to Greek and Norse religions.

In addition, there are regional aspects of Hinduism. The phrase "great and little traditions" implies tradition and texts common to all Hinduism (the "great" tradition), and those that are merely regional (the "little" tradition). But these are not in opposition. There is a tendency to rationalize, to include the regional within the greater scope of Hinduism. A regional deity may become associated with Vishnu or Siva, or even equated with him. Perhaps this can most clearly be seen in the plethora of goddesses considered as Mahadevi, or the Great Goddess. As in the philosophy, there is an attempt to forge an underlying unity out of the diversity. As previously stated, Hinduism is polytheistic, but it is also monistic.

Finally, a word about contemporary movements, many of

which had presence and influence in the United States and other Western countries from the 1920s through the 1970s. Often such are not considered to be Hindu by more mainstream Hindus. One group has even been termed as "Protestants in exotic garb." Here the strength of the religion is also its weakness: there is no official way to declare a sect or cult to be "non-Hindu." Perhaps of greater importance is the fact that popular art—calendars, prints, statuettes, videos—have enabled common people to have their own religious collections and to pursue their devotions as they wish and at their convenience.

Jainism

One of the smallest religions in the world, with about 5 or 6 million devotees, or one-half of 1 percent of the population of India, Jainism is yet also a major religion, if for no other reason than because of its antiquity. It is probably as old as Hinduism and may well date back to the Indus civilization. There is a tendency in the West to consider it a break-off from Hinduism, just as is Buddhism, but such thought confuses the respective roles of the Buddha and Mahavira, a contemporary who is often considered to be the founder of Jainism. He is not, and he did not claim to be. He considered himself a *tirthankara,* a ford-maker, providing a ford across the river of samsara; that is, an escape from the cycle of rebirth. Like the Buddha, however, he came from the aristocratic caste rather than the priestly caste. Mahavira referred to himself as the twenty-fourth in a series of tirthankaras. The twenty-third was Parsva, 250 years prior to Mahavira. That Jainism predates Mahavira is accepted by scholars.

Mahavira is a title for Vardhamana, who revived an ancient tradition that came to be known as Jainism. The title means "great hero," and he is also referred to as the Jina, or conqueror (of the senses and karma). The name *Jain* (or *Jaina*) is a derivative of Jina; hence, a follower of the Jina, or Mahavira. A schism developed between the "white clad" and the "sky clad," the latter referring to monks, who in renouncing all their possessions, go naked. The purpose of Jainism is to attain release from samsara, the cycle of rebirth. The faith is austere and highly ethical. It contains extreme emphasis on karma, and on *ahimsa,* usually translated as "nonviolence," which term does not quite convey the power of the concept. In Jainism, ahimsa is far more than merely passive refraining from violence; the word literally means "not having the desire to do violence."

In Jain belief, *all* action results in karmic bondage, which is like matter adhering to the *jiva* (the basic spiritual unit in an individual). Karma from good deeds has little, if any, lasting effect, but that resulting from violence is especially harmful. Ethical conduct can lessen the accumulation of karma. The karmic crud needs to be burned off (like burning off fat or calories from the body) through austerities and renunciation; especially helpful is to become a renouncer (monk or nun). At moksha, or liberation, when the karmic matter that weighs down the jiva is burned off, the jiva rises to the top of the universe, where it floats in infinite bliss. Means of livelihood are restricted; for example, one cannot be a farmer, for plowing would injure worms. Many Jains have become very successful merchants and bankers.

Jains have spread throughout India, but the greatest concentration is in west-central India. Mahatma Gandhi was influenced by Jains; he was raised in Gujarat, and his mother had a cousin who was a Jain monk. He may have been influenced by the Jain doctrine of ahimsa, although it is also present in Hindu and Buddhist thought and his perception of ahimsa differed considerably from the Jain doctrine. He stated that he thought it a crime to feed ants when people are starving, and when criticized for ordering a rabid dog to be killed, answered that it would be greater violence not to do so. Jains have founded remarkable animal hospitals, but they will not have terminally ill animals put down, which is viewed as detrimental for the animals' spiritual well-being. Suffering

Jain priests at Ranakpur Temple in Rajasthan (Corel)

burns off karma, and not affording a beast the opportunity for getting rid of as much of it as possible will hinder the chances to improve its lot in the next life.

Jains are, of course, vegetarian; but even plant life is respected. The ultimate act is self-starvation, which is not viewed as violence but as restraint. Mahavira starved to death at the age of seventy-two. Chandragupta Maurya (r. c. 321–297) is alleged to have renounced his throne to become a Jain monk and also starved himself to death at the age of seventy-two.

The relationship between Jains and Hindus is of interest. Although a distinct faith, Jainism is in many ways part of the greater Hindu community. Prince Ilango Adigal, author of the Tamil classic the *Shilappadikaram* (*The Anklet*), fifth century C.E., was a Jain who was brother of a south Indian king, himself a Hindu.

Buddhism

Buddhism is an offshoot of Hinduism, contemporary with and competitive to the resurgent Jainism of Mahavira. The sixth and fifth centuries B.C.E. represent an era of great intellectual, philosophical, and spiritual development throughout much of Eurasia. Buddhism and the resurgent Jainism are just two of the new movements or schools of thought of that time; it is that they survived, while others died away or were absorbed back into Hinduism. In contrast to Jainism, Buddhism became a strong missionary religion expanding far beyond its homeland, in which it eventually disappeared. Jainism, in contrast, did not expand beyond India and has had a continuous history within it.

Siddhartha Gautama was born about 560 B.C.E., the son of the leader of the Sakyas, a group on the periphery of the Gangetic plain in an area that is now in Nepal. The stories of his luxurious early life may be somewhat exaggerated, but he is considered to have been a prince and is accordingly sometimes referred to as Sakyamuni, sage of the Sakyas. As a youth he was pampered and protected from the unpleasantries of life. Four unexpected sights greatly moved him: he saw a sick man, an old man, a corpse, and a monk. The first three were each a great shock; the fourth he viewed as a path he should follow. Abandoning wife and baby (Mahavira is said to have done the same), he left home to seek enlightenment. It should be noted that the marriage was most likely political in nature, Siddhartha's wife and son would have been well-looked after, both later became followers, and this is a legend meant more to make a point than to be taken negatively.

Seeking enlightenment, he tried rigid austerities, which he rejected as being damaging to the body and the mind. When he did achieve enlightenment through long and arduous meditation (a process most people today would consider austere), he became a buddha, which is the past form of a verb meaning to wake up; he was the awakened one, the enlightened one, in short, the Buddha.

He had a very straightforward, even simple, message: *duhkha* (explained below) exists; it has a cause; because it has a cause, it can have a cessation; and the manner in which it can be overcome is by following his prescription, the eight-fold path, which is essentially right wisdom, right conduct, and right resolve.

In Buddhist thought, karma is the cause of all existence. The entire universe is karma, not a thing but a happening. The cosmos and life are ongoing events resulting from cause and effect (or, more pedantically, antecedents). What results is duhkha; or, more precisely, it is our apprehension of the process, and our involvement in it, which leads to duhkha.

It is essential to understand the nature of duhkha. Nineteenth-century Western scholars liked to translate it as "pain" or "suffering." These terms seem somewhat melodramatic today. Perhaps each generation needs to find its own equivalent, in relation to its own experience, for life is marked by duhkha. An existentialist might use the term "malaise." After September 11, 2001, "anxiety" might be a good term. "Unsatisfactoriness" has been used, but it seems too unnatural. From Western philosophers has come "disease," or *"dis-ease."*

The word was used in reference to a cart with an axle skewed or the hub out of line. Indeed, duhkha can be like taking a trip in a car whose wheels need aligning; it is uncomfortable, but it can be fixed. In this way, duhkha also can be fixed. One has first to come to terms with the *process* of karma. To a considerable extent it is the way we look at things; indeed, there really are no "things" in any permanent sense, only events; every "thing" changes. We tend to deal with dynamic reality as though "it" were an "it" and were stable. The events that make up existence—which we call things—consist of smaller events, which are part of larger events and are all interrelated and codependent. Thus, one would not speak of the universe as a thing; one would speak of it as an ongoing event, a process that *is* the universe. The point is, every "thing" (i.e., event) is transitory and related holistically to all other "things"—events. In an absolute sense there is no such thing as a thing; existence is no-thing (which should not be interpreted nihilistically; it is merely a description).

Buddhism rejects the Hindu concept of atman; it speaks of *anatman*—there is no atman. But anatman should not be taken as a substitute for atman; it does not exist. Anatman is descriptive term. It is not that I was Napoleon in a previous existence; rather, he and I are part of the same process. The particle, say the physicists, behaves like a wave; a "thing" is an "event." The only reality is process, which is what life and the cosmos interrelatedly are.

Buddhism had considerable historical and social influence in early India. Kings who were not Buddhist became patrons, and the Buddha was highly respected as a person. The Buddha himself was a product of the Upanishadic age, but he went beyond mere philosophical inquiry and denounced priestly ritual and the Vedas themselves. He popularized monastic renunciation, which was a direct challenge to the Hindu belief in stages of life with their responsibilities (treated in the next chapter). His call became far more missionary than Mahavira's. For these reasons, though the Buddha himself became a popular legend—even tied to Hinduism as one of the avatars of Vishnu—the religion became estranged from Hinduism. Yet it was responsible for architectural advances and educational centers. What may well have been its early strength, monasteries, became its Achilles heel. The monasteries became too visible and too powerful. Like the much-later Henry VIII in England, rulers began to covet their wealth and to resent their power. Most fatally, they made easy targets for the zealous invading Muslims from about 1000 C.E. on.

Buddhism reappeared in India only in the twentieth century. It represents today about 0.7 percent of the population, a far cry from ancient times. Its reentry was in part political and in part social, and to only a small degree spiritual (with the obvious exception of refugee Tibetans). The prominent leader of India's untouchables (Dalits), B. R. Ambedkar, declared himself Buddhist and thus set an example for many of his followers; however, the act could be seen as more one of renouncing caste-oriented Hinduism than of embracing a new faith.

It must be stressed that Buddhism remains very popular in other parts of Asia, and its outlook has found interest among non-Buddhist psychologists, physicists, and cosmologists. Its art, literature, and architecture have had worldwide impact.

Sikhism

Sikhs account for only about 2 percent of the population of India, but they seem ubiquitous, at least in north India. Largely Punjabi, they are tall, the males bearded and wearing turbans. They have been prominent in government and the military, in business and virtually all walks of life in India, Canada, Britain, and the United States.

Sikhism came out of the Hindu-Muslim cultural contact among certain spiritual figures. There was an intent to take the best characteristics of each religion, rejecting unfavorable features—although this theory is now rejected by some scholars. Regardless, Sikhism became and is a separate religion.

In about the year 1500 a Hindu named Nanak (1469–1539) had a spiritual experience that led him to wander, seeking religious knowledge from various sources. He became the first of ten gurus in the Sikh faith. The fifth guru, Arjan (1563–1606), built the Golden Temple at Amritsar, the center of the Sikh faith. He was martyred (as was the ninth guru, Tegh Bahadur, 1621–1675), and Sikhism became embroiled in Mughal politics. Akbar had treated Sikhs kindly, but he died in 1605. Later Mughals viewed them as a threat, and persecution tended to unite the community even more tightly, and to militarize it, with defense of the faith becoming a top commandment.

History continued to embroil Sikhs in politics, with their becoming aligned with Hindus in the bloody partition between Pakistan and India at independence (1947). In 1984, a separatist movement of Sikhs took over the Golden Temple, making it a fortress. Prime Minister Indira Gandhi in June 1984 sent the Indian army to dislodge the separatists, who had also been engaging in terrorist activities. The battle was bloody and fatal to its leaders, the Golden Temple was severely damaged, and many hitherto moderate Sikhs became radicalized. On the morning of October 31, 1984, Indira Gandhi was assassinated by two members of her bodyguard, both of whom were Sikhs. A general pogrom against Sikhs raged through the capital, which resulted in a massacre still unexplained as to the lack of protection on the part of Delhi law enforcement.

After the death of the tenth guru in 1708 there were no more gurus, the honor being assumed by the holy book, the Adi Granth, or Guru Granth Sahib. The presence of the book represents a center of devotion, even in private homes. A *gurdwara*, door of the guru, is a place where the holy book is present.

A decorated lorry carrying Sikh scriptures moving through the main streets of Calcutta forms part of a procession to celebrate Guru Nanak (1469–1539), the founder of Sikhism. (Hulton-Deutsch Collection/Corbis)

The central focus of Sikhism is love of God and the overcoming of selfish pride. For both, a Sikh needs the community; but the responsibility is his or hers alone. Sikhism is primarily a devotional faith, but there are some traditional features of behavior, especially for men: Hair should be uncut (hence, the turban), a comb should be carried for grooming; a special bangle, underwear, and dagger must be worn. Of course, not all Sikh men, especially outside of India, observe these customs, and their observance has upon occasion resulted in trouble—especially regarding the dagger in schools and on airplanes. Male Sikhs will have the honorific "Singh" somewhere among their names (but not everyone named Singh is Sikh; many are Hindu); a female, "Kaur."

Religious Violence in Contemporary India

Many places in the world are marked by violence between religious communities. Though lacking the sophisticated technology and suicide bombings employed elsewhere, communal violence in India at times takes on a savageness that is staggering not only to the perception of outsiders, but to calmer Indians as well. It is the violence between Hindus and Muslims that is most widespread, but it needs to be emphasized that such violence occurs between *some* Hindus and *some* Muslims and is generally abhorred by the vast majority of Indians. Yet the very size of India allows for a quantitative scale of violence that is bewildering.

In the summer of 2002, lengthy, in-depth studies of Hindu-Muslim violence and its causes appeared in the U.S. media, most notably National Public Radio's "All Things Considered" (July 8 and 9), the *New York Times* (July 27), and the *New York Review of Books* (August 15). Each of these accounts examined not only the history of conflict between the communities but the psychology of the grisly outbursts that can appear to be spontaneous. Although not necessarily using the term, these sources also noted the insidious nature of *hindutva*, a Hindu nationalism that equates "Indianness" with "Hinduness."

Among the tolerant or "secular" Hindus, many hasten to point out that the majority of Hindus do not like hindutva at all. Some refer to hindutva supporters as a "Hindu Taliban." Others point out that a small number of extremists have "highjacked" Hinduism, and that Hinduism is supposed to be inclusive, not exclusive. But the fact remains, as the National Public Radio report (from which the preceding observations have been taken) pointed out, for the first time since independence, extreme nationalists may have the power to carry out their agenda; thus, the education minister has spoken of the necessity to "Indianize," "nationalize," and "spiritualize" the educational curriculum.

Recent events have caused observers to express increased concern in regard to hindutva. Communal rioting goes back centuries; but the violence has often been organized, as in the assassination of Mahatma Gandhi a few months after independence—and partition—by a cabal of ultranationalist Hindu extremists, the Rashtriya Swayamsevak Sangh (National Self-Help Association), or RSS, founded in 1925 and virulently opposed to Gandhi's attempts to erase Hindu-Muslim political differences. (The current prime minister and deputy prime minister had ties with the group.) The octogenarian younger brother of the trigger man, Nathuram Godse, told a reporter for the *New York Times Magazine* (February 4, 2003) that India was in the process of renouncing Gandhi in favor of Godse. So strong is the hatred that it has lasted eight decades as an ideology.

More recently, on December 6, 1992, a mob, aided and abetted by right-wing Hindu cultural groups, tore down the Babri Masjid, a mosque constructed by the first Mughal emperor, Babur, in 1528. It had not been used for centuries, but legend had it that it was built upon the site of a demolished Hindu temple that had marked the birthplace of the god Ram (or Rama) in the sacred city of Ayodhya (in the state of Uttar Pradesh). A pogrom ensued against Muslims in the city, and communal violence erupted in a number of cities and regions.

Almost ten years later, on February 27, 2002, in Godhra, Gujarat (on the western central coast), two railway coaches filled largely with Hindu women and children returning from Ayodhya on the Sabarmati Express were set afire. Details are murky. The passengers were more than pilgrims, apparently having gone to express support for Hindu activists at the site. An altercation developed between Hindu passengers and Muslim boys selling tea at the station. After the train restarted, the emergency cord was pulled, and the train came to a halt in a Muslim neighborhood where a mob attacked it. It is unclear exactly how the fire occurred, but some fifty-eight passengers were killed. What followed were riots and slaughter. The grisly communal violence that spread through central Gujarat included rape and beheadings, pillage, and fire gutting homes and shops. Over one thousand Indians were killed, mostly Muslims. A Muslim member of the national parliament was tortured for forty-five minutes and then beheaded. Over a year later there had still been no convictions. (At a trial in May 2003, intimidated Muslim witnesses withdrew previous testimony made to police.)

The Gujarat government was run by the Bharatiya Janata Party (BJP), which also is in charge of the national government. Both the state and the national government are in alliance with several extremist Hindu groups. These groups have been supported by hindutva sympathizers outside of India. A small group of academics and professionals in the United States calling for a stop to the "funding of hate" have asserted that even U.S. corporations have unwittingly contributed to hindutva organizations operating under the pretense of charities. A similar informal group developed to challenge the charges. Most of the participants in either group are Indian Americans or nonresident Indians.

Meanwhile, a state election was held in Gujarat in December 2002. The BJP won 126 seats in the 182-seat assembly. A BJP victory had been anticipated by most observers, though probably not this one-sided. What has observers, inside and outside of India, concerned is the nature of the campaign. It far exceeded politics, especially in a campaign for an election the results of which were pretty much a foregone conclusion. It was not merely anti-Muslim, it was anti-secular and was heralded by right-wing Hindus as a "laboratory" for forthcoming elections in other states. Because in several of these states the Congress Party is in power, and many voters seem to be in an anti-incumbency mood, observers are concerned about a mixing of the issues: anti-Congress and hindutva. The Congress Party (India's most dominant, until recently) has its own baggage: the party of

Gandhi and Nehru, for decades it went almost unchallenged at the national level and often as well in many states. Further, it has been accused in the Gujarat campaign of having used a "soft" hindutva approach to voters, in spite of its strong foundation in and history of secularism. Indeed, the leader of one of the BJP's affiliates (Visva Hindu Parishad—VHP—or World Hindu Council, which styles itself as a cultural organization rather than political), remarked in regard to the election that it marked "the graveyard of secular politics," which would "extend to Delhi" (*New York Times,* December 16, 2002). He was referring to the national elections scheduled for 2004.

The VHP, although not constituted as a political party, is such a close ally of the BJP that at times it seemed to be running the campaign, saying things that the actual candidates themselves felt restrained from saying, such as that Muslims should "live like a minority," and even disparaging Mahatma Gandhi and questioning his patriotism. The cruel irony to this is that Gandhi himself was Gujarati.

The importance of the Ayodhya site has not diminished. A high court in Uttar Pradesh has ordered excavation of the site to determine whether a temple existed there before the mosque, but it put various restrictions on the method of excavation for purposes of religious sensitivities. An archaeologist stated he thought something was underneath the surface, but he did not know what it was. Then, in mid-August the Archaeological Survey of India issued a report saying (to quote the *New York Times,* August 27, 2003) that "it has found evidence that a structure may lie under the mosque." Therefore, said Hindu fundamentalists, a temple should be built on the site. Muslim groups, in contrast, called the report vague and attested that an ancient mosque lies under the rubble. The court will have to sort it out, but if the determination is that the remains are of a temple, the VHP's call for similar action at the major mosques in Mathura (the birthplace of Krishna) and Varanasi (city of Siva) will undoubtedly become shriller.

To further complicate matters, those mosques, unlike the one in Ayodhya, are still in use.

Also, the VHP has stated that it has the right to appropriate the sixty-seven acres of government land that surround the site, in order to build a temple. It issued the demand as an ultimatum, with ten thousand supporters marching on the Parliament in New Delhi and calling the national government "callous" and "godless." The VHP president has called for "rooting out secularism" (*India Abroad,* March 7, 2003). Right-wing Hindus have called for broadening the movement against mosques at holy sites in Banaras and Mathura and bypassing the courts to pressure Parliament to authorize the building of a temple in Ayodhya at the site of the previous mosque. At the funeral of a Hindu holy man in Ayodhya who had been associated with the temple project since 1949, the prime minister himself publicly avowed the building of a temple (*New York Times,* August 2, 2003).

It would seem that hindutva may have become an obsession beyond merely anti-Muslim and anti-secular expressions. The BJP chief minister (governor) of Goa—India's smallest state and a former Portuguese colony, but now with Hindus exceeding Roman Catholics in population—a few years ago took decidedly antiforeign (i.e., Portuguese and Catholic culture) stands on issues such as church restorations, particularly in regard to foreign financing. There was even a call for destruction of seventeenth- to eighteenth-century churches on the basis that they were built on the sites of ancient Hindu temples (shades of Ayodhya). Someone seemed to have recognized that the structures and culture had been tourist attractions (including for wealthy Hindus elsewhere in India) and could be more effectively promoted. The BJP governor "quietly dropped this stance" (*New York Times,* June 3, 2003).

The portents for the Indian political system could be ominous, although some observers feel the current anti-secular hindutva movement and expression to be more of an aberration than a sign of permanent change. There are factors to consider, which can provide insight not only into Indian politics, but Indian—especially Hindu—culture as well.

It is doubtful that India would ever declare itself to be a "Hindu Republic" (much as Pakistan, and later Bangladesh, declared themselves as Islamic republics). As noted earlier in this book, the primary identity of Hindus is not as Hindus as such, but with family, caste, village, and region; Hinduism does not represent a cohesive identity, except as imposed by those who want to draw a distinction from "non-Hindus" (which usually means Muslim). Even then, inclusion can be arbitrary, with Dalit (untouchable or outcaste) identity as Hindus often recognized by neither caste-Hindus or Dalits themselves. Hindus are very diverse, and most people in metropolitan areas have higher priorities—such as economic—than an imposed political-religious chauvinism focused on negatives. The very communal divide the VHP is calling for may be its undoing simply because of the various divisions inherent in Indian society.

Gujarat is an unlikely paradigm for Indian politics: the various states differ greatly in many ways. Further, there are some tensions among the groups under the hindutva umbrella. The BJP itself runs India through a coalition of parties, and it can ill afford to alienate its partners. Perhaps most important, the national government has to concern itself with highly practical problems, most especially economic. One of the strongest counterforces to hindutva may well be the technological revolution—and its likely economic benefits—underway right now.

Of course, if hindutva were somehow to capture the political process, and the BJP to win a solid majority in the national elections—and a radical ideologue to replace the aging prime minister, Atal Bihari Vajpayee, then it is a whole new ball game.

Tensions with Pakistan provide a source of political discontent that is fodder for hindutva. A Washington think tank, the Center for Strategic and International Studies, produced a report circulated in U.S. government circles, *The Role of Hindutva in Indian Politics* (reported on in *India Abroad,* February 14, 2003). The report warned of a major political threat in the next national election: "policy toward Pakistan could become more of a political football than it has been—with dangerous consequences."

On February 13, 2003, a bomb exploded on a commuter train in the Bombay (Mumbai) station, killing and wounding about seventy-five people. It was the tenth anniversary of a dozen bomb explosions at a number of sites that, according to the Associated Press, were "blamed on Muslim militants retaliating for the destruction of a sixteenth-century mosque [Babri Masjid] by Hindus, [which] killed 257 people and wounded at least 1,100."

It should be noted that a "Special Report" by the United States Institute of Peace on February 2003 presented some interesting observations in regard to the context of communal violence: "In India, lethal ethnic riots have occurred primarily in 4 of India's 28 states [now 29; the study addressed 1950–1995], and primarily in urban, not rural settings." Although rural population is large (85 percent in 1950, down to 67 percent by 1995, according to the report), eight cities accounted for 46 percent of riot-related deaths between 1950 and 1995, despite containing only 18 percent of the total population. (The cities were Bombay, Ahmedabad, Aligarh, Hyderabad, Meerut, Baroda, New Delhi, and Calcutta.) The major reasons given included polarization of communities by politicians for electoral purposes, lack of "local networks of civic engagement" (including communication between groups), and other local conditions.

It should be noted that not all political violence in India is communal in nature—much has been separatist, although the two amorphous categories can overlap. A recent example occurred on the eve of the celebration of the anniversary of independence, August 15, 2003. Reuters news agency reported the indiscriminate killing of thirty-four people by bombs and shooting in the northeast "volatile state of Tripura" in at least two locations (*New York Times,* August 15, 2003).

References
Basham, A. L. *The Wonder That Was India,* rev. ed. New York: Hawthorn, 1962.

Bouton, Marshal M., and Philip Oldenburg, eds. *India Briefing, 1988.* Boulder: Westview, 1988.

Brass, Paul. "The Gujarat Pogrom of 2002." *Items and Issues: Social Science Research Council* (winter 2002–2003). http://conconflicts.ssrc.org/gujarat/brass/ (accessed March 30, 2004).

———. *The Politics of India since Independence.* Vol. 4, part 1 of *The New Cambridge History of India.* Cambridge: Cambridge University Press, 1995.

Center for Development Economics. *PROBE: Public Report on Basic Education for India.* Delhi: Oxford University Press, 1999.

Eerdman's Handbook to the World's Religions. Grand Rapids, MI: William B. Eerdman, 1982.

Grose, Thomas. "Jewel in the Crown." *Prism Online,* October 1999. http://www.asee.org/prism/oct99/html/india.htm (accessed March 30, 2004).

Hardgrave, Robert L., and Stanley A. Kochanek. *India: Government and Politics in a Developing Nation,* 6th ed. New York: Harcourt Brace College, 2000.

Khilnani, Sunil. *The Idea of India.* New York: Farrar Strauss Giroux, 1999.

Koller, John M. *The Indian Way.* New York: Macmillan, 1982.

Manor, James. "Politics: Ambiguity, Disillusionment, and Ferment." Pp. 1–26 in Singhal, D. P. *India and World Civilization.* Calcutta: Rupa, 1993.

Teresi, Dick. *Lost Discoveries: The Ancient Roots of Modern Science—From the Babylonians to the Maya.* New York: Simon & Schuster, 2002.

United States Institute of Peace. "Special Report: Lethal Ethnic Riots, Lessons from India and Beyond." Washington, DC: United States Institute of Peace, February 2003.

Varshay, Ashutosh. "Understanding Gujarat Violence." *Items & Issues: Social Science Research Council* 4, no. 1 (winter 2002–2003): 1–5.

Waterstone, Richard. *India: Belief and Ritual, The Gods and the Cosmos, Meditation and the Yogic Arts.* London: Thorsons, 2002.

CHAPTER FOUR
Indian Society and Contemporary Issues

This chapter will examine several important issues related to Indian society, beginning with caste. It is by far the central institution of Indian society—if the word *institution* can be somewhat loosely used as a cover-term. Caste is the social fabric not just of Hinduism, but of India itself, historically and currently. It is not often spoken about in day-to-day life and is not easily noticed by casual outside observers, such as tourists; but it is pervasive throughout Indian society and is in many ways the underpinning for it. Caste is often decried and even condemned by outsiders—generally because it is not understood. There are abuses within the system, and some aspects are out of date; but it has shown itself to be resilient and adaptable to modern developments such as democratic politics and urbanization. What Western critics often do not understand is that though abuses such as untouchableness can be combated, the caste system itself cannot be eliminated—even were it desirable to do so.

The situation of women in contemporary India is ambiguous; in some ways it is related to socioeconomic class position, yet it has distinct—if not always clear—cultural historical causes. Again, a problem in sociological understanding by a Westerner is due to the natural tendency to observe and judge in terms of one's one culture and society.

Another condition of Indian society generally unknown, or at least ignored, in the West is that of the multiplicity of languages, and, by extension, regional cultures. This situation has serious political and social implications, contributing to the complex of problems in politics and society.

135

The primary sources of popular entertainment in present-day India are cinema and television. Movies especially have important social and economic impact on the society. India is the largest producer of feature films in the world and has been for decades.

The overriding and most insidious issue facing contemporary Indian society is that of ecology and its root cause, population explosion. This is a matter dealt with elsewhere in this handbook as well, for it impacts all aspects of society.

Finally, India's relations with its competitor China, the improving economic and political relations with the United States, and the volatile relationship with Pakistan are considered. The importance of the South Asian Association for Regional Cooperation (SAARC) is also noted.

CASTE

Caste is such a complex institution—or mix of institutions—that it is impossible to precisely define and nearly so to describe. It is helpful to look at two facets of what Westerners call caste (the term comes from the Portuguese word *casta*): *varna,* a mythologically based ideal uniform throughout Hindu India; and *jati,* a socioeconomic system that is not confined to Hindus and varies regionally in its order of ranking. It is a living, hence changing, set of relationships among groups.

The origins of caste are lost, although theories are put forth and argued over. Likely there are several factors involved—social, economic, and racial. One source may well have been the desire of the lighter-skinned Aryans to preserve a cultural and "racial" priority—but this, too, is arguable (as well as controversial) and will not be discussed further here.

Varna

Hinduism, if it can be referred to as an abstract unity, is based upon orthopraxy—correct behavior—and not orthodoxy—

A shoemaker making shoes from the hides of cows. As cows are sacred to Hindus, those who handle their hides are from the caste of untouchables. (Hulton Archive)

correct belief. What one believes does not matter so much as what one does, and that is determined by one's position in life: a student getting a bit tipsy and boisterous at the local pub does not carry nearly the consequences as the president of the university doing so (or mayor, or school principal, etc.); similarly, a brahmin should not eat meat (except in Bengal, where fish is allowed), but such a restriction by no means exists for the lower castes. This is a hypothetical guide for Hindu society, and it is called *varnasrama-dharma*, which means that

A Brahmin, or priest. Brahmins occupy the highest caste level in Hindu India. (Paul Almasy/Corbis)

social rank or class (varna) and stage-of-life (asrama) have their particular duties and responsibilities (dharma).

There are four varna: brahmin, kshatriya, vaisya, and sudra. The brahmin's duty is religious and learned: to study, teach, and perform sacrifices and rituals. The kshatriya is the warrior and ruler. The vaisya engages in trade or crafts. The sudra serves the first three ranks. The first three are "twice-born" in that the boys go through a sort of confirmation ceremony at adolescence, when they are invested with a sacred cord; the sudras are "once-born" and are restricted from hearing the sacred Vedic scripture: they are "unclean"; that is, ritually impure. Even more unclean are the outcastes, or untouchables, but their existence is sociological rather than philosophical, and they are not recognized in this scheme.

There are four asrama: *brahmacarin,* or student; *grhastha,* or householder; *vanaprastha,* or forest-dweller (i.e., retiree); and *sannyasin,* or wandering ascetic. The student prepares for future life, usually by living at a hermitage and studying under a guru or spiritual preceptor. The householder is the most important stage of all (and the longest in duration), as he supports other family members. This stage is when one exercises familial and civic responsibilities. In the next stage, one used to retire to the forest (with or without his wife) at a certain age, when his children were grown and his hair had turned white; it was a subjective decision, not a set time. One retired to contemplate spiritual matters, and still can, but nowadays it is more of a grandparent stage (although that does not rule out spiritual contemplation). The last stage, the sannyasin, is not for everybody. All earthly obligations must have been met, and one should be fully in control of oneself. This step is a withdrawal from society, and one abandons not only home, but name and caste and all other earthly ties. Rudyard Kipling wrote a moving short story, "The Miracle of Puran Bhagat," which sensitively and touchingly captures the spirit of this stage.

There are also four "ends," or dharma (roughly, "duty"), involved in this structure. The first is dharma itself, and it governs the other three (and will be considered in dealing with them). *Artha* means power or wealth (one leading to the other): but wealth must not be ill-gotten, and power must be exercised in a nonselfish dharmic manner. *Kama* is pleasure: poetry, picnicking, drinking alcohol (unless one is brahmin)—in moderation, and sexual pleasure (within the bonds of matrimony); dharma must govern pleasure (which cannot hurt others, nor be detrimental to oneself). The idea is balance: all work and no play makes for an incomplete person.

Artha and kama are applicable to the householder stage, not the other three. The final dharma, called moksa, is everybody's concern: it is release from the cycle of rebirth. Such release means achieving (or realizing) Oneness, one with the Absolute. It does not happen to everybody, obviously, in this particular life, but it will, eventually. The whole structure is meant to make for a smoothly running society, one that can aid in the upward trip toward spiritual release.

The position of woman in this scheme is somewhat difficult to explain. She is the partner of the male, and her dharma includes that of wife and that of mother. Her duties are womanly, not male; she is not in competition with him. (Nevertheless, it can be noted that not only India, but Sri Lanka, Pakistan, and Bangladesh have all had female prime ministers.)

All this is to be taken as a general guide, not an absolute manual. (Aldous Huxley, in *Brave New World,* showed what could happen were it to be rigidly applied.) Historically in India, there were prostitutes (courtesans were sometimes rationalized as having "contrary dharma"), along with thievery, corruption, and abuse of power; and so it is today, as in any society. But the ideal emphasized dharma, self-less duty, so that all the various socioeconomic elements could work together in a holistic and stable manner. It represents an attempt to forge unity from diversity.

The concept of dharma is so strong that it extends to all relationships: there is a son's or daughter's dharma, a father's or mother's (they would not be lumped together as "a parent's dharma"), a king's dharma, and so on. There is even *svadharma,* dharma in regard to oneself.

Jati

The term *caste* is usually applied to *jati* (literally, "birth"). It is arguable how closely varna and jati are related, but there are similarities and even some correspondences. Perhaps the biggest difference is that the structural order of varna is the same throughout India, whereas there are regional variations for the ordering of jati.

Jati reflects the group or communal orientation of Indian society, especially village society. Marriage is arranged within the jati (but out of the immediate locale) and reflects the strong sense of kinship prevalent in society. This, however, is not meant to imply that everyone in the same jati is related. Jati is often, but not exclusively, ordered along occupational lines. The brahmin, or priest, is at the top, and although accorded deference in regard to religious matters, he has little secular power. That is usually wielded by landowners. There are rankings—or subcastes—within the varna of brahmin, and landowners do not form a uniform jati of their own. Jati rankings provide the socioeconomic fabric of village India, with an ordering of craftsmen—carpenters, weavers, potters, smiths—that varies among regions. These would generally be within the vaisya varna. Laborers, such as washermen, sometimes barbers, would be sudra. In south India many of the craftsmen would also be sudra (south India has a huge percentage of sudra). The most "unclean" jobs, which are considered polluting, such as that of sweepers, are done by untouchables, or, as they are called in south India, pariahs, who are considered so because of the nature of their work, which they are born to do.

A rationale for the jati relationships is that of exchange of services, such as the potter making vessels for other jati in exchange for grain or services. This arrangement is called *jaj-mani,* which is from a Sanskrit word meaning ritual sacrifice; hence, there is a religious (some might say pseudo-religious) sanction for the system.

Even within conservative village society the jati-jajmani system is subject to change; for example, as pumps become available in homes, the need for the water-carrier's services disappears. He may move to a city, or adapt. In one curious incident, a water-carrier got a portable cooler attached to his bicycle and made the round of area villages selling Popsicles to children. In a sense, he was still a water-carrier; this illustrates the psychological depth of jati. In villages within commuting distance of a city, men may take jobs in the city—either for which they are already trained, such as members of the barber jati working as barbers (in hotels or on street corners), or new occupations, such as bus driver. Of course with increasing education, opportunities arise, such as becoming a teacher.

There is not always agreement among various jatis as to local ranking; the members of a jati may consider themselves higher in the ranking than do members of jati ranked near them. To complicate the matter further, jatis can be ethnic groups, such as the Jats, who are landowning farmers. Here again change can easily occur. If there are several sons, rather than divide the land into small parcels, one or more may move to a town or city to work for a firm or in a profession. Because they develop families separate from the extended family on the farm, the ties tend to loosen and, in the next generation, to disintegrate.

In congested urban life the physical aspects of jati tend to break down. Unlike in the village, daily life tends to be anonymous. Yet psychological features continue. Arranged marriages are still made within the jati, often even among highly successful professionals who are generations removed from any village. People with communal ties may choose to live in the same condominium complex. Perhaps most important, the distinction between caste Hindus and those doing menial work—untouchables or other low castes—is reinforced by socioeconomic class distinctions common to all societies, with the added impetus of the concept of ritual impurity.

The pervasiveness of caste is so strong that even non-Hindu groups can be absorbed into it. Thus, Muslim weavers are considered to be a caste or jati. Communal attitudes, including marriage, frequently exist among Christians and within other religious communities. Such an outlook is not exclusive to India, by any means; but its existence within a greater sense of group identity reinforces the basic nature of Indian society: individuals are primarily members of a group, the groups then coexisting to form the larger society.

Caste Today

Caste is the social fabric of India—at least of Hindu India—and it is so pervasive that it extends socioeconomically into other communities, such as Muslim and Christian. It would be impossible to abolish caste, even if it were desirable to do so. The modern concern with caste is the built-in exploitation of lower groups by higher groups and other forms of discrimination. In this sense, caste reflects the problems of a communal nature in modern (and traditional) Indian society.

The constitution of India bans untouchability. The government has established programs of an affirmative-action nature for oppressed castes, classes, and tribes. Often such programs are strongly, even violently, resisted by upper castes, especially in rural areas. But even in the cities, newspapers carry accounts of harijans (Gandhi's term for untouchables), including children, meeting death for stepping out of line. The measures by the government are not completely successful, but neither are those in regard to race and gender in U.S. society.

Caste identity can in some ways be a strength; thus, the term *untouchable* (as well as other words used to label those at the bottom of caste ranking) has to a considerable extent been replaced by one meaning "oppressed"—Dalit. The Dalits have mounted an aggressive movement of their own, seeking to improve their status—not by removing their identity, but by combating discrimination and oppression. Nevertheless, they still largely have the dirty jobs, especially in rural

*The Dalits or "untouchables" march across India annually to increase
awareness of the plight of this strata of society, considered "impure"
according to the rigid caste system still in place throughout India
today. (Antoine Serra/In Visu/Corbis)*

areas where, because of the in-born nature of the system,
they can be violently suppressed if they are viewed as getting
out of line.

It is easy enough for sanctimonious outsiders to criticize
the caste system, but nevertheless the evils of untouchableness must not be glossed over. Americans (particularly white
Americans) often become sensitive when outsiders make generalizations about racism in the United States; if anything, the
situation in regard to caste oppression in India is even more
intense. A handbook such as this is probably not the place to
get mired in this complex matter; however, a very sensible
and sensitive article—complete with Web site references—
appeared in the June 2003 issue of *National Geographic* magazine (2–39).

It might also be noted that when asked (while in Washington, D.C., on a judicial exchange program), a justice of India's

supreme court said that caste-based quotas would never end (*New York Times Magazine*, June 1, 2003, 55).

WOMEN

As might be expected in a society with such strong group identity, an Indian woman's station is generally reflected by her role, with that of mother being exceptionally high. In village culture, a young bride's position in her new home (and village—she moves to her husband's village), under her mother-in-law, is made secure when she becomes a mother, especially if the child is a boy.

Although both Hindu and Muslim traditions are generally conservative in regard to women, the actual situations vary. A sophisticated, rich urban woman may own her own boutique, be well traveled, and have a high degree of independence; or she may be curtailed by tradition, such as *purdah* among Muslims. Purdah, or *parda* (the word means "curtain"), or the sequestering of the women of the family, can be psychological as well as physical. Some women observe purdah as a matter of choice; others who would not normally observe it in the world at large may do so when they return to the family home or in a traditional Muslim neighborhood.

Hindu tradition emphasizes *stri dharma*, or womanly dharma (duty). The woman is the heart of the family, with moral duties to husband and children. She also possesses a cosmic-like power, called *sakti* (literally, "potential"), which is not unlike the powers Westerners attribute to Mother Nature, which, like sakti, can be beneficial or destructive. Women give birth, bringing us into maya (the relative world). Motherhood is highly revered in Hinduism. Some surveys indicate that the mother-son relationship is stronger than that of husband and wife. Mahatma Gandhi once counseled a group of writers to "remember that a woman was your mother before a woman became your wife"—the point being that their writing should be chaste.

Sakti can wreak righteous havoc. In the *Shilappadikaram,* a fifth-century C.E. Tamil classic, a wife destroys a king and his capital city after he fails in his kingly dharma, which results in her husband being unjustly executed. Interestingly, this destruction occurs when she rips off her breast (the symbol is obvious) and hurtles it to the ground, causing a great conflagration. She is the instrument of sakti. Indeed, sakti is greater than mortal women, but not than goddesses; indeed, the wife in the *Shilappadikaram* achieves the status of a goddess. In regard to women, the sakti often needs to be curtailed and guided—by men, of course. Like the stereotypical irrationality of women, the mysterious power can be unpredictable and devastating. In goddesses it is expected and accepted (albeit not understood); in human females it is feared and resented.

The concept of sakti has implications for women's sexual nature as well, which is often viewed with disquiet and alarm. As a sexual being she is often insatiable in the folk literature. In one morality tale, as soon as a husband leaves town on business, his wife entertains to the extent that men are lined up at her door. Numerous men are misbehaving, but only one woman; nevertheless, the blame is placed upon her.

Furthermore, woman's allure is dangerous, for folk wisdom has it that loss of semen weakens a man, physically and spiritually. It is arguable how widely spread this belief is, but it is there. As wife she is temptress, but as mother she has risen above mere womanhood. Nevertheless, feminine beauty is highly appreciated throughout India, especially in dance and art. To add to the curious ambiguities, in the epic and classical literatures female characters are often—perhaps even usually—far more complex and interesting than their male counterparts, sometimes achieving amazing inner strength. Yet, an ancient law code states that a woman must be protected (or restricted): as a girl by her father, as a wife by her husband, as a widow by her son. The injunction regarding widows can be contradicted by other customs, as will be seen below.

Another feature regards the belief in menstrual uncleanliness. Among some groups in some regions even a mother must remove herself from her family during menstruation.

There is an old saw followed by some that a girl should be married before her first period. This is a likely source of child marriage, although other features, such as forging ties between two families, must also play a part. Child marriage is against the law, but in many areas the law is not enforced or cannot be enforced because of the sheer quantity of such marriages. Further, "the recommended age"—eighteen for women, twenty-one for men—is simply unrealistic in village India. Detection would be difficult anyway, as Hindu marriages are often not recorded but only ritually observed by the families involved.

As in many cultures, female infanticide in India has a long history. The use of modern ultrasound scanning equipment to determine the sex as well as the health of a fetus has lately resulted in a swelling of female feticide throughout India. The 2001 census recorded a drastic drop in the ratio of females to males under seven years of age: 927 females per 1,000 males; the number was 945 females per 1,000 males in 1991. Women's advocates have been caught in a bind: though against gender-related abortion, they understand the plight of a family that already has several daughters. In India, a daughter is basically raised for someone else; she marries and moves into another household, working in another family. Worse, a dowry must be raised. Several dowries can bankrupt a family.

Dowry is against the law. So, the word is not used. The groom's family asks for "gifts." The practice of making the bride a commodity has instigated "dowry deaths," most frequently by "bride burning." Figures are hard to come by, but the National Crimes Bureau, Home Ministry, recorded 5,199 in 1994, ranging from zero in some states and territories to that of 1,977 deaths in Uttar Pradesh, the most populous state. The capital, Delhi, had 132. The national governmental figures for the year 2001 were about 7,000. However, many such deaths go unreported or are unrecorded, staged to appear as accidents. Even when the facade of an accident is seen through, convictions can be difficult to obtain. An unofficial estimate is that 25,000 Indian brides are killed or maimed yearly.

The scenario is something like this: The bride's new family is unhappy with the "gifts" or perhaps wants a new set of gifts, which means another bride. While working in the kitchen (which is usually set off from the rest of the house and constructed of noncombustible material), she is burned to death when the kerosene cooking stove "explodes"; actually, she is doused with kerosene and set on fire. It can happen so fast as to catch her unaware. Even if she has suspicion, there is not much she can do, unless her own family is willing to take her back. Institutions such as shelters are woefully inadequate, and the socioeconomic situation of the bride is one of almost complete dependency.

A tactic for increasing dowry can involve a sort of blackmail: The groom's family claims, at the last minute, to have discovered that the prospective bride had an affair in college (the groom's sexual history never seems to be an issue), and so demands more money. Such a situation occurred in the middle of May 2003, in a suburb of Delhi. At the last minute—with 2,000 guests already dining and the bride attired in bridal red, the groom's family demanded the equivalent of $25,000. This was in addition to the already agreed-upon dowry of "two televisions, two home theater sets, two refrigerators, two air conditioners and one car" (*New York Times,* May 17, 2003). A brawl developed, and the bride called police on her cell phone. "By calling the police, Nisha Sharma, a 21-year-old computer student, saw her potential groom land in jail and herself land in the national spotlight as India's new overnight sensation." Newspapers, in English and in Hindi, declared her to be "a New Age woman and seen as a role model to many," as one put it, showing a drawing of her wearing a sari with a sash reading "Miss Anti-Dowry."

Women's leaders hailed her bravery and determination. But while the media made a field day of her act, the police reportedly dragged their feet in apprehending any of the family. As far as the expenses of the failed wedding, her parents were relieved. Her father expressed that she could have been killed in such a marriage, and said, "I thought, let the money go." According to his daughter, "My father was thrown out of his house because he didn't take the dowry when he got married in 1980." She herself was interviewed for CBS News magazine *60 Minutes* (*India Abroad,* June 27, 2003).

Another unenviable role is that of the widow. Some castes, in some areas, used to have the widow burn on the husband's funeral pyre (although this was never as widespread as many critics of Hinduism like to think). She was literally a *sati* (suttee), or "true woman." Sometimes the action may have been voluntary, for as a living widow she would be cut off from society and even family. More often, the pressure—including physical—was likely just too great. Today there are institutions in places like Varanasi (Banaras) for widows of certain castes. Sati has been outlawed in India for centuries, but once in a great while it occurs in an isolated place.

Sati is fairly much relegated to history; when it does occur, it is an anomaly. Unfortunately, trafficking in women is a major problem in India, and it involves mainly girls of age twelve and thirteen. Both boys and girls can become part of the child-bondage system, providing cheap labor in factories for silk, rugs, brass, and other industries such as making *bidis* (cheap cigarettes) and matches. They do domestic service, both in Indian metropolitan areas and in the Middle East. The majority of the girls are forced into prostitution in the big cities and in certain tourist areas. They are, of course, largely poor, rural, and low caste. Some of the older ones are abandoned wives. In spite of such trafficking being a criminal offence, it is a thriving industry, with such terms as *trafficking belt* and *routes* used to describe it. Not all the girls are from India: thousands, yearly, come from Nepal and

Bangladesh. Some are sold by parents, both unwittingly and knowingly in regard to the future that awaits them. Some have relative freedom—to the degree that a prostitute can have such; some are mere slaves.

As alarming and heinous such information is, it needs to be stressed that such activity is most certainly not restricted to India, but is a worldwide problem (an excellent reference on modern slavery can be found in the September 2003 *National Geographic* magazine). Prajwala is a nongovernmental organization involved in many activities throughout India, including rescue, rehabilitation, and reintegration programs for prostitutes and their children. It is estimated that 95 percent of the children in the Prajwala shelter for children of prostitutes have HIV. The Prajwala shelter is in the state of Andhra Pradesh (southeast India), from which comes the single largest percentage of trafficked women—40 percent was the estimate in a 1997 survey by the National Commission for Women. Rehabilitation includes education, but Prajwala has plans to implement prevention for the next generation, so that they may avoid becoming victims of trafficking.

This bleak picture of Indian women, like Western morbid curiosity in sati (e.g., *Around the World in Eighty Days* and *The Far Pavilions*), can be misleading. Indira Gandhi was twice prime minister of India, which may indicate that class and family are more important than gender. Of course, she had to have personal strength to win her battles. There are many such women, all over India, and at all levels of society. Many of these have taken up the fight for women's causes, and they include lawyers, doctors, educators, and journalists. An example is *Manushi,* founded in 1978 as "a serious journal which aims to bridge the gap between academic/scholarly writing and popular culture."

Manushi puts women's matters in the larger context of political, social, and economic issues—and abuses. The March–April 2002 issue, for instance, contains an article on "The Politics of Communal Polarisation," including an exam-

Indira Gandhi (1917–1984) was the first and only female prime minister of India and showed remarkable strength in leadership, if at times somewhat controversial. She was assassinated by her personal body guards on October 31, 1984. (Bettmann/Corbis)

ination of the hypocrisy between political clichés and actions (or lack thereof). When such issues as "bride burning," dowry, and female feticide are examined and developed in relation to the larger social, political, and economic context of India, they are better understood and more effectively confronted.

Thomas Friedman, in his column in the *New York Times* on March 14, 2004, posited that a major difference between India and certain ultraconservative Islamic societies is that "women are [becoming] empowered" in India. One outstanding example is the Self-Employed Women's Association (SEWA), founded in Ahmedabad and registered as a trade union in 1972. In 1974, 4,000 self-employed women established a bank with a capital of 60,000 rupees. According to a UNESCO Web site (http://www.unesco.org/most/asia1.htm) the bank had "51,000 depositors and working capital of Rs. 10 million crores" (100 million rupees; there are about 45 rupees per dollar) by 1995. The annual report for 2002–2003 lists the working capital as 849,095,000 rupees.

According to its Web site (http://www.sewabank.org), "the SEWA Bank is a unique institution in that it is primarily owned by, led by and established for self-employed women in low-income communities." It now operates in rural districts of Gujarat, covering 175,000 "clients." Its headquarters, with a staff of seventy, is fully computerized. Financial counseling is offered to bank members, but the aim in regard to poor women is to "pull them out of vicious circle and enable them to become self-sufficient." In addition to loans (with a recovery rate of 92 percent), the bank offers a number of services, enabling women to "have control over their own income" and "have their own hand-carts, sewing machines, looms and tools of carpentry and blacksmithy." The bank has been innovative and a catalyst for change, putting assets in the name of women, sponsoring projects such as improving drinking water, and going beyond symptoms of poverty to involve poor women in various financial activities and institutions.

LANGUAGE AND REGIONALISM

India is a land of many languages, which often coincide with regional cultures and state boundaries. Yet within a major geopolitical region, or state, there can be minority cultures and languages as well. This is one reason why new states have been carved out of older states. India's political map has been quite fluid since independence, and regional cultures are political and emotional issues.

The census lists eighteen "scheduled" (or officially recognized) languages and ninety-six "others." The issue is complicated by the vexing problem of what constitutes a dialect, as opposed to a separate language. As a result, one reads of almost astronomical numbers of languages in India. These reports can confuse and dismay the outside observer about the "exoticness" of India. The major language families are Indo-Aryan (a branch of Indo-European), largely in the north, and Dravidian, largely in the south. Numerous scripts are employed for the written forms. Each state has a major ("scheduled") language, but usually with significant percentages of speakers of other languages. The figures referred to here are from the 1991 census (as tables for the 2001 census were not released at the time this book was published).

If one were to draw a line about two-thirds of the way down the Indian subcontinent, he or she would have roughly marked the division between the Indo-Aryan languages and the Dravidian languages. The four southern states and their respective languages are: Andhra Pradesh on the east coast, Telugu (about 56 million speakers); Tamil Nadu, southeast tip, Tamil (about 48 million speakers); Karnataka, west coast, Kannada (about 30 million speakers); and Kerala, southwest tip, Malayalam (about 28 million speakers). Each of these languages has speakers in other states as well, and each of the states contains significant numbers of speakers of other languages.

The Dravidian family of languages seems to be unrelated to any other language group. Attempts have been made to find correspondences with Basque and Finnish, among others, but the Dravidian languages stand by themselves. One supposition among some scholars is that the Dravidian peoples are descendants of the Indus Valley civilization.

In the northern part of southern India and in central India, there are several "tribal" languages, as there are also in northeastern India. These include Bhili (about 5 million speakers) and Gondi (2 million), as well as several others (from thirty thousand to six hundred thousand).

The Indo-Aryan family, largely in the north (interestingly, Sinhalese, the major language of Sri Lanka, is Indo-Aryan), contains a large number of languages: Hindi (337 million), Bengali (70 million), and, in lesser numbers, Nepali, Urdu, Gujarati, Sindhi, Punjabi, Assamese, Marathi, and Oriya. In general, each language is primarily associated with a state and that state's culture (for example, Bengali, Bengal; Oriya, Orissa; Marathi, Maharashtra). The "national" language was supposed to be Hindi—as mandated in the constitution—which has the largest number of speakers and is the primary language in the capital, Delhi, and several states. However, Hindi is officially considered the main language of the states of Bihar and Rajasthan, but Bihari and Rajasthani speakers are likely to consider their languages as separate rather than as dialects of Hindi. This shows the difficulty of defining one language in a country of so many.

The Indo-Aryan languages are often categorized as coming from Sanskrit; this is not quite correct. Sanskrit is an Indo-European language, as can be discerned from cognates with English, such as *matr* (mother), *duhitr* (daughter), *bhartr* (brother), *do* (two, dual), and *trin* (three). When the Aryans made their incursions into India, they did so in waves. They spoke languages styled as *prakrta* (or prakrits), which means "natural"; *samskrta* (sanskrit) means "cultivated." An ancient linguist, Panini, took one dialect of prakrit, wrote a descriptive grammar, and "froze" it so that it became the language for philosophy, science, and other learned matters. This is classical Sanskrit. It did not develop as a spoken language (not that certain scholars and religious figures do not memorize and "speak" it, but in such a sense it is an "artificial" language). The language works well for its intended cause. But it was never a "living" language, which situation has resulted in certain advantages in regard to the study of philosophy and religion.

From about the fifth century C.E., with the demise of the Gupta empire, northern India broke up into regional states, each of which developed its own language out of the prakrits, which in turn developed into modern Indian languages, complete with their own literatures and contributing to the development of regional cultures. Although related, the languages are nonetheless distinctive; the situation is analogous to the language pattern of Europe and to that of south India.

There has been strong resistance to the instituting of Hindi as the national language, which had been a move strongly pushed by Mahatma Gandhi, even though his native tongue was Gujarati (although he was fluent in both Hindi and English). He felt Hindi was the natural choice, as the largest language. But it has never been a majority language, and its proposed imposition was resented by people from other languages and cultures within India. The interesting fact is that when Gandhi communicated with Charkravarti Rajagopalacharya (who was to become India's governor-general and Gandhi's son's father-in-law) it was in English, as Rajagopalacharya was a Tamil speaker. Indeed, after the British left, English remained as the lingua franca and still is. As Nehru, India's first prime minister, once put it, English is India's window on the world. He also noted that it would not make sense to translate physics textbooks, for instance, into multiple languages, some which lacked the vocabulary for such an undertaking—not to mention the cost to do so. Two obvious results are that Indians are extremely proficient in computers and other technologies, and most educated Indians are not just bilingual, but often at least trilingual. Further, India has had an impressive number of Nobel Prize winners in the sciences.

One might think that the diversity of languages would tend to pull the country apart. But with the British gone, English has largely become neutral, and indeed is the primary language of higher education. It is also the language of international business. It is so pervasive that one can see Hindi business signs with English words included. Although more Indians speak Hindi than English, educated Hindi speakers are often English speakers as well. English is probably the language most used in print, and it is used in government and politics, albeit considered officially as an "assisted" language. Political considerations in a former imperialist colony really prohibit any further recognition of what is actual. Some fine newspapers have all-India editions, both in newsprint and on internet (http://www.samachar.com and http://www.indonet.com each carry a number of examples).

MOVIES AND TELEVISION

Films have been made in India for more than a hundred years. The first talkie appeared in 1931. The center for filmmaking has from the beginning been Bombay (Mumbai), hence the nickname "Bollywood" (in reference to Hollywood, California, where most U.S. films are made). Most films are done in Hindi, but a wide range of languages is also used, although on a much smaller scale than the quantity made in Hindi. Estimates for recent years range for a total of about 800 to 1,000 films a year. In 2001, a total of 1,031 films were made in India, compared to 739 in Hollywood, and they earned a total of $1.3 billion, compared to $51 billion for U.S. movies (*India Abroad,* March 14, 2003). Most of the Bollywood films are frankly escapist, with repetitive dance and romance format, and are designed purely for the domestic market.

Stellar exceptions to the formula films of Bollywood are the Bengali films of Satyajit Ray (1921–1992), which have won a number of international awards. His films largely were made in Bengal and produced in Calcutta, not Bombay. Shortly before his death he received the Academy Award for lifetime achievement. He observed at the time that it was the foreign market, not the Indian market, that had made it financially possible for him to make films. The style of his films makes an interesting contrast to that of the much more popular Bollywood films. His subjects are more serious and his treatment more sophisticated, dealing humanistically with themes of social change and tragedy. His budgets were small, resulting in an almost Spartan, yet poetic, treatment. Bollywood films are becoming more extravagant in production and costs, and a few are starting to gain some attention internationally and to break away—to a degree—from the negative stereotype conveyed by the label of Bollywood. One, *Lagaan,* was nominated for the Academy Award for best foreign film in 2002. Another, *Monsoon Wedding,* shown mostly in art film houses, grossed $13 million in North America; yet many U.S. films have totaled more on their opening weekends. Their successes seem to have come largely from "non-desi audiences" (that is, not from the expatriate Indian communities), prompting one Indian observer to state that they "are not Bollywood films." To that end, a Los Angeles firm, Cinebella, has initiated a program of films for release in North America, called "Beyond Bollywood." So far, "crossover appeal" from Indian Americans to the general population of U.S. moviegoers seems very limited. Even so, some Indian film-makers are eyeing markets beyond India.

An Israeli observer and student of Indian films recently produced a photographic documentary of the movie industry in relation to contemporary culture in *Bollywood Dreams* (New York: Phaidon, 2003). He told *India Abroad* (May 9, 2003) that film, not religion, is the dominant culture, that religions remains separate as film has nothing to do with

Posters for Bollywood movies (Catherine Karnow/Corbis)

religion. Using three popular actors as example, he stated, "Someone who hypothetically has strong, say negative views about Muslims could be a fan of the three Khans—Shah Rukh, Salman, or Amir." Whether true or not, the observation does show the power of film on the culture. Furthermore, films have provided an avenue into politics, including high elected office, for a number of actors and actresses.

A social issue has emerged from the murky financing of films in the rapidly growing and increasingly expensive, and profitable, industry. The Indian Mafia (a term used by state authorities) has become involved. In addition, mobsters have attempted extortion and have become friends with some film stars. So much money has been generated, profits and stars' salaries have become so lucrative, and the underground economy has achieved such strength that gangster inroads into the movie world seem almost to have been inevitable. Ironically, gangsters are sometimes portrayed in Indian films, especially as comic relief.

Finally, the industry is facing international competition; for example, *Men in Black II* was released in India—dubbed in Hindi, Tamil, and Telugu—about a month after its release in the United States.

Foreign competition has also changed Indian television, which just a few decades ago was monopolized by the government-owned Doordarshan network. Doordarshan was adjunct to All India Radio, historically akin to the British situation with BBC. As in Britain, competition has appeared not merely through liberalization of the system, but because of satellite TV, including MTV Asia, BBC, CNN, ESPN-Star, and NBC Asia. There are also entertainment channels in Hindi, movie channels, and music channels. New channels become available frequently, due to what has been termed "the satellite revolution in India." Another development has had negative influence on film revenues: illegal showing of films over subscription cable systems, which are small enough to make detection difficult.

Portrait of Indian film director Mira Nair (Arici Graziano/Corbis Sygma)

There has been complaint about suppression of journalists, domestic and foreign, both by regional groups within India and by the central government. According to *India Abroad* (April 11, 2003), the Committee to Protect Journalists ("a New York–based media watchdog") in its annual report accused the government of "targeting its critics in the media as a matter of policy." Incidents involved a journalist with the *Times of India* being beaten by police while covering communal violence, and the New Delhi bureau chief of *Time* magazine being threatened with expulsion for an article calling into question the health of the prime minister. Attacks on reporters in various regions included the murder of a journalist "by a local religious sect."

POPULATION AND ECOLOGY

In the first Indian census taken after independence, in 1951, the population of India was slightly more than 361 million. Today it is well over a billion. Arguments are made, with various figures presented, that the rate of growth has been declining. The problem is that with almost a tripling in a little over fifty years, any increase contributes to the ecological deterioration that in some ways can be said to be progressing at geometric rates, or at least in a holistic manner. For example, population increase in India's rural mountainous areas results in greater increase in demand for fuel. Village women have to walk much farther to get the fuel—and, of course, carry it as far to get home. There have as well been commercial demands on wooded areas (with villagers at times moved to protect trees by hugging them—known as the chipko movement). In addition, increased population places increased demand on the land for farming, which leads to clearing away trees and brush on the hillsides, which leads to erosion, which deposits more soil on river bottoms, which increases the severity of flooding.

Increased population means increased need for dams. These come at a price. The Sardar Sarover dam on the

Farmers from the village of Sikka survey the swollen Narmada River, under which there was agricultural land just two days prior. (Tom Pietrasik/Corbis)

Narmada River submerged 248 villages. The proposed Mahesh-war dam on the same river, according to *Environmental Defense* (September 2002), "would have flooded 61 villages, displaced 35,000 people, and devastated local ecosystems." It would have affected the lives and livelihoods of countless more. Since 1995, thousands have made protests aimed at preventing construction, which have led to arrests and police attacks.

India's large cities also have increased in population, in most cases in greater proportion than the national increase. Many newcomers are refugees from the countryside unable to make a living there; others are descendants of refugees from the partition at independence (1947) who have nowhere else to go. The result is staggering slums. The problem of clearing the slums is resettlement; Bombay and Calcutta especially are just too crowded. People are homeless, living on sidewalks, in cardboard boxes, and in whatever they can find or construct. Sanitary conditions are nonexistent. Yet the people persevere.

Slum dwellers in front of their shacks near the Victoria Memorial in Calcutta. (Jeremy Horner/Corbis)

In Bombay, many slum women do domestic work for the wealthy in nearby condos and apartments. Calcutta is virtually bankrupt, with barely enough money to get the ancient and decrepit sewers ready to handle the annual monsoon. Communal tensions can easily erupt in such conditions; indeed, it is surprising that the violence is not more widespread.

The increase in population also has been accompanied by an increase in the middle class, which involves increase in the desire for material goods—alarmingly so by those just on the lower fringes of the middle class. Dowry deaths are in part a symptom of this want for more amenities. With the opening of the economy, more goods are available, and though not affordable to most, have become more noticeable as a result of communications and technological advances. A *New York Times* article observed that "India's rapidly growing economy has fueled demand for consumer goods like jewelry" (January 30, 2004) and in an *India Abroad* article,

"Indians shop until they drop . . . the spending power of India's 300-million strong middle class is transforming the nation" (February 27, 2004). There are some very wealthy people in India, but the extent and depth of the poverty, along with population increase and urban ecological damage (e.g., the severity of smog in Delhi has become intense), could eventually increase socioeconomic discontent. At the very least, the dramatic increase in population could significantly add to the problems of governability.

Then there is the matter of expectations. The economic advances being brought about by privatization and technological developments are sure to increase wants, including automobiles and other pollution-causing manufactures, being pushed by companies like General Motors and Honda. The director general of the Tata Energy Research Institute, Rajendra K. Pachauri, has stated that major companies are gearing toward building sports utility vehicles in India: "They see it as a major market. They have the buzz of the people. This is something that should cause real concern." Even the traditional use of kerosene for lighting and cooking, he observed, kills about 600,000 women yearly through asthma and other diseases (*New York Times,* August 20, 2002).

Developing countries tend to see Western demands for restraint as hypocritical (much as in previous years they viewed Western preachments on birth control). This is connected with cost. At a conference in New Delhi, October 2002, Prime Minister Vajpayee stated that India could not replace fossil fuels as an energy source because of cost, nor should it be expected to, as "our per capita greenhouse gas emissions are only a fraction of the world average" (*New York Times,* October 31, 2002).

In contrast, the prime minister on July 26, 2003, called for an "undelayed response" in regard to AIDS, with 4.58 million Indians affected by the end of 2002. Men made up 61.5 percent, but 1 percent of the total were pregnant women. This might not seem all that major in a population of over a billion, except that the increase was from 3.97 million the previous year (*New York Times,* July 26 and 27, 2003). A study funded by the Bill and Melinda Gates Foundation observed: "The spread from high-risk behavior groups to the general populace is another key indicator that HIV/AIDS in India has reached epidemic proportions." In October 2003, the foundation promised $200 million toward fighting AIDS (*New York Times,* November 14, 2003).

Hygienic conditions have for obscure reasons (i.e., village life, climate, tradition) been problematic. Mahatma Gandhi lamented that Indians seemed to be more concerned about ritual purity than sanitation. Before a seminar in New Delhi, Nobel Laureate Amartya Sen remarked, almost in passing (it was not the focus of his address), on "the dreadful state of healthcare in India" (*India Abroad,* August 15, 2003). Just one example: An Associated Press article in the *San Francisco Chronicle,* June 8, 2003, reported that polio is festering in the slums of Calcutta, and that India had experienced a six-fold increase in cases from the previous year. The reasons provided by health workers were distrust in the government, funding shortfalls, rumors about infertility resulting from vaccination, and the inability of illiterate mothers to administer the oral vaccine properly. One could also mention the abominable sanitation and hygienic conditions in the slums. Again, the problem is one of encroachment of people—too many people, and neither enough space nor proper living conditions to accommodate them.

The encroachment of people also means loss of habitat—or at least serious infringement thereon—for India's wild animals. This has been particularly disastrous for tigers. Colonel John Wakefield, an octogenarian born in India and director of the Kabini River Lodge in south India, has observed that population, rather than poaching, is the tiger's major enemy. He feels that India's wilderness areas will soon give way to the necessity for more houses and farmland. Historic sites within India are also falling risk to population pressures. A *National*

Geographic article (October 2002) listed twenty-three "In Danger" sites, including the Ajanta Caves and the Ellora Caves (with their ancient cave drawings), Humayun's Tomb (Delhi), and the Taj Mahal (Agra), as well as a fort, monuments, parks, and even the Darjeeling Railway (a narrow-gauge passenger train in the foothills of the Himalayas, affectionately referred to as "the toy train"). The Ajanta and Ellora Caves are suffering from an overabundance of tourists, while Humayun's Tomb, and especially the Taj Mahal, are deteriorating from industrial pollution in the air.

A nongovernmental organization worthy of particular note is the Centre for Science and Environment (CSE), which dispenses information through several Web sites (available through http://www.google.com) and books, including a series labeled as *The State of India's Environment: A Citizens' Report,* commencing in 1982; the most recent book in the series is the fifth, which a CSE Web site describes as "a comprehensive dossier on environment issues, events, policies and practices, along with statistics on environment-related facts presented in a reader-friendly way." Besides the most obvious concerns, also examined are such matters as increase in consumption of plastics and bottled water being contaminated by pesticides in groundwater.

Pesticides have even been detected—in "high quantities" (according to an August 5, 2003, report by the CSE)—in Coca-Cola and Pepsi products purchased in India, though the charge was dismissed by the companies. Nevertheless, Parliament was outraged (banning Coke and Pepsi machines in parliamentary buildings), and the matter went to the courts. Meanwhile, the government ran new tests on twelve samples, concluding that nine samples showed "marginally higher levels of pesticide" than allowable in the European Union, but nevertheless were acceptable under Indian law (*New York Times,* August 22, 2003). Still, the negative publicity was out. The government, meanwhile, is considering raising the standards to match those of the European Union. Although there have been street protests, there doesn't appear to be any serious call to expel Coca-Cola and Pepsi from India. On the positive side, they are viewed as symbols of globalization; but to some people that is a negative representing a threat and loss of control in opening the economy to foreigners. The issue is likely more serious in terms of ecology than economics. As Amy Walder of the *New York Times* speculated (August 23, 2003), "If pesticides were indeed present in soft drinks, it would probably be because they had soaked into the groundwater used to make them."

Yet, if the social problems that inevitably result from increased population can be managed, India's economic outlook may be very good indeed, according to officials with the global investment firm Morgan Stanley. They predict that India will be the next trillion-dollar economy and by 2020 the fourth-largest world economy (*India Abroad,* April 18, 2003).

INDIAN RELATIONS WITH
THE OUTSIDE WORLD

Since independence, India has enjoyed warm relations with Great Britain, which is to a considerable extent because of the nonviolent nature of the independence struggle. The two female prime ministers of the respective nations, Indira Gandhi and Margaret Thatcher, respected each other and were friends. The Indian navy had a sizable contingent at Lord Mountbatten's funeral; indeed, the degree of respect for him is indicated by the fact that after independence, India asked Mountbatten to stay on through the transition period as governor-general (a position later replaced in the constitution by that of president). India is a member of the Commonwealth, which consists of nations of the old British empire, now on a basis of equality in regard to political and economic bases. Relations with Britain are still very cordial.

During the Cold War, India remained neutral, and it styled itself as the leader of the bloc of neutral nations—at least until

1962, when military hostilities developed with China in the Himalayas. Ever since then, relations with China have been at best lukewarm, although today those relations, while competitive, are more economic than military or political. Both countries now seem more concerned with internal problems than with each other.

Nevertheless, the Chinese defense minister extended an invitation to Indian Defense Minister George Fernandes to visit China, which he did for a week, during April 20–27, 2003. The invitation was seen by observers as an indication of China's desire to bury the past (*India Abroad,* May 2, 2003). There were several issues of concern, if not outright anxiety: the competition "in the race to dominate Asia"; the border conflict, still unresolved although somewhat less festering; India's perception of Chinese military support and nuclear aid to Pakistan; Chinese resentment about India providing refuge for the Dalai Lama (the head of Tibetan Buddhism) and his entourage; and suspicions about India's attitude toward Tibet, which China invaded in the 1950s and continues to govern. There were probably others as well—for example, the degree of political stability in Nepal, the Himalayan kingdom wedged between the two Asian giants.

Fernandes's trip was followed by a visit of Prime Minister Vajpayee to Beijing on June 27 of that year, after which he and his entourage of businessmen then visited other Chinese cities. Trade between India and China is up from a few hundred million dollars less than a decade ago to more than $5 billion today. Vajpayee's visit allegedly focused on trade, but sensitive issues were unofficially discussed, and some issues (e.g., border disputes) were agreed upon to be explored in the future. The important matter is that the talks represented a change of attitude by both nations.

Despite its pronounced policy of Cold War neutrality, India developed with the Soviet Union a "friendship" that included a friendship pact but never a military treaty. There were several reasons for this arrangement: deep concern with U.S.

support for Pakistan (still a concern, albeit much less so), fear of China's intentions and military power (the Soviet Union and China had by that time become estranged), and the on-again off-again relationship with the United States, which was usually more off than on. The Soviets also provided some economic aid (as did the United States, but that aid was not viewed with the same sense of gratitude as was the former). Perhaps most important, Indian leaders tended to feel that the Soviet Union gave India more respect than did the United States—a nation perceived of as not understanding India and not caring to do so. India's relationship with Russia today is cordial but not as strong as it once was; nor is there need for it to be so.

Which brings us to the India–United States relationship. The world's two largest democracies have a history of ambivalence toward each other. On one hand was the Cold War attitude on the part of the United States that "you're either with us or against us." For its part, India's concern was with its own problems, not the U.S.-USSR conflict. On the other hand, perhaps because the United States has a democratic form of government, it seems to have been held to a higher standard than was the Soviet Union, with its difficult history of violent government both before and after the Communist revolution. Nevertheless, Indian leaders were always warmly received in the United States, and U.S. officials likewise in India.

Recent developments have increased both warmth and trust, especially the visit of President Bill Clinton to India toward the end of his presidency, and a return visit of Prime Minister Vajpayee to the United States. The Bush administration has continued to foster warmer relations and has adroitly maneuvered policy in regard to retaining Pakistan's support in the war against terrorism while not losing India's trust. Interestingly, when India does disagree with U.S. policy in regard to the Kashmir struggle and Pakistan, it does so by contending that the United States does not understand the nuances of the situation, and not by impugning its motives (as it likely would have done a couple of decades ago). For example, Indian ambassador Lalit Mansingh chided one hundred senators and representatives at the annual Indian American Friendship Council dinner in Washington, D.C., on July 15, 2003, for U.S. "pandering" to Pakistan. He was not complaining about economic aid, which he said India approved of "because a stable Pakistan is good for India's security." His concern was with $1.5 billion of weaponry, "because historically, every time U.S. weapons have been supplied to Pakistan they have been used against only one country—that is, India." His remarks came a mere seven months after a three-hour meeting between the Indian and U.S. national security advisers, Brajesh Mishra and Condoleeza Rice (December 9, 2002, in Washington), in which Mishra vehemently complained of U.S. tolerance toward Pakistani incursions and violence, which he termed as a double standard in regard to "cross-border terrorism." Yet by early February 2003, Foreign Secretary Kanwal Sibal, visiting Washington, D.C., told the press that a "U.S. tilt toward New Delhi is now evident" (*India Abroad,* December 20, 2002; February 14 and July 25, 2003). As spring—and the U.S. intervention in Iraq—wore on, some Indian officials began to express the opinion that Pakistan should be attacked—even by the United States—for being a terrorist state. The U.S. war in Iraq renewed the charge of a double standard. To add impetus to India's claim, in late April 2003, U.S. ambassador Robert Blackwill, announcing his early resignation effective the following June, observed that the war against terrorism could not be won until "terrorism against India ends permanently" (*Christian Science Monitor,* April 29, 2003). India also threatened to retaliate after the next attack in Kashmir or elsewhere, stating that its patience was wearing thin. In unofficial circles, talk of a preemptive strike was increasing. Then came a surprise announcement by Prime Minister Vajpayee that he wished to work toward the restoration of relations with Pakistan.

Yet, on May 7, 2003, Mishra was conciliatory in an address—

"India, United States, and the New World Order: Prospects for Cooperation"—before the Council of Foreign Relations in New York City. He put the matter of the history of U.S.-India relations succinctly: Cold War ideologies provided a context in which "India and the United States were not really allies. Nor were they enemies." The events of September 11, 2001, he said, changed that (although the warming of relations had previously started with President Clinton's visit toward the end of his term). The perception by each in regard to their relationship moved from regional (i.e., confined to South Asia) to global.

The Henry L. Stimson Center, a Washington think tank, speculated about a possible U.S.-India entente in regard to confining the increase of Chinese power. (Ironically, when Prime Minister Vajpayee visited China, there was speculation as to the thawing of India-China relations leading to a counterbalance of U.S. power in Asia.) Columnists in both India and the United States expressed concern in regard to the American obsession with Iraq that ignored increasing tensions between India and Pakistan.

On the positive side, the move toward privatizing the Indian economy has had a mellowing effect on the two countries' attitudes toward each other. Further, September 11, 2001, had great impact upon the Indian outlook, especially as just a few weeks later a deadly terrorist attack took place on the Indian Parliament. Encouraging and complimentary comments regarding U.S.-India relations have been voiced by leaders such as President Bush and the majority leader in the House of Representatives, Tom DeLay. Joint U.S.-India military exercises occurred late in 2002, in Alaska and at Agra, and the U.S. Congress now has a bipartisan caucus on India. India had 66,836 students in 2001–2002 attending U.S. universities; this figure represented 12 percent of all international students, the largest contingent (China was second with 63,211).

Perhaps underestimated is the influence of Indian Americans and nonresident Indians (NRIs). These include Indian academicians at U.S. institutions (e.g., Nobel laureate for economics Amartya Sen), computer scientists, and many professionals. Arguably the most famous and the most appreciated—a heroine in both countries—was Kalpana Chawla, astronaut on the space shuttle Columbia. Although an U.S. citizen, she kept close contact with her hometown, Karnal, Haryana, arranging for students there to visit the United States and the Houston Space Center. A few weeks before she was killed in the Columbia tragedy, the leading news magazine *India Today* ran her picture on the cover of a special issue on the success of "the Indian diaspora" (as the Indian émigrés are often collectively referred to). The headline read "Making Us Proud." Upon her death, headlines in Indian newspapers ran along lines such as, "India cries for Kalpana Chawla." President A. P. J. Kalam, formerly a scientist and executive in India's space program, pronounced: "We in India had been especially proud that our own Kalpana Chawla was part of this space mission. Alas, we have tragically, though heroically, lost her."

The move toward privatizing the Indian economy also has had a mellowing effect on the two countries' attitudes toward each other, as did the aforementioned terrorist attacks of September 2001.What would be most warming to relations, however, is if India could secure a permanent seat on the United Nations Security Council. Indeed, it is somewhat amazing that the second-largest nation in the world presently does not have such a seat. With India having become a nuclear power, it is receiving more attention and—such is the nature of international politics—more respect.

There are, of course, recurring problems: Americans upset with jobs moving abroad—now, white-collar jobs connected with communications and information technology; American jobs of technological specialization lost to immigrants, causing a stir in Congress (with proposed legislation to change immigration and visa policies) and even in some state legislatures. India is not the only target of concern, but because of its very success in technological education, it is a primary one.

Although U.S.-India trade has drawn increased interest, it has a long way to go: exports to China in 2002 were more than five times those to India. Undersecretary of Commerce Kenneth Juster told the twenty-eighth annual meeting of the U.S. India Business Council in New York that India ranked twenty-seventh in terms of U.S. exports—behind, for instance, Ireland and Jamaica (*India Abroad,* June 13, 2003).

Then there are nongovernmental issues, such as the determination of at least one Indian group to see a moratorium on foreign adoption of children. The concern is, in part, that the adoption procedures in India are often corrupt, and adoption by foreigners encourages poor families to sell baby girls (burdensome because of dowry). Of course Americans seeking a child for adoption don't see the matter in terms of quantity or an imperfect system. To such individuals, in the words of a lengthy feature article in the *New York Times* (June 23, 2003), "the only number that counts is one—the child they are seeking." Of course, there could well be a postcolonial psychology at work here as well.

Perhaps most notably, "the era of globalization" has opened up India to the world. In a column in the *New York Times* (September 22, 2002), Thomas L. Friedman, having recently returned from India, noted a developing social mobility that offers some hope of lifting millions out of "abject poverty" through the acceptance of economic liberalization and cooperation with globalization—including preparation for the inevitable ups and downs; in short, in taking advantage of the emerging global economic development. Tied to global economy, India is becoming increasingly involved in the outside world.

Pakistan and Kashmir

Prime among India's primary foreign policy problems are its dealing with its neighbors, especially Pakistan. The birth of Pakistan at independence (1947) was one of violent severance from India (ironically, and tragically, the birth of Bangladesh in 1971 was to be, as well, one of violent severance from Pakistan). The historical roots go back to the Muslim takeover of government by invaders from central Asia in the late twelfth century. In retrospect, this historical development can seem as overstressed, but the emotions about the period run long and deep and can be raw and ugly. The new nation of Pakistan was (and is) no match for India in terms of hegemony in the region and military prowess.

Kashmir is claimed by both nations. A line of demarcation, resulting from the conflicts right after independence, leaves about one-third of Kashmir in Pakistani control, the other two-thirds in Indian control. It is the only "majority Muslim" state in the Indian union. On that basis, and the nature of the conflict immediately after the partition between the two nations, Pakistan claims all of Kashmir. India will not relinquish it for a number of reasons, chief of which is that to do so might well set off an avalanche of separatist demands for withdrawal from the union: such is present among ethnic groups in northeast India and has but recently been defused in Punjab state. There are other potential situations of separation in a nation so ethnically and culturally diverse as is India. Indians use the example of the Civil War in the United States, which—as they point out—was fought to preserve the union.

India has been at war three times with Pakistan: in 1947 over Kashmir; in 1965 over Kashmir; and in 1971 in regard to the independence movement in Bangladesh. Likely yet another war would have occurred in 2002 but for the nuclear concern and the diplomatic intervention of Britain and the United States. The prime irritant for India is the terrorist attacks in Indian Kashmir, launched from the area controlled by Pakistan. The Pakistani government likely is not directly responsible for the attacks, but the Indian view is that Pakistan should control such incursions and may even be aiding and abetting them. India tends to blame Pakistan for much—

or at least insinuates blame—such as the attack on Parliament in December 2001 and an attack on a Hindu temple in Gujarat in September 2002, as well as other terrorist activities within India. Tensions have been so strong that a quick flashpoint could occur and war between two nuclear powers could erupt. Such a development would not only be disastrous for the region, but also have worldwide consequences.

A study in the November 2002 *National Geographic* offered the following graphic comparisons between the two nations: Population—Pakistan, 144.6 million (Muslim 97 percent, other 3 percent); India, 1.03 billion (Hindu 81.3 percent, Muslim 12 percent, Sikh 1.9 percent, Christian 2.3 percent, other 2.5 percent); Economy—Pakistan, $282 billion; India, $2.2 trillion); Troops—Pakistan, 620,000; India, 1.26 million; Nuclear weapons—Pakistan, 35–50? India may have more, and "reportedly has accumulated enough weapons-grade material to make 100 to 150 nuclear bombs." What is really frightening is that once launched, a missile could not be recalled, and that warning time for major cities would be five minutes.

The results of Kashmiri legislative elections in early October 2002 seem initially encouraging in that the party of the family dynasty that had run Kashmir for more than fifty years, and was vehemently opposed to discussions with Pakistan, was defeated. Both parties of the likely coalition in the legislature favor talks. At the same time as the Kashmiri elections, however, national elections in Pakistan strengthened militant Islamic fundamentalists, which may well make it very difficult for President Musharraf to engage in meaningful dialogue on the Kashmir issue.

Further, the Indian government has historically been intransigent on Kashmir, refusing to include Pakistan in any proposed discussions with militants (India views it as an internal, not bilateral, problem). To make matters worse, a leading militant (Abdul Majeed Dar) who advocated dialogue with the Indian government was assassinated in Kashmir on March 23, 2003.

Coincidentally or otherwise, the next day elsewhere in Kashmir a group of Pandit (high brahmin) families were attacked. They were eleven of the families left in a village from which forty other families had fled. Their Muslim neighbors had assured them of their safety. The attackers were outsiders wearing Indian army uniforms. Of the fifty-two family members in the village, twenty-four were killed, including eleven women and two children. With the United States embroiled in Iraq, fears spread that the violence would increase. The Indian deputy prime minister, L. K. Advani, was dispatched to the site, where he expressed his displeasure not only with Pakistan but with the United States as well for the lack of containment of the violence. The next day Pakistan and India each test-fired nuclear-capable missiles, and India denounced Pakistan as an "epicenter of international terrorism" (*New York Times,* March 23–26, 2003.) On March 27, National Public Radio reported that the U.S. secretary of state and the British foreign minister condemned the act of violence and declared their two nations ready to intercede to help India and Pakistan resolve their differences over Kashmir. It was doubtful either country would agree, especially India, and sure enough, as the *New York Times* reported (March 29, 2003), India "reacted angrily to suggestions from American officials that the two countries should resume a dialogue." Meanwhile, on March 28, "Men believed to be Islamic militants cut off the noses of six villagers" (a time-honored method of punishment to show disgrace). The Muslims were believed to be agents of India.

Then, just when the situation seemed more hopeless than ever, with U.S. deputy secretary of state Richard Armitage on his way to try again to prevent an eruption of hostilities, Prime Minister Vajpayee indicated he wanted one more try at peace—his last chance, he announced (elections were to occur in 2004, and his health seemed to be precarious). This time, however, rather than a summit, a series of steps were to be employed, starting with the resumption of air travel and diplomatic ties. Pakistan responded warmly, Prime Minister Mir Zafarullah Jamali telephoning Vajpayee to invite him to Pakistan. (In India the power lies with the prime minister; in Pakistan, with the president. Relations between Vajpayee and President Musharraf were severely strained from a previous summit, and India did not want a summit atmosphere to develop.) Infiltrations from Pakistan continued, and Pakistan claimed one on the part of Indian soldiers into Pakistan-held territory—perhaps in response (the claim, that is) to Indian accusations that militants wanted to disrupt the process toward rapprochement. In an astute move, the Indian prime minister announced that Pakistan could not be held responsible for all such attacks.

Almost immediately, speculation developed in regard to hard-liners on each side attempting to sabotage the talks. They have the potential to do so because of divisions within the power structure of each country. The Carnegie Endowment for International Peace recently published an analysis, *Spring Thaw in South Asia,* forewarning of stern opposition from the right-wing allies of the Indian prime minister, who, the report predicted, would insist on cessation of all terrorist activities within Kashmir (*India Abroad,* May 30, 2003). Such concerns seem to have been defused by American pressure on both sides through the visit of Deputy Secretary of State Armitage and by the positive response of Pakistani hard-liners. Quick action by the Indian government in regard to restoring diplomatic, communication, transportation, and cultural ties helped immensely. The *Christian Science Monitor* (August 12, 2003) noted: "It's hard to say whether this is the turning point from antipathy to peace. But the moment has clearly changed."

At least two other factors were at work. Foreign policy observers within India began to become frustrated with India's fixation on Pakistan. As one expert, Brahma Chellaney, put it, India's obsession with Pakistan had detracted from its emerging role as a world power, "negatively focusing

its attention and squandering its energies in a semi-failed, terrorist ridden nation next door" (*India Abroad*, June 13,
2003). In short, and put colloquially, it's time to move up and
play ball with the big boys, like China and the United States;
or, in Chellaney's words, "to take India out of the narrow con-
fines of the subcontinent [and] make it into a respected
power in Asia and the world, and in its own eyes." He used the
term "the Pakistan trap" for the delimiting quandary "in
which it finds itself."

The second factor seems to be one of human nature (or at
least as it should be). People on both sides are becoming sick
and tired of needless violence and repetitive, extremist terrorism, which are seriously hindering and damaging the
chances for progress. More human issues have surfaced, sym-
bolized perhaps by the coming together of Pakistani and
Indian physicians and surgeons in regard to Fatiman Noor, a
little Pakistani who underwent heart surgery in Bangalore,
India. In the words of *India Abroad* (August 8, 2003), "The
baby's operation became a catalyst for the Action Group of
Physicians of South Asia." As one physician put it, "We had at
the time no idea what we would do, but we knew it was time
to get to know each other, to explore ways and means of working together."

All this—from the brink of nuclear war, to open talks and
positive steps toward sincere seeking of peace—in just a year.

It seemed too good to be true, and it may be, for on August
25, 2003, two major car-bomb blasts in Bombay killed at least
fifty-two people. The consensus was that the culprits were the
Lashkar-e-Toiba, a Pakistan-based terrorist group active in
Kashmir, and the outlawed Students Islamic Movement of
India. The deputy prime minister, L. K. Advani, long considered a hawk (especially in comparison to Prime Minister Vajpayee), in no uncertain terms blamed Pakistan directly, citing
the failure to turn over to India twenty people wanted for the
1992 Bombay blast that killed over 260, and stating that Pakistan was jealous of India's democracy and economic progress

and hence was determined to destabilize Indian society. Yet, India seemed to continue to exercise patience and a determination to ease tensions and to reestablish basic relations.

There is an avenue for a possible further relaxing of tensions: SAARC. The annual meeting of SAARC provided such an avenue in early January 2004. Vajpayee requested a visit with Musharaff, which was granted; the two met privately the next day, and India agreed to put Kashmir on the agenda for discussions on decreasing hostilities. For his part, Musharaff praised Vajpayee and promised to crack down on terrorists (who had staged two assassination attempts on him in the previous two weeks).

South Asian Association for Regional Cooperation (SAARC)

In April 1981, after previous consultations, the foreign ministers of the seven nations of South Asia—Bangladesh, Bhutan, India, Maldives, Nepal, Pakistan, and Sri Lanka—agreed to form an association for regional cooperation in five nonpolitical areas: agriculture; rural development; telecommunications; meteorology; and health and population activities. Those areas have since deepened and broadened in scope. In December 1985 the heads of government (or state) met for the first time. The charter calls for their meeting annually (three times this has not occurred). There are two important general provisions: unanimous agreement on all decisions; and the exclusion of "bilateral and contentious issues . . . from the deliberations of the Association."

In short, the purpose of the association is to discuss socioeconomic issues and to promote cooperation in those areas. Politics and bilateral relations are not matters for inclusion on the agenda. Yet, SAARC annual meetings offer a stage for such discussions. Although the more public deliberations occur, heads of government can meet privately to explore problems, without such an unofficial meeting seeming to be a "summit."

*Foreign ministers of the South Asian Association for Regional
Cooperation (SAARC) member countries link hands in unity after
signing agreements at the closing ceremony of the summit in
Islamabad on January 6, 2004. (Mian Khursheed/Reuters/Corbis)*

At the 2002 meeting in Katmandu, Nepal, Prime Minister
Vajpayee refused to meet with President Musharraf of Pakistan, even though the latter was receptive to such a meeting. Although the meeting was not scheduled, it was anticipated by observers, and the failure of its occurrence made a
statement.

Ministerial meetings have, since 1986, been held on the following topics: international economic issues, children,
women's issues, environment, disabled persons, youth,
poverty, housing, agriculture, commerce, tourism, information, and communications. Regional centers have been established for agricultural information, tuberculosis, documenta-
tion for various sciences and developmental matters,
meteorological research, and human resources development.
Commerce ministers have met periodically since 1996
regarding matters of trade, especially preferential trade

arrangements. Tourism, energy, and the role of private-sector investment have also been issues in discussions.

SAARC has had consultations with a number of regional and international organizations: the EC (European Commission), ASEAN (Association of Southeast Asian Nations), UNCTAD (United Nations Conference on Trade and Development), UNICEF (United Nations Children's Fund), APT (Asia Pacific Telecommunications), ESCAP (Economic and Social Commission for Asia and the Pacific), UNDP (United Nations Development Program), UNDCP (United Nations Drug Control Program), ITU (International Telecommunications Union), CIDA (Canadian International Development Agency), WHO (World Health Organization), and UNIFEM (United Nations Fund for Women). From these consultations have resulted signed memoranda, agreements, frameworks for cooperation, and conferences (e.g., through the auspices of CIDA, SAARC experts in 1998 participated in a workshop on NAFTA/SAFTA—the North/South American Free Trade Agreement—SAFTA also can imply South Asian Free Trade Area).

Finally, through the years SAARC technical committees have been established in the following sectors: agriculture; communication; education, culture, and sports; environment and meteorology; health, population activities, and child welfare; prevention of drug trafficking and drug abuse; rural development; science and technology; tourism; and women in development.

The impressive record of agenda items, the international cooperation, and outreach to other international agencies, have, of course, not solved all the region's problems; but SAARC has strengthened the ties among the nations of South Asia and has raised their stature in the world beyond the area. Although consensus (unanimity if a matter comes to a vote) is the hallmark for decisions within SAARC, India—by its sheer size and relative power—obviously has the hegemony in the area. As a result, while all nations have benefited, India perhaps has so the most.

References

Akbar, M. J. *Riot after Riot: Reports on Caste and Communal Violence in India.* New Delhi: Penguin, 1991.

Baker, Sophie. *Caste: At Home in Hindu India.* Calcutta: Rupa, 1991.

Bumiller, Elisabeth. *May You Be the Mother of a Hundred Sons: A Journey among the Women of India.* New Delhi: Penguin, 1991.

Elder, Joseph. "Enduring Stereotypes about South Asia: India's Caste System." *Education about Asia* 1996 (fall): 20–22. Also available at http://www.dalitusa.org/es.html.

———, ed. *Lectures in Indian Civilization.* Dubuque, IA: Kendall/Hunt, 1970.

"Global Campaign Halts India's Giant Maheshwar Dam." *Environmental Defense* 2002 (September): 8.

Johnson, Gordon. *Cultural Atlas of India.* New York: Facts on File, 1996.

Koller, John M. *The Indian Way.* New York: Macmillan, 1982.

Lewis, Oscar. *Village Life in North India: Studies in a Delhi Village.* New York: Vintage, 1958.

Mishra, Pankaj. "Kashmir, the Unending War." *New York Review of Books,* October 19, 2000, http://www.nybooks.com/articles/13850. Updated February 27, 2003.

Mohanti, Prafulla. *My Village, My Life: Nanpur: A Portrait of an Indian Village.* London: Transworld, 1975.

O'Reilly, James, and Larry Habegger, eds. *Travelers' Tales India.* San Francisco: Travelers' Tales, 1995.

Wiser, William, and Charlotte Wiser. *Behind Mud Walls.* Berkeley: University of California Press, 1971, 2000.

Web Sites

Film: http://www.indiaonestop.com/film.htm
Media: http://www.indonet.com
National Geographic: http://magma.nationalgeographic.com/ngm/0306
Newspapers: http://www.samachar.com
South Asian Association for Regional Cooperation: http://www.saarc-sec.org
Television: http://www.dinesh.com/india/television.shtml

PART TWO
REFERENCE MATERIALS

Key Events in Indian History

3000 B.C.E.	"Start" of Indus, or Harappan, civilization (c. 2300–1750 B.C.E.)
1500 B.C.E.	First of invading waves of Aryans (Indo-European speakers)
500 B.C.E.	Buddha; historical recordings; philosophical challenges to Brahminism
326 B.C.E.	Alexander at the Beas, tributary of the Sutlej, hence, Indus
321 B.C.E.	Chandragupta Maurya founds Maurya dynasty (321–185 B.C.E.)
260 B.C.E.	Asoka defeats the Kalingas; promulgates "dhamma"
320	Chandragupta I founds Gupta dynasty (C.E. 320–480 or 490)
400	Gupta (and Indian) Golden Age; Chandragupta II (C.E. 380–415)
606	Harsa's (d. C.E. 647) accession ("Camelot")
711	Muhammad ibn Qasim in Sind
1000	Mahmud of Ghazni commences series of invasions/raids
1185	Muhammad Ghuri conquers Lahore
1206	Commencement of Delhi Sultanate (i.e., "medieval India")
1206–1290	Slave dynasty
1290–1320	Khilji dynasty
1320–1413	Tughluq dynasty
1414–1450	Sayyid period

1450–1526	Lodi dynasty
1526	Commencement of Mughal empire
1526–1530	Babur
1530–1556 (in exile 1540–1555)	Humayun
1556–1605	Akbar
1600	East India Company chartered
1605–1627	Jahangir
1612	First company "factory" (post) at Surat (moved to Bombay in 1674)
1627–1658	Shah Jahan
1640	Company post established in Madras
1658–1707	Aurangzeb
1690	Company post established in Calcutta
1707–1857	various
1773	First of several parliamentary acts seeking to regulate the company
1858	Transfer of government following the Sepoy Mutiny
1877	Queen Victoria declared empress of India
1919	Amritsar massacre
1947	Partition and independence
August 15, 1947	Establishment of the Republic of India
January 30, 1948	M. K. Gandhi assassinated
May 27, 1964	Jawaharlal Nehru dies
October 31, 1984	Indira Gandhi assassinated
May 21, 1991	Rajiv Gandhi assassinated

Significant People, Places, and Events

The culture of India is so vast, its history so long and in many ways regional, that the selection of items for a glossary is necessarily somewhat arbitrary. The problems of inclusion-exclusion have been faced with the primary criterion in terms of perceived significance for Americans. To further keep the list manageable, only Indians have been included (hence, Louis Mountbatten is excluded).

Advani, L. K. (1928–) Deputy prime minister; probably the most important power within the Bharatiya Janata Party, of which he was a cofounder in 1980 and was president for ten years. He once appeared in a campaign in imitation of the god Rama (Ram), complete with bow and arrows—a clear appeal for the oft-touted return of the Ram Raj—Hindu rule.

Ajanta Caves Cave temples with fresco-like paintings and religious sculptures cut out of rock, discovered by a company of British soldiers on maneuver in 1817, in south central India in a gorge near the source of the Waghora River. Painted by Buddhist monks from the fourth to the seventh centuries C.E., the wall paintings are surprisingly secular in appearance, with themes taken largely from the jataka tales—folk morality stories based upon previous lives of the Buddha. According to art historian Benjamin Rowland (*The Ajanta Caves: Early Buddhist Paintings from India*, UNESCO, 1963, 5), "The styles of Buddhist painting in Tibet and Nepal, Central Asia, China and ultimately Japan all have their beginnings in the classic mode represented by this series of murals."

Ambedkar, B. R. (1891–1956) Leader of the Dalits
(untouchables) and "the prime architect of the Constitution
of independent India" (http://www.ambedkar.org), Ambedkar
is one of the most important figures of twentieth-century
India. He studied economy at Columbia University and
received a law degree in London. Repeatedly discriminated
against, he once observed, "I was born a Hindu, but will never
die a Hindu," which was prophetic as just a couple of months
before his death he converted to Buddhism. He is revered
among Dalits more than any other person.

Amritsar A city in Punjab, site of two "massacres" and the
holy Golden Temple of the Sikhs. In April 1919 troops under
General Reginald Dyer opened fire without warning on a
crowd assembled against curfew restrictions, on a holiday, in
an open area (but hemmed in by surrounding buildings)
called Jallianwala Bagh. Official figures estimated about 1,600
casualties from 1,650 rounds fired, 379 of which were fatalities; an unofficial but reliable estimate was 530 fatalities. The
result was a hardening of attitude by Indians, with leaders
shifting from a demand of home rule to that of full independence (*purna swaraj*).

In June 1984 the Indian army was dispatched by Prime
Minister Indira Gandhi to dislodge Sikh separatists from the
Golden Temple, from which they had been launching terrorist attacks. Their leader was martyred and the temple badly
damaged. That October, Indira Gandhi was assassinated by
two Sikh members of her bodyguard. A massacre of Sikhs followed in the capital.

Aryan/Indo-Aryan *Aryan* is a linguistic term for the Indo-
Aryan branch of Indo-European languages, of which English,
Sanskrit, and north Indian languages are all members; thus,
the Sanskrit *matr* is obviously related to English *maternity*
and *mother*. The word *Aryan*, also related to "Iran" and
"Eire," has become laden with racism because of Nazi appro-

priation of the term without recognition of its basic meaning and function.

"Aryans"—i.e., speakers of proto-Sanskrit—entered India in waves, through several centuries (c. 1500–1000 B.C.E. or so). They probably came from central Asia, although a recent revisionist school of thought insists that the Aryans did not come from outside but were within India, possibly even in the Indus civilization. So far, this theory is untenable. Regardless, the Aryan speakers carried with them, through memorization, the Veda, which is the oldest collection of hymns and documents in any Indo-European language.

Ayodhya   Devotees believe that the god Rama (or Ram) was born in this northern Indian city. About 1528 the first Mughal ruler, Babur, built a mosque on the site that some have claimed to mark Rama's birthplace. In December 1992, zealots tore it down, although it had not been used for centuries. Widespread attacks on Muslims followed in the city and elsewhere, and the attack as well as the brutalities that followed took on a Hindu chauvinist aspect. The issue has become taken under consideration by Parliament and the courts.

Bollywood   A term combining "Bombay" and "Hollywood" to label India's film capital. Between eight hundred and one thousand films are produced annually, almost all in Bombay (Mumbai), and most in Hindi. As might be expected, a subculture has developed around the film industry, including some unsavory characteristics.

Bose, Subhash Chandra (1897–1945)   A national hero in his native Bengal, Bose was described by his political nemesis M. K. Gandhi as "Patriot of Patriots." On the theory that "the enemy of my enemy is my ally," Bose raised troops (the Indian National Army) and allied with the Germans and then the Japanese. He had little influence on either nation and was used by each for propaganda purposes. His death is alleged to have been in an airplane accident near the end of World War II, but the specifics have never been fully confirmed.

Buddha (c. 566–480) Born in Lumbini (now in Nepal), Siddhartha Gautama was the son of a leader of the Sakyas, a tribal republic. He is also termed Sakyamuni, or Sage of the Sakyas. According to legend he was pampered and raised in luxury. Disturbed by seeing a sick man, an old man, and a corpse, and then seeing a monk, he left home and family to seek enlightenment. Upon enlightenment, he became a buddha; literally, awakened. He saw the true nature of existence and spent the rest of his life spreading the message. He also counseled King Bimbisara and his son and successor, Ajatasatru.

Chanakya, or Kautilya Adviser to Chandragupta Maurya (India's first emperor), Chanakya wrote (or perhaps more accurately compiled) the *Arthasastra,* or *Treatise on Power* (c. 300 B.C.E.), which has been compared to Machiavelli's *The Prince* for its amoral realpolitik. It is an amazing work, delineating how to run a kingdom in a bureaucratic and quasi-totalitarian manner. There is even a section on courtesans—whose rights, by the way, are steadfastly defended, even to the point of calling for capital punishment if a courtesan is forced to engage in sex after she has said no.

Dalits *Dalit*—"oppressed"—is the term used by the people who have historically been referred to as untouchables, outcastes, and pariahs. They are mostly poverty ridden and are castigated for no reason other than the heritage of their birth. They have gathered strength in urban areas and as a result of governmental affirmative-action programs, which have been met with vicious opposition in some areas. They still are underprivileged.

Dravidian   The term is used for a people and a culture, but it is actually a linguistic label for languages of the four south Indian states: in Andhra Pradesh, the Telugu language; in Tamil Nadu, Tamil; in Karnataka, Kannada; and in Kerala, Malayalam. There also are twenty lesser Dravidian languages; one, Brahui, is found near the Indus River sites in the northwest, which adds support to the theory that Dravidian speakers are descendants of the Indus civilization, pushed south by the invading Aryans. There are significant cultural differences and tensions between the north and the south, so the use of the term in a cultural sense fits.

East India Company   A private organization chartered by Queen Elizabeth I on December 31, 1600. It was responsible for the establishment of the port cities of Madras (Chennai), Calcutta (Kolkata), and Bombay (Mumbai). The political vacuum left by the disintegration of the Mughal empire caused the English merchants to become conquerors, and the company unwittingly (at least at first) found itself on the road to empire. By 1773, Parliament had become concerned with the company's growing political and economic power, and abuses resulting therefrom, and started putting restraints on it. In 1858, Parliament abolished the company and itself took over direct rule of India.

The Emergency (1975–1977)   A complex political and matter-of-state situation in which virtual martial law was declared and put upon the country during the premiership of Indira Gandhi. The provision under which it was done was entirely legal (if questionable in application), left over from the days of the British Raj and not removed after independence. This emergency was declared in regard to internal enemies of the state—not external dangers. Political opponents of the government were imprisoned, and local police used the situation to suit their own agendas.

Gandhi, Mohandas Karamchand (1869–1948) Primary leader of India's independence movement and developer of satyagraha, a method of seeking social (including political) change through nonviolent methods. Satyagraha influenced movements in the United States, Africa, and Europe. Indeed, Gandhi developed the theory and method while in South Africa. He was assassinated by a militant right-wing Hindu conspiracy.

Goa "Golden Goa" is a true fusion: Indian and Portuguese, "fully Westernized—with bars, clothiers, milliners, and jewellery and perfumery stores brimming with foreign goodies" (Mario Cabral E Sá and Amit Pasricha, *Goa: Pearl of the East,* New Delhi: Lustre Press, 1996; p. 19). The Portuguese were the first Europeans in modern times to occupy India (1498) and the last out (1961, being dislodged by the Nehru government). Their influence is shown in Goa's 167 Roman Catholic churches and abundance of Portuguese surnames and place names. Situated alongside the Arabian Sea in southwest India, Goa is a popular tourist destination for Indians and non-Indians alike.

Gupta Dynasty (c. 320–469) The Gupta dynasty did not achieve the imperial status of the Maurya dynasty; the bureacracy was not as pervasive, and conquests of territory often were supplanted by areas of "influence" rather than ones of total domination. The founder was Chandragupta (r. c. 320–335), whose domain was the east central Gangetic plain. His son, Samudragupta, in his long reign (c. 335–375) extended conquests along the east coast of India and into the interior, as well as increasing his power in the tributary states. The glory of the dynasty, however, lies in the reign of Chandragupta II (c. 375–415), India's so-called golden or classical age (although there were similar such reigns and periods in the south). It was an era of great art and literature. After the death of Chandragupta II's grandson in 467, the imperial days were all but over, with even the coinage for which the dynasty was justly renowned becoming debased, and the territory becoming fragmented.

Humayun's Tomb   Before the stairwells were cemented up by the government, if one went to the top of "Humayun's Library" in the Old Fort (Purana Qila) of Delhi, he or she could see in the distance, near the Jumna, a breathtaking sight: the tomb of the second Mughal emperor, Humayun (d. 1556). The tomb itself is open to the public and is far less crowded than the Taj Mahal, of which it is a precursor. It is especially delightful in that there is a huge amount of greenery—probably more than in the Taj—and affords at times a sense of privacy. It offers, from the platform above the graves but below the dome, a panoramic view of the capital city.

Independence   On August 15, 1947, India received her independence from Great Britain, although it was more a matter of having been won by the Indians than granted by Great Britain. Because of the nonviolent approach led by M. K. Gandhi, the British left—to paraphrase Walter Cronkite—with cheers rather than jeers. Unfortunately, the partition of British India at independence, which resulted in two nations—Pakistan as well as India—also resulted in millions migrating and hundreds of thousands killed. Nevertheless, India became the world's largest democracy, and a secular one at that.

Indian National Congress/Congress Party   Founded in 1885 almost as a discussion society, the Indian National Congress was transformed by Gandhi and others into the instrument that wrested independence from the British. After independence it was the ruling party from 1947–1977, 1980–1989, and 1991–1996; since 1996 it has been the largest minority party, hence leader of the opposition. Through most of its history since independence, the party has been led by a member of the Nehru (or Nehru-Gandhi) family.

Indus (Harappan) Civilization (c. 3000–1500 B.C.E.; heyday, 2500–1700 B.C.E.) Ancient civilization of many cities centered in the Indus River system but extending well beyond the drainage area of the system. When more is learned about it through archaeological research, it may well prove to be the largest and most impressive of all ancient civilizations. Its city-planning and sophisticated drainage system are particularly impressive.

Kabir (1440–1518) Poet and religious synthesizer, older contemporary and precursor of Guru Nanak (1469–1539), the founder of the Sikh religion. He insisted that it did not matter what name one used for God, that all true devotees, no matter what religion, could find God within their hearts. His poetry reflected and advanced his message, and when he died, his disciples allegedly argued over how to dispose of his body—with Hindus arguing for cremation, and Muslims for burial. When his disciples later entered the room where the body had been lying in state, in its place they found a dozen roses. The legend goes that the Hindus burned their half-dozen and the Muslims buried theirs.

Kalidasa Even less is known about India's greatest literary figure than is known about Shakespeare, to whom he is often compared because of his superb poetic talent and dramatic genius. He probably lived during India's golden classical age, the reign of Chandragupta II, 380–415, although even that has been disputed. Of his surviving works, the most famous is *Abhijnanasakuntalam* (or simply *Sakuntala,* after its heroine), "The Recognition of Sakuntala." This work is justly acknowledged as one of the finest pieces in world literature. Kalidasa took a brief incident from the *Mahabharata,* lengthened it greatly, and enriched it into a powerful poetic drama, transforming the heroine into such a vivid character that she has been extolled by Indians and non-Indians, including Goethe. His narrative and lyrical poetry makes metaphorical connections between nature and people (particularly lovers) and is richly romantic without becoming syrupy.

Kumbha Mela With origins in or before the seventh century C.E., this festival is held every twelve years (as determined by astrological configurations) at the city of Allahabad, located at the confluence of the rivers Ganges, Jumna, and the mythical Saraswati. It is the largest pilgrimage festival in the world and was last held in 2001. Somewhat "lesser" kumbha melas are held in three other locations, three years apart from one another, accounting for a cycle of four over a twelve-year period.

Madurai Now a city of about 2 million, Madurai is an ancient temple and festival center about 2,500 years old. It played a large political and cultural role as capital of the Chola and Pandya kingdoms and represents a classical period of south Indian art and architecture—perhaps the epitome of Dravidian culture, as represented in the Tamil epic *Shilappadikaram.*

Mahavira (c. 540–468) A contemporary of the Buddha, Vardhamana was likewise a noble who left home and family to seek enlightenment; after accomplishing this, he was known as Mahavira, Great Hero, and as Jina, Conqueror (of the cycle of rebirth). He is not considered by Jains to be the literal founder of Jainism, but the twenty-fourth in a series of *tirthankara,* or a builder of the ford that leads across the stream of rebirth. At least one predecessor, Parsva, is considered as historical.

Maurya Dynasty (c. 320–181 B.C.E.**)** A young adventurer named Chandragupta Maurya gained the imperial dream from Alexander of Macedon, whom he met (probably) when Alexander was encamped at the Beas, a river in the Indus system. He returned home to Pataliputra and replaced a decaying and unpopular dynasty, commencing to build an empire that reached its height—the greatest of any empire in pre-British India—under his grandson, Asoka (r. c. 268–233).

Asoka developed a policy called *dhamma,* based on Hindu dharma, or duty, which called for restraint and cooperation among his subjects. It was a "paternal despotism," but this was a far kindlier rule than was common in ancient times. To promulgate his philosophy he had a series of edicts carved upon rocks and pillars throughout the empire. The empire was huge in area, its bureaucracy complex; Asoka's abilities were considerable and his reign long. The logistics of running such an extensive empire seems to have been beyond the capabilities of his successors, and the empire—and with it, the concept of dhamma—withered away.

Monsoon The monsoon—actually, there are two, the summer one being of more importance—assures India of a harvest. The monsoon is the sustenance not only for people and crops, but for rivers as well. It has great psychological impact, most especially for city-dwellers, for it breaks a long spell of almost unspeakable heat. Its impact has been aptly related by Alexander Frater in *Chasing the Monsoon* (New Work: Knopf, 1991) and an ABC television production based on the book.

Mughal Dynasty (1526–1857) The great Mughal rulers of early India were Babur, the founder of the dynasty (1526–1530); Humayun (1530–1556), who spent most of his reign in exile; Akbar (1556–1605), who built the empire, making it possible for his son Jahangir (1605–1627) and grandson Shah Jahan (1627–1658) to pursue cultural interests and safely delegate administration to subordinates; and Aurangzeb (1658–1707), whose exploits trying to conquer southern kingdoms in the last two decades of his life effectively bankrupted the empire. Those who followed were weak and ineffective, with the last deposed by the British after the Sepoy Mutiny, by which time the emperor was facetiously referred to as "the king of Delhi," so much had the Mughal territory shrunk.

Nagarjuna (probably first century C.E.) Nagarjuna was perhaps the most important figure in regard to Buddhist thought (except, of course, for the Buddha himself), yet, as one source puts it, "there has been hardly another personality so elusive as his" (K. Venkata Ramana, *Nagarjuna's Philosophy,* 1975). He is believed to have been a south Indian brahmin who converted to Buddhism, and his works explore the nature of reality—*sunyata,* or "no-thing-ness," and *pratitya-samutpada,* or "interrelatedness." His thought forms the basis of "the middle way," which rejects extremes in regard to the description of reality.

Nanak (Guru Nanak) (1469–1539) The founder and first guru of the Sikh faith (a guru is a "spiritual teacher"; a sikh is a "learner"). Selected features of Hinduism and of Islam were adopted and adapted; others were rejected. Nanak was born in the Punjab, where today in Indian Punjab (the province was split at Partition), Sikhism is strongest. Although only composing about 2 percent (or about 20 million) of the population of India, Sikhs can seem far more numerous, especially in the north. This is in part due to their agricultural, financial, and political power in Punjab; their roles in cities, ranging from professionals to taxi drivers; and their formidable appearance, often larger than other Indians and with the men wearing distinctive turbans.

Nanak's rejection of idols and enunciation of the equality of believers—along with Mughal persecution of the community and martyrdom of some leaders—has led to a strong sense of community among Sikhs.

Nehru Family The Nehrus were the most influential family in twentieth-century Indian politics. Motilal Nehru (1861–1931) was a powerful, wealthy lawyer and a leader of the Indian

National Congress and the independence movement. His son Jawaharlal (1889–1964), also an important independence leader, was the first prime minister (1947–1964) of independent India. Jawaharlal's daughter, Indira (1917–1984), was India's third prime minister (1966–1977; 1980–1984). She married Feroze Gandhi (1913–1960, a Parsi and no relation to M. K. Gandhi) in 1942. Her son Rajiv (1944–1991), who was an airline pilot rather than a politician, was selected to succeed her as prime minister (1984–1989) in concern for continuity and unity after her assassination. He was assassinated by Sri Lankan Tamil Tiger terrorists for his support of the Sri Lankan government during the guerrilla war in Sri Lanka. Rajiv's widow, Sonia, is currently leader of the Congress Party.

Collateral members of the family have been of importance as well (e.g., B. K. Nehru, Motilal's nephew, a diplomat; Vijaya Lakshmi Pandit, Motilal's daughter, a diplomat; and Nayantara Sahgal, Motilal's granddaughter, a novelist). Rajiv's younger brother, Sanjay (1946–1980), was active as adviser to his mother before his death in the crash of his private airplane; his widow, Manika, has been active in political parties in opposition to the Congress Party.

Panini (fifth century B.C.E. or earlier) Panini's grammar provided the standard for classical Sanskrit, setting a structure for the language that has not changed and that has provided the medium for literature, philosophy, religious discourse, and science. His grammar of the Sanskrit may well have been the first work in linguistics.

Partition At independence on August 14–15, 1947, British India was divided into two new nations: India and Pakistan, the latter of which had west and east wings, separated by 1,500 miles of India. The idea was to prevent, or at least minimize, violence, and to provide a homeland for Muslims. The dislocation was devastating. Muslims fled northern India to Pakistan while Hindus and Sikhs fled into India. Between

200,000 and 1 million are estimated to have been killed during the migration (it was so chaotic that a more precise estimate is unlikely). The socioeconomic dislocation, massacres, and rapes have been recounted in many novels, one of which, Khushwant Singh's *Train to Pakistan,* has been in print for decades. In 1971 a bloody civil war, which resulted in Indian intervention, brought about the independence of the eastern wing, now Bangladesh, from the western wing. Both wings have experienced various military coups.

Pondicherry   As Goa is of Portuguese flavor and influence, Pondicherry is of French. Located along India's southeast coast just south of Madras, the town was started in 1673 (although some settlement existed since Roman times) by the French as a trade center. The Dutch took it in 1693 and gave it back to the French in 1699. France's greatest figure in India, Joseph François Dupleix (1697–1763; he has been characterized as "the greatest enemy the East India Company ever had"), had it in mind as the capital of the French empire in India. But in a series of wars—in Canada and Europe as well as India—the French lost to the British. In 1761 Pondicherry was razed by the British, but it was reconquered by the French in 1765. In 1954 France ceded Pondicherry to India—six years after the British had left, but seven years before the Portuguese departure.

Pondicherry is famed as the spiritual center of Sri Aurobindo Ghosh (1872–1950), a Bengali terrorist against the British who was given asylum by the French on the provision he renounce political activism. His philosophical and literary works have developed respect from scholars, and his religious ideas resulted in a number of followers and a series of establishments in the United States and elsewhere.

Raziya   Ruler of the Delhi Sultanate from 1236 to 1240, Sultana Raziya (the spelling of her name varies in English) is one of the most romantic—and tragic—figures in Indian history and culture. In some ways she seems more legend than history. Allegedly appearing before the Friday mosque in a fiery red dress after her father's death, she rallied the Delhi nobles for her claims to succeed him. She was unmarried and is reputed to have been ravishingly beautiful. As a result, she was courted both for her beauty and her throne, and when she did choose, the results were not only the loss of her throne but of her life. Buried in an unmarked grave, she remains not only a mystery but perhaps the first woman—at least in South Asia—to rule a Muslim kingdom.

Roy, Ram Mohan (1772–1833) Hindu reformer and catalyst for the Bengali Renaissance. Roy was instrumental in encouraging the British to institute social reform, especially in regard to *sati* (suttee), or widow immolation on the husband's funeral pyre (a practice not really widely practiced, but abhorrent nonetheless). Interested in Christian and Islamic thought, he used Western ideas for Hindu reform. He thus represented a synthesis between East and West, perhaps the first such in the Raj.

Sankara (788–820) Important religious philosopher central to the important school of Advaita Vedanta (nondualism, or monism), affecting—perhaps even effecting—the philosophical development of Hinduism to this day. His impact not only made advaita the dominant philosophy within Hinduism, it effectively countered Buddhist philosophy within India. Further, it had considerable impact on certain American and European thinkers.

Sepoy Mutiny, a.k.a. the "First War of Independence," or the Rebellion of 1857 Exactly what this event should be called is a sensitive issue, one bordering on political correctness. Many historians feel the uprising to have been basically reactionary in character, with regional powers concerned about loss of privileges and principalities. Savage carnage occurred on both sides, and rupture between the two was complete: they would never trust each other again. The East India Company was dissolved, as was the fiction of what remained of the Mughal empire. The immediate cause was the distribution of cartridges coated in grease to Indian soldiers (sepoys) in the hire of the East India Company. The coating was thought to be pig fat or cow fat, or both, thus anathema to both Muslims and Hindus. At Meerut, north of Delhi, the soldiers slew their officers and marched on Delhi, pronouncing the pathetic old Mughal emperor to be their leader. Although the conflict was largely confined to north-central India, the damage in relations was irreparable.

Shankar, Ravi (1920–) Composer, virtuoso, master teacher, Ravi Shankar is heralded in his country and abroad. He has written film music (for such hits as *Pather Panchali*, 1955) and has established associations and institutions to propagate interest in Indian classical music. In a sense, he introduced the world—from the Beatles to Woodstock—to the sitar. Objecting to drugs and misrepresentation of Indian culture, he moved from pop festivals to composing and performing jazz (such as with Bud Shank and the Pacific Coast Jazzmen) and classical music (with Andre Previn and Zubin Mehta). He has won many honors, including Grammy Awards. In recent years he has performed at fewer concerts, but his two daughters are each very active in music: Norah Jones, the popular pop singer and 2003 "Grammy Queen," and Anouska Shankar, sitarist who on September 21, 2003, at Avery Fisher Hall in New York City "performed the premiere of 'The Offering,' a piece by her father . . . based on a raga originally used for prayers" (*New York Times*, September 23, 2003).

Tagore Family The Tagore (Thakur, in some accounts) family has been called "the leading family of the city"—that is, historically so, most especially in a cultural sense. Within three generations of this remarkable family were many, many prominent figures—too many to list here—in art, philosophy, literature, and social and religious reform. Perhaps the most prominent and well-known were the patriarch, Dwarkanath (1795–1846), merchant and businessman; Devendranath (1818–1905), religious and social reformer; Rabindranath (1861–1941), poet, dramatist, novelist, painter, and 1913 Nobel laureate for literature; Gagendranath (1867–1938), perhaps most known for his sketches and caricatures of social commentary; and Abindranath (1871–1951), trend-setter for the Bengali school of Indian painting. Many of the Tagore women were interested and active in social change and cultural advancement but, perhaps because of the times, did not achieve the individual prominence of the men.

Taj Mahal Probably India's greatest tourist attraction—deservedly so—"The Taj" (in Agra) surpasses all of the many lovely Mughal architectural achievements. It is a cliché, but true, that even the most beautiful photograph cannot do the Taj justice. It was built by the emperor Shah Jahan for his favorite wife, Mumtaz, who died in 1631 after bearing fourteen of his children. He is also buried there, having spent the last years of his life incarcerated in a fort overlooking the Taj from across the Jumna River. The Taj was listed in the October 2002 issue of *National Geographic* as among fifteen world cultural sites in serious environmental danger (in the case of the Taj, from acidic atmosphere caused by pollution).

Vajpayee, Atal Bihari (1926–) Prime minister of India since 1999 and veteran statesman, having served as external affairs minister and almost thirty years in parliament. As a student he joined the Quit India Movement (directed at the British) in 1942. He has also been a journalist and social worker and is a poet, writing in Hindi.

Varanasi, a.k.a. Banaras Varanasi is the ancient and current name of the city the British called Benares; it is still affectionately referred to as Banaras. It is a holy city for Hindus, on the sacred Ganges River. Perhaps the oldest continuously lived-in city in the world (the Buddha went there after his enlightenment, as it was already known as an ancient center of learning and spirituality), it is also a modern city with a renowned university and first-rate tourist facilities. Still, most of all it is a pilgrimage center, one to which some devout people go to await death, to have their remains cremated on the banks of Mata Ganga—Mother Ganges. Because of its location, age, and continuity, Varanasi has special significance for India and for Hinduism in particular.

Indian Languages, Food, and Etiquette

*"The more fragmented the world gets,
the more desperate we are for etiquette."*

—Amy Dickinson (successor to Ann Landers at
the *Chicago Tribune*) in an interview with the
New York Times Magazine, July 27, 2003

India is so geographically vast and culturally diverse that generalizations in regard to etiquette and food are almost impossible. Food preferences depend upon religion, caste, and region, as well as, of course, personal likes (e.g., many Indians are vegetarian out of choice, not due to religious restrictions). Etiquette, too, can differ in regard to tradition, social status, and degree of Westernization.

LANGUAGES

The complexities and perplexities of the language situation in India are astounding and cut across several levels. First is the large number of languages. The census of India recognizes ninety-six languages—eighteen scheduled (constitutionally recognized as major languages) and seventy-four nonscheduled. The decision in regard to scheduled and nonscheduled was in a sense political, with the scheduled languages having specific identity with certain states. Three of the nonscheduled languages have more speakers each than four of the scheduled languages but are without a broad state basis.

The scheduled languages, followed by the top twenty nonscheduled languages (in terms of number of speakers) are listed in the tables on pages 208 and 209. These data are from the 1991 census, because the language census data from the 2001 census was not available as the time when this book went to press. The number of speakers listed beside each is in terms of those who declared that language as their mother tongue, for 19.44 percent of the population (1991 census) is bilingual, which represents a steady increase since the 9.70 percent in the 1961 census. Many people also claim to be trilingual. Due to political unrest in Kashmir, figures for that state were not available.

To complicate matters further, linguistic inclusion or exclusion is not always clear. Hindi has a number of dialects, some of which seem clearly to be dialects, others are arguable. This problem is reflected in the wide range of figures given as the actual number of languages: Language in India (http://www.languageinindia.com) concludes from the data of the 1991 census that there are 114 languages (even though only 96 are listed). It also states that "Hindi includes around 48 languages, dialects, or mother tongues," which in itself reflects the murky nature of the language situation. The census itself mentions 216 "mother tongues" (perhaps a term that diffuses the language-dialect issue). Two other figures for the number of languages in India, given by Culturopedia (http://www.culturopedia.com) and Ethnologue Report for India (http://www.ethnologue.com) are 407 and 850, respectively.

There are social implications as well. Caste and class variations will occur within a language, not unlike national variations within English (e.g., Canadian, Australian, Scottish, Indian) or regional dialects within American English (e.g., New England, the South). There is also the matter of diglossia, or sociolinguistic codes in regard to status and class differences of speaker and hearer. Thus, there are three levels of the pronoun *you* in Hindi: formal, intimate, inferior. Urbanization, education, and especially newspapers have had effect on languages. In regard to Hindi, for example, some papers opt for a "Sanskritized" vocabulary (use of Sanskrit words for the more vernacular counterparts).

Then there is the matter of scripts. Technically, scripts are not languages, for they are written whereas languages are spoken. Someone may be trilingual, but illiterate; and scripts can be adapted for a particular language (as in the case of Sanskrit). Nevertheless, scripts express the language in writing—the spoken word becomes the written word. As such, they are associated with one or more languages. Even the number of scripts is hard to ascertain, for as with languages, it is not always easy to decide which is a separate script and which is a variation rather than a derivation from another script. Malayalam, Kannada, and Telugu all have their own scripts, each being a modification of the Tamil script. Suffice it to say there are probably about a dozen scripts.

The history of language development is also complex. The two major language families in India are Dravidian in the south and Indo-Aryan in the north (except for Sinhalese, the primary language of Sri Lanka, which is Indo-Aryan). Indo-Aryan languages are a branch of Indo-Iranian, itself a branch of Indo-European.

The modern Indo-Aryan languages (as listed in the table on page 208) are Hindi, Bengali, Marathi, Urdu, Gujarati, Oriya, Punjabi, Assamese, Sindhi, Nepali, Konkani, Manipuri, Kashmiri, and Sanskrit (which is likely listed for purposes of prestige and politics—it really is not a modern language developed from its classical roots). These languages are descended from variations of the ancient Vedic Sanskrit (or early prakrits), which was prior to classical Sanskrit. The antecedents to the modern languages were brought into India with the waves of Aryan incursions. The prakrits then developed into apabhramsas, the medieval or early forms of the modern languages, which, of course, became the modern languages. The languages are reflective of the particular cultures that developed, resulting from the political diffusion that occurred prior to the conquest of Muslim groups from central Asia (c. 1185). There are other anomalies. Konkani, spread along the southwest coast, was influenced by the Dravidian Kannada and

Malayalam languages. It was for a time derisively considered a dialect of Marathi (thus, it has been strongly affected by the larger languages in the area). Missionaries and others were able to depict Assamese as a "sibling" language to Bengali, rather than a dialect. A 1968 bill passed by the legislature of Manipur resulted in the inclusion of a language of the Tibeto-Burman family being included with Manipuri, an Indo-Aryan language; thus, politics superceded linguistics. Two different languages, from different language families, became politically assimilated.

Another example of historical impact is Urdu (the word is cognate with English "horde"), or "the language of the camp,"

Top Eighteen Scheduled Languages in Descending Order of Strength (1991 Census)

1. Hindi	337,272,114	39.85%
2. Bengali	69,595,738	8.22%
3. Telugu	66,017,615	7.80%
4. Marathi	62,481,681	7.38%
5. Tamil	53,006,368	6.26%
6. Urdu	43,406,932	5.13%
7. Gujarati	40,673,814	4.81%
8. Kannada	32,753,676	3.87%
9. Malayalam	30,377,176	3.59%
10. Oriya	28,061,313	3.32%
11. Punjabi	23,378,744	2.76%
12. Assamese	13,079,696	1.55%
13. Sindhi	2,122,848	0.25%
14. Nepali	2,076,645	0.25%
15. Konkani	1,760,607	0.21%
16. Manipuri	1,270,216	0.15%
17. Kashmiri	n/a	n/a
18. Sanskrit	49,736	0.01%

Source: Office of the Registrar General, India. 2002. *Top Eighteen Scheduled Languages in Descending Order of Strength (1991 Census).* September 2. Available at http://www.censusindia.net/results/eci11_page4.html (accessed March 17, 2004).

which became a means of communication between the conquerors from central Asia who set up the Delhi Sultanate and the people of the Delhi area. It started out as a "hybrid" Hindi. Structurally, Hindi and Urdu are the same (hence, Hindi-Urdu), but the learned and literary vocabularies differ (Hindi using Sanskrit words, Urdu using Persian words). Also, Urdu uses a modified Arabic script (nastaliq), Hindi the popular script of northern India (devanagari), which it shares with Marathi, Nepali, and Sanskrit—which of course wouldn't make any difference to an illiterate villager.

Actually, in some ways, the above implies more clarity

Top Twenty Nonscheduled Languages in Descending Order of Strength (1991 Census)

1. Bhill/Bhilodi	5,572,308	0.66%
2. Santali	5,216,325	0.62%
3. Gondi	2,124,852	0.25%
4. Tulu	1,552,259	0.18%
5. Kurukh/Oraon	1,426,618	0.17%
6. Bodo/Boro	1,221,881	0.14%
7. Khandeshi	973,709	0.11%
8. Ho	949,216	0.11%
9. Khasi	912,283	0.10%
10. Mundari	861,378	0.10%
11. Tripuri	694,940	0.08%
12. Garo	675,642	0.08%
13. Kui	641,662	0.07%
14. Lushai/Mizo	538,842	0.06%
15. Halabi	534,313	0.06%
16. Korku	466,073	0.05%
17. Munda	413,894	0.04%
18. Miri/Mishing	390,583	0.04%
19. Karbi/Mikir	366,229	0.04%
20. Savara	273,168	0.03%

Source: Office of the Registrar General, India. 2002. *Top Twenty Non-Scheduled Languages in Descending Order of Strength (1991 Census).* September 2. Available at http://www.censusindia.net/results/eci11_page4.html (accessed March 17, 2004).

than exists. Two examples are two mother tongues, which are not officially recognized even as nonscheduled languages. Rajasthani speakers are apt to bristle at the description of their language as a dialect of Hindi; Bihari has been described as a dialect both of Hindi and Bengali. It is situated between Bengal and a Hindi-speaking state (Uttar Pradesh) geographically and is similar to each linguistically. It also produced one of India's greatest poets (Vidyapati, c. 1352–1448).

The situation with the Dravidian family of languages is not as complex, but perhaps more perplexing. There are four scheduled languages, each predominant within a particular state: Tamil in Tamil Nadu, Telugu in Andhra Pradesh, Kannada in Konorak, Malayalam in Kerala. There are a number of other Dravidian languages in the south as well, but which lack the political linking as a state language. It has been posited that the language (or perhaps languages?) of the cities of the ancient Indus civilization may have been Dravidian, in part because of a linguistic pocket of a Dravidian language, Brahui, in the Indus area (now in Pakistan); and, because of perceived similarities between the Indus civilization and Tamil culture. The matter is complicated by the fact that what Indus writing has survived has not been "cracked," or deciphered; we know next to nothing of the language of this civilization.

Attempts have been made to connect the Dravidian family of languages with other non-Indo-European languages, such as Basque and Finnish, but to no avail. It seems to be a family decisively from the subcontinent, concentrated in south India. Tamil, the oldest, has a rich literary tradition. All four languages possess outstanding poetry, particularly religious and devotional poetry. The other three languages are offshoots of Tamil (which has a recorded history of two thousand years): Telugu first, then Kannada, and Malayalam.

Other language groups are also represented in India—such as Tibeto-Burman in the northeast—but are seldom dominant enough to have much cultural impact, and certainly not to the extent of Indo-Aryan and Dravidian. So-called tribal or aboriginal (adivasi) languages remain from pre-Aryan and perhaps pre-Dravidian times.

Finally, it needs to be stressed that language can be a very emotional issue (as can be seen at times even in the United States). At times, violence can erupt, especially whenever talk arises about implementing the constitutional provision that Hindi be made the national language. People in non-Hindi states, with their cultural and linguistic distinctions from Hindi, have rioted. Even within the various states there are lesser language groups. Thus, it is possible for a child to speak one language at home, the state language in school, and yet perhaps have to learn Hindi as well if he or she wishes to pursue a particular career. Most courses of study in universities will require English as well. Indeed, it is almost paradoxical that the language of the former imperial masters has become not only what Nehru called India's "window on the world," but its lingua franca as well.

FOOD

Food is eaten with fingers (right hand only), with flatware, and sometimes with chopsticks (Chinese restaurants abound in India). Even with fingers, eating is mannerly and decorum prevails: graciously mix the items on one's plate and lift the food to the mouth. React to the situation by watching one's fellow diners.

The types of food are myriad: rice preferred at one place, wheat at another; very hot and spicy in the south, less so in the north; Hindu food, Mughal food, British food, Chinese food—and restaurants to match. Beef is generally not available, and not advised when it is; in contrast, water buffalo can be very tasty. Pork is generally not served. What is called mutton is very often goat, which when cooked in a pressure cooker (an indispensable kitchen item) with appropriate spices can be quite tasty; it is often served as a curry dish. Vegetarian meals, whether in a vegetarian restaurant or home, can be so delectable that even confirmed meat-eaters will be pleased. Curry is not the powdered combination of spices as sold in the West, but any of a variety of sauces prepared to accompany selected dishes. Chicken and fish may be the most frequent meat dishes and are especially popular as tandoori—cooked with a blend of spices in a *tandoor,* a charcoal-fueled clay oven. Rice is prepared in a number of ways: pilaf (of pilao), biryani (a single-dish meal with meat and spices), plain or spiced, and some areas agglutinating (sticky).

There are many types of bread; some regional, others national in popularity. Perhaps the most popular are roti or chapati (like a tortilla), puri (a puffed-up bread snack), naan (a puffed bread cooked in a tandoor), and kulcha (a soft, round bread stuffed with spiced vegetables or meat).

Potatoes are popular, but really are not a staple as in the United States, or as rice is in India. Often they are stuffing in snacks, which are very popular, expecially the pastry-type samosa. A very popular and widespread staple is daal, a lentil dish (reminiscent of canned condensed green-pea soup in appearance).

Sweets are also popular, especially those made from milk. There is a myriad of regional options, served in homes and sold in streets. Condiments are more of a necessity than a frill; chutneys, relishes, and pickles are made in the home as well as commercially.

Indian cities are a veritable menu of foods and places to eat them, from five-star restaurants to street-side stalls. Street stalls can be safe and offer good food, though some should be avoided. A good way to determine is by checking out the clientele; if in doubt, walk on. Western travelers may wish to vary their diet by alternating British food with the more traditional Indian meals. The food on trains is generally very good, with a variety of choices for those with dietary restrictions.

BEVERAGES

Beverages are diverse, but tea and coffee are staples. There are two types of tea: regular tea (Assamese, Darjeeling, and Nilgiri—named for the areas in which they are grown); and chai, a spicy mix of assorted varieties, which is also becoming popular in the United States. Chai is not made from regular tea, but is prepared similarly to regular tea in that one generally adds a great deal of milk and sugar to the drink. Coffee also usually contains much milk and sugar. South India is noted for its tasty—and strong—varieties, both as crop and a beverage. Soda pop, both Indian and American, is popular and easily available. Drinking water should be boiled; this is done in the more expensive hotels, but not always in restaurants. Lemonade/limeade and phosphates are served in restaurants.

Fruit drinks are popular, but sometimes are altered by the addition of salt, sugar, or spices such as cumin. Also popular are milk drinks, especially lassi, a drink made from yogurt or curds. There are many varieties of lassi—it's often flavored with bananas, mangoes, various nuts and spices, and as combinations of any of the above. Though it's usually drunk cold, some varieties can be heated.

Several types of alcoholic beverages are available. There are frequent mandated dry days, and liquor stores are not conspicuous, so travelers wanting alcoholic drinks would be wise to plan ahead. Foreign whiskies (especially scotch) are expensive and much appreciated by well-to-do Indians. Indian liquors generally do not suit the Western palate, although Indian gin is mild and of a lower proof (sixty) than U.S. or English gin. Indian wines have improved over the decades, but it has been observed that they tend not to complement the hot, spicy Indian food. Be that as it may, an Indian graduate of Stanford University, Rajeev Samant, has founded a winery in central India (at Nasik, northeast of Bombay). It is quite an undertaking in a country "where annual wine consumption works out to one teaspoon per person"

(*New York Times*, June 16, 2003). Nevertheless, after six years, he says, "We keep running out of wine," in spite of doubling the output every year (since 2000) and despite a national ban on the advertising of alcoholic beverages. His market is "affluent young Indians," including women (for whom it is chic to be seen holding a glass of wine, unlike the derogatory connotation when she holds a cocktail). Samant's partner and adviser is a California winemaker, and other wineries are being established. Prices are $9 to $15 per bottle in restaurants, and the wines have received favorable reviews abroad, including from *Wine Spectator*.

Indian beer is a generally unknown treat, resulting from British-Indian partnerships during the colonial period. There are many brands, which, unlike American beers, are not stratified as to quality (e.g., microbrew, supermarket brands); they are all generally of the same high quality. Beer is readily available in hotels and urban restaurants, usually in bottles and is drunk with meals or separately—as in the United States. The poor cannot afford even beer, let alone liquor, and resort to palm toddy or some other harshly distilled drink, some of which are literally deadly.

ETIQUETTE

There are some general observations on etiquette that can be made in a "better-safe-than-sorry" mode.

Do not take, pass, or eat food with the left hand, which is the one used for after-toilet cleansing. It is best to follow this dictum even in a home with Western-style toilets and toilet paper. In Westernized tourist hotels and restaurants, this is not a serious matter and generally can be ignored.

Limit body contact, especially across genders—even in Westernized social functions.

It is advisable for women to avoid provocative clothing, again even in what would appear to be Westernized social functions. What is provocative is, of course, dependent upon the social or cultural context, but generally shorts and short skirts should be avoided. Men, too, might avoid informal clothing.

Be careful in initiating conversational topics, especially in regard to sex, politics, and religion; it might be better to leave such subjects alone and let someone who lives in the culture steer the conversation.

Senses of humor vary among cultures; be careful in regard to jokes and remarks that might be taken as flippant, in poor taste, or even rude.

Before bringing a gift to a host or hostess, check on what might be appropriate and what might be taken as offensive (e.g., Western liquor would be very much appreciated by some, disapproved by others). Candy is usually a welcome gift, but it should be stressed that gifts are usually neither necessary nor expected. Greeting may include—in a Westernized setting—hand shakes between men (never across gender lines), but the folded hands "Namaste" greeting is safest, even if at times a bit awkward for the Westerner.

Check out the local custom in regard to tipping; Americans are often criticized for overtipping.

People can be very inquisitive, especially on trains, in regard to topics that may seem highly personal to Westerners (e.g., family, salary). The intent is usually well-meaning. Yet, as anywhere, one must be careful in regard to friendships pushed by strangers; even when the purpose is above-board, such incidents can lead to very awkward situations. Women traveling or staying alone need to be on guard as to men's intentions. Some assume Western women, especially when unaccompanied, to be promiscuous.

Recognize that India is a nation of many cultures, customs, classes, social habits, and perceptions in regard to a *vilayat—* foreigner. Also recognize that the vast majority of Indians one meets are hospitable and helpful. One's instincts can usually be relied on, with caution as the key.

Above all, do not be brash. It is unlikely that rudeness will be commented upon; but it will be remembered.

India offers a number of foods, beverages, and related concoctions that a Westerner may well wish to avoid: chilies, curds, lassi (a drink generally of yogurt or buttermilk, but which might contain anything—even tobacco). But generally speaking, India provides many gourmet treats. Still, the usual precautions in regard to change of climate are advisable for foods, if they are new to one's digestive system. If one does become ill with "Delhi belly" or some other intestinal malady, Indian pharmacies ("chemists") are inexpensive, trustworthy, and easily available.

References
Kingsland, Venika. *The Simple Guide to Customs and Etiquette in India.* Kent, England: Global Books, 1996.
Kolanad, Gitanjali. *Culture Shock! India.* Portland, Oregon: Graphic Arts Center Publishing, 2001.
World Food: India. Lonely Planet Food Guide Series, 2001.

Indian Impact on the
West and American Culture

For several millennia India has had contact with, and influence upon, civilizations East and West. Some of these impacts are fairly clear, such as the cultural absorption and modification of the ancient epics, the *Ramayana* and *Mahabharata,* in Thailand and in Indonesia, or that of Buddhism in Thailand and Hinduism in Bali, and of Sanskrit in languages and names (e.g., Sukarnoputri, or "daughter of Sukarno," the president of Indonesia and daughter of a previous leader). But in other cases the degree of cultural impact is less clearly ascertained, if it can be at all, or if it even ever existed; for example, the idea of rebirth or reincarnation, or the ideas of fluidity (or existence as process) and atoms among ancient Greek philosophers. Then there is always the problem of common source, such as the Indian folktale of the woman who leaves the baby protected by a loyal mongoose as she goes to fetch a jug of water. When she returns, the mongoose comes running to greet her, blood on its muzzle and claws. She jumps to the conclusion that it has killed the baby, and she kills it by crashing the jug full of water on its head. When she goes inside, the baby is asleep with a dead cobra near it. The same tale exists in Irish folklore, with cultural differences: a hunter instead of the mother, a wolfhound instead of the mongoose, and a wolf in place of the snake. When one takes into account that the name Eire—or Ireland—is cognate with Aryan, and that the respective languages of Sanskrit and Irish are related, the connection becomes clear. But where was the origin? Perhaps neither in India nor Ireland. (Some direct borrowings, however, are thought to have entered from India into Aesop's fables.)

The point of all this is that influence is not absolute, and it can be reciprocal and cyclical. Thus, Gandhi was influenced (to a degree) by Emerson and Thoreau, who had been influenced (to a degree) by ancient Hindu Upanishads and the Bhagavad Gita. In turn, Gandhi influenced (to a degree) the American civil rights movement and its leaders, especially Martin Luther King Jr.

With that in mind, this section takes a brief look at Indian influence on Western civilization in general, and on U.S. culture in particular, in terms of two broad topics: intellectual culture and popular culture. A third category, nonviolence, is treated separately. All this, by nature, is somewhat amorphous. The influences will be noted rather than explained (that would be a book in itself).

INTELLECTUAL CULTURE

Within the topic of intellectual culture, or thought, are a number of necessarily overlapping categories: religion and philosophy (the distinction between these two is by no means as clear in India as in the West), math, science, cosmology, linguistics, and literature.

Western philosophy is usually considered separately from religion and sometimes has stood in opposition to it, even very early on, as with Anaximander (sixth century B.C.E.). Later, as perhaps best exemplified by Galileo, religion and science stood in open hostility to each other. The current evolution-creationism controversy is evidence of such. This bitter dichotomy between religion on the one hand and philosophy and science on the other is unnatural to and hardly existent in ancient Indian thought.

That there was interchange between India and the pre-Alexandrian Mediterranean world is accepted. But the degree of direct Indian influence upon Greek culture (and vice versa) has to be largely speculative. Much, just as with languages and folk tales, could have come from a common cultural source.

This is paralleled by the strong similarities among the pantheons of gods in ancient Indo-European cultures.

The most significant Indian contribution to the West is likely *sunya,* or zero, which not only is the basis of Indian mathematics but is central to Hindu and Buddhist philosophies as well (most especially Mahayana Buddhism). It is a concept (and symbol thereof) that transcends dualities, just as zero exists in relation to positive and negative numbers. "It is," in the words of the comparative historian D. P. Singhal (*India and World Civilization,* 1972), "simultaneously the All and the None." The Indians also recognized its function as "place-value notation," in which regard it became the basis of the decimal system. The ten-place numbering (or decimal) system was transmitted from India to the West.

Ancient Indians also developed the idea of atoms as the basis of matter, in several schools of thought. Their approach, although through philosophy rather than experiment, has attracted the attention of some contemporary physicists and cosmologists, whose popular writings often reveal amazing similarities to cosmological ideas in ancient India (even when dismissing the ancient Indian speculations as mysticism); for example, out of nothing, everything; from the One, many; multiple universes. This most likely is due to great minds thinking alike, but the ancient Indian thinkers were millennia ahead of the modern physicists.

In about 500 C.E., Aryabhatta estimated the year to be 365 days, 6 hours (he tacked on a superfluous 12 minutes and 30 seconds). His work was translated into Latin in the thirteenth century, so it may well have had influence on European thinking. He also showed insight in regard to the apparent rotation of the planets (he said it was the earth that rotated), the luminosity of the moon, and eclipses. He was but the most outstanding of many ancient Indians dealing in astronomy. There are other examples in the physical sciences and technology as well. The problem is, observes historian Gyan Prakesh (*Another Reason,* 1999), "Hindu science was ineluctably different" in approach, theories, and concepts—even though "the Hindu scientific method resembled Western reasoning." *Reasoning*, not experimentation, was the key.

Early in the colonial period, William Jones (1746–1794), a man of many talents in the service of the East India Company in Calcutta, noted that Sanskrit was akin to Greek and Latin—hence, to the vast majority of other European languages. Thus was the modern science of linguistics born; however, Panini, fifth century B.C.E., may well have been the world's first linguist for the comparative observations made in his Sanskrit grammar.

Jones did something that may be even more significant. He translated into English the Sanskrit classic *Sakuntala (Abhijnana-Sakuntalam,* or *The Recognition of Sakuntala).* It was an immediate hit, especially with Goethe and German Romanticists: The nature-girl appealed to dreams of their mythological past. But the image changed, especially among English intellectuals as imperialism became explicit as well as a force needing to be rationalized: Indian culture was deemed to be inferior to European—especially English—civilization. For James Mill (exponent of utilitarianism and author of a negative study of India, *History of British India,* 1817), the play was primitive and irrational. New translations and critical articles followed, with the judgment that the play reflected a static culture, in contrast to the dynamic English society.

Not all English-speaking intellectuals were so negative. In the United States interest arose in ancient Indian religious literature and philosophical thought, in part because of William Jones's support for the American colonies and the subsequent young nation. Americans became interested in what he wrote, which focused largely on Indian classical culture. In addition, British intellectual study of Indian culture sparked interest among U.S. intellectuals. And some American colonists, who were, after all, members of the British empire, traveled to India and became aware of Hindu reformers and synthesizers such as Ram Mohan Roy. By the 1830s, classical Hindu thought was being seriously studied in the United States. Before the end of the nineteenth century, Sanskrit was being taught at Yale and Harvard universities. Ralph Waldo Emerson, Henry David Thoreau, and Walt Whitman were influenced by the Upanishads and the Bhagavad Gita. Emerson's essay "The Oversoul" showed a marked influence by the Hindu concept of Brahman, or the Absolute.

Meanwhile, a Russian mystic, Helena Blavatsky (1831–1891), with American Henry Steele Olcutt (1832–1907), developed and propagated a cult called the Theosophical Society. The purpose of the society was the "championship of Hindu ideals and . . . India's past" (R. K. Gupta, *The Great Encounter,* 1987). Although "Theosophy was a murky stew," as put by Gillian Darley (*London Review of Books,* April 17, 2003), it had almost inexplicable influence as a forerunner of the myriad movements that seem to have exploded in the twentieth century—with swamis in the 1920s and gurus in the1960s—almost as though Indian spiritual merchants could sense a ripening market in the United States. There were so many, at so many levels (from the sincere to hucksters), with such a wide range (from neo-Hindu to neo-Sikh; from meditators to Hare Krishnas), that the impact still has not been sorted out. Beyond the phenomenon of what the late Agehananda Bharati (Austrian-born anthropologist at Syracuse University) referred to as Protestants in exotic garb, increasing interest arose in academia. From the 1960s to the 1990s, this interest moved from the neospiritual phenomenon to increased serious academic study and teaching at the undergraduate level in the humanities and the social sciences. Federally subsidized graduate programs were instituted at a number of major U.S. universities, and fellowship programs were established in Indian modern languages by the U.S. Department of Defense. Graduates from these programs were then hired into undergraduate schools, and the teaching of Indian culture and society became part of the mainstream curriculum.

Two years after Madame Blavatsky's death, a Hindu monk, Swami Vivekananda, visited the Chicago Parliament of Religions, in 1893. The son of a middle-class commercial Calcutta family, he had become enthralled with a Bengali mystic, Sri Ramakrishna. Vivekananda's appearance in the United States was a resounding success, resulting in a number of Ramakrishna Society temples in major cities and spinoffs and imitations by other yogis and swamis. In retrospect, the attraction seems to have been a mix between sincere spiritual intention and desire and the lure of the exotic. Some of it in the 1960s probably was due to social and political discontent fueled by the Vietnam War. Although separate from the Theosophical Society, neo-Hinduism paralleled it, and, with later developments such as the Hare Krishnas (ISKCON, or International Society of Krishna Consciousness) and other questionable organizations (and some not even at the level of questionableness, such as Bhagvan Rajneesh in Oregon), all became lumped together in the U.S. consciousness. However, the influx of Hindus, as Indian Americans, into mainstream U.S. society—socially, economically, and politically—seems to be helping to sort it out and likely will continue to do so for the foreseeable future. Indeed, Indian American organizations such as the Indian American Education Foundation (http://www.iaefseattle.org) are trying to convey a correcting image of Indian culture within the U.S. educational system.

There also was serious response from U.S. intellectuals and creative writers (often of British origin): Christopher Isherwood, Gerald Heard, and Aldous Huxley, among others. Much of this thought was fostered by the Ramakrishna Order or Society, established by disciples of Swami Vivekananda. These swamis were largely responsible for the intellectual movement they termed *Vedanta* (which others have labeled as neo-Vedanta). Vedanta means "end of the Veda"; that is, the philosophy of nondualism that was espoused in the Upanishads—the religio-philosophical discourses placed at the end of the sacred Veda texts. Spiritual talks and intellectual essays by Western intellectuals and Indian swamis, published by various sources, were collected by the Vedanta Society of Southern California (in Los Angeles) and published in two anthologies (*Vedanta for the Western World,* 1945/1960; *Vedanta for Modern Man,* 1962). In 2004, the essays seemed to some to have hit a dead end: intellectual writings exploring Eastern thought for Westerners (as the two titles suggest) are now old hat. But their impact was far more than the frivolous pop-culture pied-piper approach of the self-styled gurus of a later generation. They reflected a new inclusion in U.S. culture and U.S. thought, and they contributed significantly to the serious inquiry and interest in all things Indian.

It is perhaps Huxley's *The Perennial Philosophy* (1944/1970) that is the most pronounced exposition of an attempted synthesis of Western and Hindu thought—at least as done by a Westerner. The work is inquisitive, and almost an anthology with its lengthy quotes. How successful it is, is questionable (as, it can be supposed, would be any such study); it may in fact be too eclectic. But it is honest, penetrating, and influential.

The same approach, or outlook, underlies many of Huxley's novels, especially *Island* (1962). But India also attracted writers like Somerset Maugham (who may have been even more interested in East Asia). Both Huxley and Maugham wrote travel essays on India, but whereas Huxley was almost a seeker, Maugham was an observer (albeit a very insightful one). The title of his great novel *The Razor's Edge* (1944) is from an Upanishad (the *Katha* Upanishad) and applies the idea and experience of "seeking," of trying to find *the answer* (which Huxley examines in *The Perennial Philosophy*), to a Westerner in a Western context, in Western society.

There are many others who, for purposes of space, cannot be noted. But a little-known one who should be pointed out here is Lewis Thompson (1909–1949), a sort of precursor to the seekers of the1960s, written about by Ruth Prawer

Jhabvala, among others. He was a mystic-poet who died in Banaras of sunstroke. Seemingly naive in some ways, his poetry (*Black Sun,* 2001), aphorisms (*Mirror to the Light,* 1984), and unpublished journals reveal a strong synthesis in regard to Western and Indian psychological spiritual thought. It is perhaps arguable how deeply he got beyond Western superficial understanding of Hindu spirituality, but he lived very much in the Indian milieu, and his writings show an inquisitiveness about India that is unique for his time.

India may not seem to hold the same sort of literary interest for Westerners now as it did in the early and middle twentieth century, or such interest may just be not as noticeable. With global travel, global television, and global contact via computers, the old exoticism is gone—or, perhaps more accurately, assimilated. Western filmmaking, from movies as diverse as *Gandhi* and *Octopussy,* show an attraction for India, and there has been even more noticeable impact on other aspects of pop culture, superficial as it may seem to be at times.

CONTEMPORARY POP CULTURE

Popular cultural influence is not easy to measure, especially in the era of globalization. Yet recently in four noticeable areas Indian culture has had considerable influence on U.S. culture (excluding pseudo-culture of neo-gurus and hippy followers): music, food, fashion, and yoga.

The impact of Indian music is perhaps best exemplified by the great sitar artist and composer Ravi Shankar, who struck chords—along with many, many of his fellow musicians, Muslim and Hindu—which slowly but surely reverberated into Western music, classical with Yehudi Menuhin, jazz with Bud Shank, and popular with the Beatles. Indian music became popular as a soundtrack for motion pictures, and it became absorbed into background music.

Interest in Indian cuisine has increased to such an extent in recent decades that in major cities it is no longer really exotic. Indian restaurants have gone from fad to status: the food to eat, the place to go, in some ways overtaking what Chinese restaurants had been a few generations ago. Perhaps most interesting in the food fascination is chai. When Hindi began to be taught in U.S. universities about half a century ago, the textbooks (often merely dittoed sheets) translated *chai* as "tea." A recent issue of *India Abroad* (March 7, 2003) did also. But as that issue showed, and as American converts to the spicy, milky brew have come to realize, the term covers a wide variety: one can buy "Quik Tea" (including Elaichi and Supreme Masala) from New Jersey (albeit with a New York address) by telephone or e-mail, or "Oregon Chai," available at espresso stands and groceries. How authentic are these and other chais? A better question would be, Is there an "authentic" chai?

Recently Indian fashion in women's clothing has made an appearance on the American scene, primarily with Indian fabrics and shapes being incorporated into clothing. It is, as with all fashion, questionable how lasting the effect will be. It certainly caught the attention of the Indian American newspaper *India Abroad,* with major illustrated articles (May 9, June 13, and August 8, 2003). The *New York Times* (May 13, 2003) and *People* magazine (June 16, 2003) also noted the trend.

The in-depth article of May 13 in the *New York Times* warrants particular attention. The article starts with the observation: "Considering that it is the country historically credited with giving the world paisley, seersucker, calico, chintz, cashmere, crewel, and the entire technique of printing on cloth, it is anybody's guess why India barely registers on the global map of fashion" (that is, until the present time). The author could have added to his inventory madras and pajamas. The major focus, though, is cottons, which go back to the Indus civilization of 2500 B.C.E. Without them, the Indus civilization may not have survived; and many Americans feel that affinity today, although, ironically, artificial fabrics are quite popular in India.

Three factors are involved here: Quality of Indian design and manufacture has tremendously improved; marketing has become sensible, and sensibly aggressive; and tastes in fashion have tilted toward Western tastes yet retained Indian bases. To illustrate the interplay, right under a mid-article subhead, "A nation's new looks on Fifth Avenue," is a small color photograph of a woman strolling down a sidewalk in jeans and a somewhat-cropped peach jersey (albeit far more modest than observable on many U.S. college campuses), with belly button showing. The caption reads, "A young Indian woman strolls in a shopward direction in New Delhi." The entire scene, in this little photograph and the article in which it is enmeshed, would have been not only impossible, but unthinkable, merely a few decades ago. So, as "opening up" has helped the industrial economy, it may well be doing so for fashions as well. Yet one wonders how this new fashion would play in the villages (it wouldn't) or even in India's smaller towns. Nonetheless, there appears to be an interchange between Indian and U.S. tastes in women's fashions.

In addition to the swamis and gurus noted earlier, yoga was an early twentieth-century import from India. At first somewhat frivolous (it may well have caught popular attention as the nickname for the Baseball Hall of Fame catcher Larry "Yogi" Berra), it soon became seriously accepted. The term indicates a classical Hindu philosophy and a form of physical discipline (Nehru practiced it). Now, in the United States, it has largely become an alternative for aerobics. The word *yoga* is cognate with English *yoke*—it was (and is) a path or discipline to which one yoked oneself: a commitment.

The physical aspect of yoga is what has appealed to many Americans; that is not to say it does not involve a type of commitment, but it is not one of the intensity implied in traditional Hinduism. In the United States it also has become a business.

The Sunday travel section of the *New York Times* of June

22, 2003, had a long article on "Meditating at Sivananda Yoga Retreat, Paradise Island," in the Bahamas. Needless to say, the retreat is expensive. Another intesive retreat has been developed in the Yucatán, which, in a lengthy article, the *New York Times* labeled as "a yoga epicenter for tourists" (February 27, 2004). The "Escapes" section of the *New York Times* of January 31, 2003, had an article (entitled "Have Yoga Mat, Will Travel") on how to get from one coast of the country to the other and yet be able to have daily yoga sessions. Indeed, the article mentioned that Bikram Choudhury has "nearly 400 [yoga studios] across the country." The article accredits him with having "invented Bikram yoga," which, he says, "is like a gas station" (it fills your tank).

One of the most renowned names in regard to yoga in the United States is the octogenarian B. K. S. Iyengar, who, as quoted by the *New York Times* (December 10, 2002), stated that "Iyengar means yoga. Yoga means Iyengar. They are synonymous terms." Since the various practices of the various yogas are, for the most part, millennia-old, Iyengar's self-appreciating observation is questionable. The point is, yoga has become popularized, if not even Americanized.

Nevertheless, yoga has made an impact both in terms of fad and health. Thus, from a regional newspaper, the *Spokesman-Review* (Spokane, Washington), two items in the month of September 2003 can stand as examples. The first (September 7) was a travel item about a hot-springs resort on the Flathead Indian Reservation in western Montana: besides a hotel and spa, RV hook-ups, hot springs, and mountain bike rentals, "Yoga classes are also offered." The second (September 13) involved a heart-transplant patient at Sacred Heart Medical Center in Spokane, who before the surgery "watched TV, took up yoga, [and] spent hours wandering through Sacred Heart's healing garden." It seems to have helped. The sixty-three-year-old came through the operation fine.

It is perhaps all too easy to attribute fads—healthy or otherwise—entirely to another culture, as though they are photocopies. An observation made by Jhumpa Lahiri, Pulitzer Prize–winning fiction writer who is of Bengali heritage, is helpful here. In an interview in the *New York Times Magazine,* September 7, 2003, she said, "Nobody I know in India practices yoga. You don't have people rushing home from their jobs to make it to the 6 o'clock yoga class. And I'm amused to see Indian clothing becoming popular—I rebelled against it as a kid because I wanted to wear jeans."

GANDHIAN NONVIOLENCE

Mohandas Karamchand Gandhi (1869–1948), London-educated lawyer from Gujarat, developed his concept and method of *satyagraha* (a term he coined), literally "grasping toward Truth [or God]," during the Indian resistance to white governmental oppression in South Africa early in the twentieth century. Its chief components are *satya,* "Real or Absolute Being" (implying Truth and God); *ahimsa,* possessing the desire not to do violence, and implying nonselfish love (Martin Luther King Jr. compared it to agapé); and *tapasya,* rigid self-discipline and willingness to sacrifice.

Among the many influences that led him to develop satyagraha was the concept of "turning the other cheek," from the Sermon on the Mount, which he determined could be applied on a mass basis, not merely on an individual basis. But of even greater importance was that of ahimsa, a principle central to the ancient religion of Jainism, the greatest concentration of which was in the area where Gandhi grew up. The concept was simple, even mechanical: *himsa* (violence and the desire to do it) results in bad karma, which is a metaphysical cement that accumulates and weighs one down. So the Jains conceived that the negative, ahimsa, avoids such a metaphysical state. To the Buddhist, violence should not be employed nor desired, out of compassion (sort of a golden rule: "Do not do to others . . ."). For Hindus, violence disturbs *rta,* or cosmic harmony. To this Gandhi added the interpretation that if one does not wish harm to his fellow being, he must wish him well, out of compassionate love.

To Gandhi, satyagraha was a philosophy, a commitment, a way of life. To others, such as Motilal Nehru and his son Jawaharlal (India's first prime minister), it was more a tactic. Regardless, it was the method largely responsible for the achievement of India's independence. And it spread far beyond South Africa and India in the twentieth century (described by Peter Ackerman and Jack Duvall in *A Force More Powerful: A Century of Nonviolent Conflict,* 2000). This is not to imply that nonviolence or ahimsa was new to the twentieth century. Gandhi himself insisted that it was "as old as the hills." It comes in different shapes, forms, degrees, and designs, and has throughout history (as has been thoroughly examined in Gene Sharp's extensive study—funded in part by the U.S. Department of Defense, by the way—the *Politics of Nonviolent Action,* 1973). Its connection with the U.S. civil rights movement is very well-documented, very clear, and very dramatic.

There were modern antecedents of course, particularly Thoreau. But Thoreau was white and a New Englander. The interest in him among blacks could arguably be said to have been largely confined to academics. In regard to Gandhi, the U.S. black interest was direct and practical. It has been noted in many works, both by academicians—e.g., Dennis Dalton's *Mahatma Gandhi: Nonviolent Power in Action* (1993) has a chapter on Gandhi, Malcolm X, and Martin Luther King—and by participants or freedom fighters, perhaps most outstanding of which is John Lewis's *Walking with the Wind* (1998). Lewis's memoir, in addition to acknowledging the importance of Gandhi's influence in general on the civil rights movement, develops the important role of James Lawson (especially in preparation for the Nashville lunch counter sit-in) in training people in Gandhian tactics. Many of the events in the civil rights movement can be effectively compared to particular satyagraha events (e.g., the Salt March) in the Indian independence movement.

Another example of civil rights activists describing their debt to Gandhi occurs in the very first paragraph of the first interview in Howell Raines's classic oral history *My Soul Is Rested* (1977), in which James Farmer recalls in 1941 sending a memorandum to A. J. Mustie, "executive director of the Fellowship of Reconciliation, proposing that FOR take the lead in starting an organization which would seek to use Gandhi-like techniques of nonviolent resistance—including civil disobedience, noncooperation, and the whole bit—in the battle against segregation." Later in the interview he refers to Krishnalal Shridharani and his classic book *War without Violence,* the topic of Shridharani's Ph.D. dissertation at Columbia University just before the outbreak of World War II. In the introduction to the Indian paperback edition, Shridharani in January 1960 wrote that "perhaps to the surprise of my Western readers, Satyagraha seems to have more in common with war than with Western pacifism." He also notes, without reference to the incipient U.S. civil rights movement, "My contact with the Western world has led me to think that contrary to popular belief, Satyagraha, once consciously and deliberately adopted, has more fertile fields in which to grow and flourish in the West than in the Orient."

There are any number of writings and talks wherein Martin Luther King Jr. acknowledged the inspiration and practicality of Gandhi to the movement. In *Stride Toward Freedom: The Montgomery Story* (1958), King provided six points of nonviolence, which may well be the finest and most concise presentation of the essentials of satyagraha—and he did so without use of Indian terminology.

Raising Up a Prophet: The African-American Encounter with Gandhi, by Sudarshan Kapur (1992), is the most important book in regard to this section on nonviolence, and hence has been reserved until last. A similar and much longer work, which refers extensively to Kapur's work, is Mary King's

Mahatma Gandhi and Martin Luther King Jr.: The Power of Nonviolent Action (for UNESCO, 1999). Both are out of print. Kapur notes three channels for Gandhi's influence: black newspapers, black churches, and black colleges. There were several reasons, in the early twentieth century, for African American interest in Gandhi: he was not white, and, as Kapur put it, was held in "low esteem . . . in white America at large." Although he was not Christian (which was a concern for many), he was rationalized as "Christ-like" and a leader of oppressed people. His stand against untouchableness was as important as his stand against the British. He stressed practice of nonviolence more than theoretics, and told black leaders (including Benjamin Mays, later a mentor to King) who had gone to India to meet him that "a minority can do much more in the way of nonviolence that a majority," a reference to the primary difference between the U.S. and Indian scenes. The point was that a minority can be more cohesive. Although his spirituality was appreciated, his religious inclusiveness was even more so. The spiritual grounding of satyagraha, the stress on winning over the adversary through love and truth, and its perceived relevance for the U.S. scene attracted attention and approval. Gandhi's assassination resulted in martyr status for him, and black leaders such as Mordecai Johnson and James Lawson went to India to study his methods. (For that matter, Indian leaders, both before and after independence, had been meeting with American blacks and speaking at black colleges.)

Early in 1950, King heard one of Johnson's lectures; he consequently bought books about Gandhi and began to study him in earnest. James Lawson, probably the most unappreciated of the civil rights leaders, was of seminal influence in the 1950s at workshops and retreats on nonviolence and Gandhian tactics. Kapur put it this way: "The post-1954 movement led by African-Americans did not emerge out of an historical vacuum."

In closing, it should also be noted that Cesar Chavez,

leader of the United Farm Workers, also acknowledged his debt to Gandhi's influence. Chavez, like Lawson, is terribly underrecognized and underappreciated. He made an amazing Gandhian statement within a U.S. context: Chavez once said in an interview that if there is a gun involved, he would rather the other fellow had it and thus be the one having to make the choice.

India-Related Organizations and Web Sites

BUSINESS AND ECONOMICS

Asia Business Today
Web site: http://www.asiabusinesstoday.org

A resource of the Asia Society (see below under Education), the Asia Business Today Web site provides information on government, market information, trade organizations and business councils, weather and travel, and a variety of other top news stories related to Asia. It is an internet resource for numerous banks and commercial interests.

Associated Chamber of Commerce and Industry (ASSOCHAM)
2nd Floor, Allahabad Bank Building
17 Parliament Street
New Delhi, India 110001
Telephone: (+91)-(11) 336-0704; 336-0749; 336-0779
E-mail: raghuraman@sandad.nic.in
Web site: http://www.assocham.org

ASSOCHAM's stated mission is "to impact the policy and legislative environment [in India] so as to foster balanced economic, industrial, and social development."

Business Information Services Network
Web site: http://www.bisnetindia.com

This site contains economic news, a products directory, information services (e.g., Women Business Centre), and Indian financial, commercial, and governmental links.

Business Standard
Nehru House
4 Bahadur Shah Zafar Marg
New Delhi, India 110002
Telephone: (+91)-(11) 237-20202
Web site: http://www.business-standard.com

Business Standard is a major Indian financial newspaper with a strong opinion page.

Central Board of Excise and Customs
Director (Customs)
North Block
New Delhi, India 110001
Telephone: (+91)-(11) 301-3908
Fax: (+91)-(11) 301-6475
Web site: http://www.cbec.gov.in

This site contains excise and customs information, especially valuable for information on tourist restrictions.

Confederation of Indian Industry (CII)
Central Office 23, 26
Institutional Area, Lodhi Road
New Delhi, India 110016
Telephone: (+91)-(11) 462-9994
Fax: (+91)-(11) 463-3168 or 462-6149
E-mail: tradecii@sai.cii.erant.in
Web site: http://www.ciionline.org

The CII is India's premier business association.

Consulate General of India
3 East 64th Street
New York, NY 10021

Telephone: (212) 774-0600
Fax: (212) 861-3788
E-mail: indoccgny@aol.com
Web site: http://www.indiagny.org

This site contains directories and links to Indian trade organizations and chambers of commerce, corporate Web sites, trade directories, banks, and real estate.

Council of EEC Chambers of Commerce in India
Y. B. Chavan Centre, 3rd Floor
Nariman Point
General Jagannath Bhosale Marg
Mumbai, India 400021
Telephone: (+91)-(22) 282-6064
Fax: (+91)-(22) 288-5403

This site lists access to numerous chambers of commerce (e.g., Delhi Chamber of Commerce).

Doing Business in India
Web site: http://www.indiaserver.com/biz/dbi/dbi.html

This site has advice on "doing business in India"—basic information (e.g., population, government, agriculture), a list of organizations (such as the Indian Investment Center), as well as links to tours.

Export Bank of India (EXIM)
Centre One, Floor 21, World Trade Centre
Cuffe Parade
Mumbai, India 400005
Telephone: (+91)-(22) 218-5272
Fax: (+91)-(22) 218-2690
Web site: http://www.eximbankindia.com

This site contains export-import information.

FAIDA
Web site: http://www.infobanc.com

This site offers a subscription to a free weekly newsletter on business opportunities in India and proclaims itself as the "One-stop source of business information."

Federation of Indian Chambers of Commerce and Industry (FICCI)
Federation House
Tansen Marg
New Delhi, India 110001
Telephone: (+91)-(11) 331-9251; 331-9261; 331-5442
Fax: (+91)-(11) 332-0714 or 372-1504
Web site: http://www.ficci.com

Basic information such as "FICCI's Economic Agenda for the next five years," railway budget, and exhibit of trade with Pakistan can be found here.

Federation of Indian Export Organizations (FIEO)
PHD House (3rd Floor)
(Opp. Asian Games Village)
New Delhi, India 110016
Telephone: (+91)-(11) 685-1310; 685-1312; 685-1314; 685-1315
Fax: (+91)-(11) 686-3087; 696-7859
E-mail: fieo@nda.vsnl.net.in
Web site: http://www.fieo.com

The FIEO represents over 100,000 exporters across India. Its Web site includes addresses of regional offices.

India Business
Web site: http://www.indiabusiness.com

This Web site is a facilitator for business services in India.

India Business, Culture, and Travel

Web site: http://www.internetindia.com

Interesting cultural information such as odd habits, health matters, and the like, can be found here.

India Business Center

Web site: http://www.asiadragons.com/india/business_center/

Here, one can find business updates and classified directories online.

India Business Law Guide

Web site: http://www.singhania.com/lawguide/

Detailed information is available on this website, such as on financial institutions, including the Industrial Development Bank of India, the Industrial Finance Corporation of India, the Industrial Credit and Investment Corporation of India, and the Industrial Reconstruction Corporation of India.

India Business Protocol

Web site: http://worldbiz.com/bizindia.html

Business briefings, business database, and predeparture country reports are available at this Web site.

India Business Reports for International Executives and Corporate Intranets

Web site: http://today.worldbiz.com

Business customs, business negotiations, business travel is the basis of this site.

India Finance and Investment Guide

Web site: http://finance.indiamart.com/

This site offers links to exporters, importers, and a business directory, among others.

India Mart

Web site: http://www.dir.indiamart.com

This site provides business directories and yellow pages as well as business catalogs for a large number of industries, services, and products, with links.

India One Stop

Web site: http://www.indiaonestop.com

Here, one can find out about development, search engines, news, and business leads.

India Server

Web site: http://www.indiaserver.com

India Server contains information on business, business culture, business directory.

Indian Business Network

Web site: http://www.ib-net.com

Indian Business Network contains categorized links to a large number of Indian and India-related Web sites.

Indian Merchants Chamber

Web site: http://www.imcnet.org

The Indian Merchants Chamber dates to 1907 as part of the independence movement. Today the chamber is involved in helping the business community in liberalization and globalization.

Indian Trade Promotion Organisation (ITPO)

Web site: indiatradepromotion.org

This Web site includes Indian Merchants' Chamber of Bombay (Mumbai), calendar of meetings, and information.

Indo-American Chamber of Commerce

Web site: http://www.indous.org

The chamber fosters business among Indian and U.S. businesses.

Industrial Credit and Investment Corporation of India, Ltd. (ICICI)
163 Backbay Reclamation
Mumbai, India 400020
Telephone: (+91)-(22) 204-5190 or 202-2535
Fax: (+91)-(22) 204-6582
Web site: http://www.icicibank.com/

Bombay and investment information as well as on-line services are found here.

Industrial Development Bank of India
IDBI Tower, Cuffe Parade
Colaba, Mumbai, India 400005
Telephone: (+91)-(22) 218-5320
Fax: (+91)-(22) 218-8137
Web site: http://www.idbi.com

Information and resources regarding financial products and banking services is available here.

Industrial Finance Corporation of India (IFCI)
Web site: http://www.cleantechindia.com

This site contains information and programs regarding industry and the environment.

Investment Map of Indian Federations
Web site: http://investmentmap.com/indianfederations.htm

Links to industrial and trade associations are the strong points of this Web site.

National Centre for Trade Information
Web site: http://www.ncti-india.com

This site deals with trade information and reports, including with specific Indian firms.

PHD Chamber of Commerce and Energy
PHD House, 3rd Floor
(Opp. Asian Games Village)
New Delhi, India 110001
Telephone: (+91)-(11) 686-3801; 686-3804; 686-6810;
686-6814
Web site: http://www.pdhcci.org

This Web site offers information and services for a north Indian regional chamber of commerce, with 1,500 members.

Reserve Bank of India
Web site: http://www.rbi.org.in

This extensive site provides a detailed profile and explanation of the bank, its functions, and branches.

SAMACHAR
Web site: http://www.samachar.com or http://www.dhan.com

"The only bookmark on India you'll ever need." The site contains the internet editions of a variety of newspapers and magazines, on a number of topics, including business news and publications, as well as other services. It is extremely comprehensive.

Securities and Exchange Board of India
Web site: http://www.sebi.gov.in/

Press releases, legal framework, investor guidance, reports and documents, and public issues are available at this Web site.

U.S.-India Business Council
Web site: http://www.usibc.com

The premier policy-development organization promoting American economic interests in India and formed in 1975 at the request of the Indian and U.S. governments, its primary mission is to foster a bilateral dialogue between key business and government decision makers in both nations. The council represents about seventy of the largest U.S. companies with trade and investment interests in India.

GOVERNMENT

Census of India
Web site: http://www.censusindia.net
This is the site for the official census of India.

Consulate General of India, Chicago
455 North City Front Plaza Drive
NBC Tower Building, Suite 850
Chicago, IL 60611
Telephone: (312) 595-0405
Fax: (312) 595-0417
E-mail: congenindia@aol.com
Web site: http://www.IndianConsulate.com

This site contains general consulate information.

Consulate General of India, Houston
1990 Post Oak Boulevard, Suite 600
Houston, TX 77056
Telephone: (713) 626-2148
Fax: (713) 626-3450
E-mail: egi-hou@swbell.net
Web site: http://www.egihouston.org

This site contains consular services as well as official and unofficial information on India.

Consulate General of India, New York
3 East 64th Street
New York, NY 10021
Telephone: (212) 774-0600
Fax: (212) 861-3788
E-mail: indoccgny@aol.com

Web site: http://www.Indiacgny.org

This site contains consulate information as well.

Consulate General of India, San Francisco
540 Arguello Boulevard
San Francisco, CA 94118
Telephone: (415) 668-0662
Fax: (415) 668-7968
General E-mail: Info@IndianConsulate-sf.org
Consular Queries: vcpv@IndianConsulate-sf.org
Web site: http://www.indianconsulate-sf.org

Consulate information on, business, education, culture, and tourism is located here.

Government of India Directory of Official Web Sites
Web site: http://goidirectory.nic.in

This site is a comprehensive directory for financial institutions and various organizations within India.

Indian Diplomatic Missions in the United States
Embassy of India
2107 Massachusetts Avenue
Washington, DC 20008
Telephone: (202) 939-7000
Fax: (202) 265-4351
E-mail: indembwash@indiagov.org
Web site: http://www.indianembassy.org

This is the site for the embassy of India to the United States. It contains much up-to-date information, including, for example, details on the 2004 election.

EDUCATION

American India Foundation (AIF)
East Coast Office:
American India Foundation
c/o McKinsey & Company
55 East 52nd Street, 29th Floor
New York, NY 10022
Tel: (212) 891-4654
Fax: (212) 891-4717
Email: aparna.sinha@aifoundation.org

West Coast Office:
American India Foundation
647 E. Calaveras Blvd.
Milpitas, CA 95035
Tel: (408) 934-1600
Fax: (408)934-1612
Email: tania.ashraf@aifoundation.org

India Operations Office
American India Foundation
N 183 Panchshila Park Second Floor
New Delhi 110 017
Tel: (+91)-(11) 2649-5042; 2649-5043
Email: gurvinder.singh@aifoundation.org
Web site: http://www.aifoundation.org

With offices based in New York, California, and India, The AIF was started on the instigation of President Clinton and Prime Minister Vajpayee. It provides grants for education and livelihood projects in India and also sponsors development and information technology projects.

American Institute of Indian Studies
1130 East 59th Street
Chicago, IL 60637
Telephone: (773) 702-8638
Fax: (773) 702-6636
E-mail: aiis@uchicago.edu
Web site: http://www.indiastudies.org

A consortium of about sixty U.S. universities and colleges promoting teaching and research about India, with research and language-training centers in India.

Asia Society
725 Park Avenue
New York, NY 10021
Telephone: (212) 288-6400
Fax: (212) 517-8315
Web site: http://www.asiasociety.org

The goal of the Asia Society is to foster understanding of Asia and communication between Americans and the peoples of Asia and the Pacific. It is a national nonprofit, nonpartisan educational organization that sponsors art exhibitions and performances, films, lectures, seminars and conferences, and provides publications and assistance to the media, and materials and programs for students and teachers.

Asia Source
Web site: http://www.asiasource.org

A resource of the Asia Society, the site has an education section that includes information for students and educators, as well as on studying abroad.

Associated Colleges of the Midwest
Whitney Kidd, Program Associate
ACM India Studies Program
205 West Wacker Drive, Suite 1300

Chicago, IL 60606
Telephone: (312) 263-5000
Fax: (312) 263-5879
E-mail: wkidd@acm.edu
Web site: http://www.acm.edu/india

The ACM India Studies Program takes place mid-July through mid-December at Pune, including a five-week orientation in India, language study, and independent study.

Association for Asian Studies (AAS)
1021 East Huron Street
Ann Arbor, MI 48104
Telephone: (734) 665-2490
Fax: (734) 665-3801

The Association for Asian Studies is a scholarly nonpolitical, nonprofit professional association with a national academic meeting and several regional ones each year. It is responsible for several publications yearly, including the *Journal of Asian Studies* and *Education about Asia.*

Fulbright Program
United States Department of State
Bureau of Educational and Cultural Affairs
Web site: http://www.iie.org/cies

This site provides information on the Fulbright Student Program, Fulbright Scholar Program, and related programs.

Project South Asia
Karl J. Schmidt
Editor, *Teaching South Asia*
Director, Project South Asia
Missouri Southern State College
Joplin, MO 64801-1595
Web site: http://www.mssc.edu/projectsouthasia

This site provides teaching resources about South Asia for

colleges and universities, along with the online journal *Teaching South Asia*.

University of Virginia/Emory University
Semester-in-India Program
Center for South Asian Studies
University of Virginia
110 Minor Hall, P.O. Box 400169
Charlottesville, VA 22904-4169
E-mail: southasia@virginia.edu
Web site: http://www.virginia.edu/~soasia

Center for International Programs
Kristi Hubbard
Study Abroad Adviser
Emory University
Telephone: (404) 727-9279
E-mail: khubba@emory.edu

Dr. Joyce Flueckiger
Director of Asian Studies
Emory University
Telephone: (404) 727-7598
E-mail: reljbf@emory.edu

The universities offer a semester program in Jodhpur, Rajisthan, open to third- and fourth-year undergraduates enrolled in U.S. or Canadian universities.

University of Wisconsin
Study Abroad Programs
University of Wisconsin
Madison, WI 53706
Telephone: (608) 262-2851
Web site: http://www.wisc.edu/studyabroad/asia

A program of study in Varanasi or Madurai, with the preceding summer in Madison. It is open to all undergraduates at junior and senior level with a grade point average of 2.5 or above.

WWW Virtual Library: History: India

Web site: http://www.unkans.edu/kansas/india/india.html

This site has a plethora of links to research tools, articles, and centers.

WWW Virtual Library: India

Web sites: http://www.india.com.ar or http://www.columbia.edu/cu/lweb/indiv/southasia.cuvl

A great many links on a great many topics and places are provided by these sites.

TOURISM

Fodor's

Web site: http://www.fodors.com

This is the site of the famous travel guides and provides information on hotels, restaurants, bookings. It has a section on bargains (hotels, flights, vacation packages).

Incredible India

Web site: http://www.tourismofindia.com

Site of the Department of Tourism, Government of India, it contains guidelines for tour operators and travel agents, a list of tour operators, information on planning a trip, sections on "useful stuff" and "fun stuff," and FAQs among other items.

Lonely Planet

Web site: http://www.lonelyplanet.com/destinations

The website of the outstanding travel guide Lonely Planet, it is as complex, informative, and useful as the guide itself.

Trade Wings Travel
Web site: http://www.tradewingstravel.com

An extensive site of a joint venture between an international travel agency and an Indian one. It has information about India, travel, travel services, tours, and much more.

Annotated Bibliography

BOOKS

The following books, with one exception, are all in print at this writing. The exception, a collection of literary excerpts, each in a cultural setting and with information and insight beyond the literary (Wightman, Simon, ed., *Traveller's Literary Companion: Indian Subcontinent,* 1996), is easily available (e.g., through http://www.amazon.com) and is so valuable and unique as to warrant inclusion.

The categories in the book section of the bibliography are as follows: Culture; Society, Politics, and Economics; History; Etiquette, Food, and Cooking; Travel; and Gandhiana. The placement of titles by category is necessarily somewhat arbitrary (thus, at least one book on cooking could justifiably be placed in the history category), as is the division and labeling of the categories.

Culture

Aitken, Molly Emma, ed. *Meeting the Buddha: On Pilgrimage in Buddhist India.* New York: Riverhead, 1995. 370 pages.

An anthology of observations of almost fifty travelers to various Buddhist sites in India, the book also includes editorial commentary and descriptions of each spot listed. Illustrated, with handsomely drawn maps, this is also a good literary work.

Armstrong, Karen. *Buddha.* New York: Penguin, 2001. 205 pages.

There are many biographies of the Buddha, some more spiritual than objective, which is not surprising because most of what is "known" about the Buddha is mythological. This work puts the Buddha's life into a cultural and historical context and incorporates his philosophy and its development in an easily accessible manner. It is sympathetic but objective, presented in a manner appealing to the contemporary curiosity.

Arnett, Robert. *India Unveiled,* 2nd ed. Columbia, GA: Atman, 1999. 216 pages.

The Indian American Education Foundation (http://www.iaef-seattle.org) has provided more than 1,500 public high schools with copies of this book. The major purpose of the foundation is to increase knowledge about India in U.S. education. The avenue of using this book would seemingly be very effective. The book is divided into six chapters, each dealing with a particular region of India: central, east, north, northwest, west, and south. Although the division of the states into these particular regions might be somewhat problematical, it is an effective way to present the cultures of India not only to high school students but to college undergraduates and the general public as well.

Two primary attributes make this book so attractive and advantageous: the text is personalized—sympathetic yet objective; and the photographs are magnificent and humanistically sensual. One feels the ambience. At $50 it is an expensive book—yet not when the quality and value are considered.

Basham, A. L. *The Wonder That Was India: A History of the Indian Sub-Continent before the Coming of the Muslims,* 3rd ed. London: Sidgwick and Jackson, 2000. 568 pages.

Originally published in 1954, this is probably the most popular introductory text on Indian culture ever published. It is a classic and only slightly dated (e.g., Basham predicted the end of the caste system in a generation). It is arranged in ten chapters (introduction, prehistory, history, the state, society, everyday life, religion, the arts, language and literature, and epilogue: the heritage of India) and twelve short appendices (cosmology and geography, astronomy, the calendar, mathematics, physics and chemistry, logic and epistemology, weights and measures, coinage, the alphabet, prosody, the Gypsies). There are abundant examples and illustrations.

Brians, Paul. *Modern South Asian Literature in English.* Westport, CT: Greenwood, 2003. 171 pages.
A straightforward account of a number of twentieth-century South Asian fiction writers, mostly from India. Written primarily for the general public and high school and community college students, this highly readable and interesting narrative explicates some of the most important recent writers in the rich fiction of modern India. A particular work of each author is treated in the context of his or her corpus of works as well as the cultural milieu. Writers dealt with are Rabindranath Tagore, Raja Rao, Khushwant Singh, R. K. Narayan, Attia Hosain, Anita Desai, Bapsi Sidhwa, Bharati Mukherjee, Salman Rushdie, Shyam Selvadurai, Rohinton Mistry, Anudhati Roy, and Michael Ondaatje.

Bumiller, Elisabeth. *May You Be the Mother of a Hundred Sons: A Journey among the Women of India.* New Delhi: Penguin, 1991 (New York: Fawcett, 1991). 306 pages.
The author (now with the *New York Times*) spent four years in India in the mid-1980s as a reporter for the *Washington Post.* Extremely readable, the book has been praised for capturing the diversity of Indian women, although one critic felt it to have fallen short in capturing their strength, and another has discerned stereotypes in it. Both criticisms are subjective, for Bumiller was an observer, not a member of any Indian community, and the work provides feeling and insight remarkable for a foreigner in such a complex culture, treating the subjects with humanity and individuality. The title represents a traditional well-wishing.

Craven, Roy. *Indian Art: A Concise History.* London: Thames & Hudson, 1997/1976. 256 pages.

This book is a title in the publisher's World Art Series, which consists of concise and extremely reasonably priced introductory studies. Using an historical approach, the author presents explications of art from the prehistoric Indus civilization through the Pahari (Himalayan foothills) miniatures in the late eighteenth and early nineteenth centuries, in eleven chapters plus an epilogue on the modern period. He takes into account regional developments and, to a degree, aesthetics. Well-illustrated, it is an excellent compact introduction in unusually handy format for an art book.

Dalrymple, William. *The Age of Kali: Indian Travels and Encounters* (American title and edition). Oakland: Lonely Planet, 2000. 394 pages.

———. *At the Court of the Fish-Eyed Goddess: Travels in the Indian Subcontinent* (Indian title and edition). New Delhi: HarperCollins, 1998. 323 pages.

A great travel writer with considerable insight into, knowledge about, and experience in India, Dalrymple brings an objective yet slightly oblique view to his splendidly written articles and books. This collection, slightly rearranged in the American edition from the Indian, is informative and delightful. Its focus on the play of human nature in society and politics makes for interesting, entertaining, and valuable reading, even for a reader with little or almost no knowledge of India. Dalrymple has aptly been described as a raconteur.

Flood, Gavin. *An Introduction to Hinduism*. Cambridge: Cambridge University Press, 1996. 341 pages.

By its very nature Hinduism is complex almost to the point of incomprehensibility: no founder or founding date, no code by which to differentiate "heterodox" from "orthodox," no single or clear definition. As this book's introduction states, "'[W]hat is Hinduism?' This is a complex issue, as the term 'Hindu' has only been in wide circulation for a couple of centuries and reading 'Hinduism' into the past is problematic."

Also problematic is finding good texts in print that clearly deal with Hinduism. Although this is definitely a textbook, it is quite readable, encompassing the vastness of "Hinduism" in a very organized and clear manner. The structure is fascinating: Points of Departure, Ancient Origins, Dharma [a central feature too often underplayed in many texts], Yoga, Vaisnavism, Saivism, Mahadevi or the Goddess, Ritual, Philosophy, and The Modern World.

This text can be very rewarding for one who has the time and inclination. Further, it incorporates the extensive terminology of Hinduism in a manner that informs but does not alienate.

Knipe, David M. *Hinduism: Experiments with the Sacred.* San Francisco: HarperSanFrancisco, 1991. 171 pages.

Dealing more with Hinduism as a religion than a philosophy, this compact study has focus on the religion's history, mythology, devotionalism, outlooks on the universe, "dimensions," and "dynamics." Particularly advantageous is the book's remarks on Hinduism today, its extensive glossary and list of deities, powers, and deified heroes.

Lannoy, Richard. *Benares: A World within a World.* Varanasi: India Books, 2002. 419 pages. A revised text of the $100 photographic exposition *Benares Seen from Within* (published by the University of Washington Press, 1999).

This excellent account of the world's oldest continuously inhabited city, which is also considered to be the holiest city of Hinduism, places Benares (Banaras, Varanasi) into the larger contexts of Hindu religion (theory and practice) and culture, as well as Indian history. The long segmented chapter "Glimpses of History" (pages 195–348) is especially valuable. This remarkable paperback (available at a fraction of the cost of the earlier, larger work—albeit without the quantity of photographs in the larger volume) provides sensitive insight into a traditional but changing city, by a writer and photographer who is very familiar with it.

Mehrotra, Arvind. *History of Indian Literature in English.*
New York: Columbia University Press, 2003. 320 pages.
An expensive ($75) but fundamental collection of essays deal-
ing with Indian literature in English—poetry, novels, drama,
and nonfiction (science and social science), from 1800 to
2000, arranged chronologically by author, movements, and
sources. The author takes the designation of "Indian literature" more contextually than ethnically (e.g., Rudyard Kipling
is included).

Moorhouse, Geoffrey. *Calcutta.* New Delhi: Penguin, 1994
(London: Weidenfield and Nicholson, 1971). 393 pages.
Novelist Paul Scott ("The Raj Quartet") referred to this fascinating narrative as "the best book on modern India I have
read." Moorhouse is a professional writer, and the book shows
it. It is a literary and topical study (poverty, wealth, migrants,
etc.), dealing with Calcutta in its own right as well as placing
it in the larger context of modern Indian history.

Naipaul, V. S. *India: A Million Mutinies Now.* New York:
Viking, 1990. 521 pages.
Although the book is based upon experiences and interviews
in the late 1980s, it remains a fine, lucid presentation in
which the author finds, in his travels through India, "scores of
particularities" of regional and cultural nature. Of Indian
descent, Naipaul was born in Trinidad; his earlier book on
India—*An Area of Darkness*—based on his first visit to India,
in 1962, was scathing in its criticism. This one is more sensitive, controlled, and optimistic, and it reveals the power of
insight and intelligence of this great travel writer and novelist.
The violence of caste and religious conflicts since the book's
publication might well temper his optimism somewhat today.

O'Reilly, James, and Larry Habegger. *Travelers' Tales: India.*
San Francisco: Travelers' Tales, 1995. 459 pages.
A collection of perceptive articles by Westerners (mostly

American) in a variety of circumstances and places in India—with a variety of responses to the culture. Their observations are open, sometimes naive, enriching, and just plain good reading! The book includes a bibliography, glossary, and map. The anthology is divided into five broad topics, perhaps more to break up the length than to direct the reader. Yet, as with any good anthology, the reader can start anywhere.

Prakash, Gyan. *Another Reason: Science and the Imagination of Modern India.* Princeton: Princeton University Press, 1999. 304 pages.

This work is a study linking Indian tradition with modernity, through science and colonialism. The incongruity between British domination and the use of science and technology has, in the author's view, a liberating influence that helped to synthesize Indian thought and Western ideas and contributed to nationalism (through a sense of unity), which reinforced the drive to independence.

Spear, Percival. *Delhi: Its Monuments and History,* updated and annotated by Narayani Gupta and Laura Sykes. Delhi: Oxford University Press, 1997. 182 pages.

The original edition of this guidebook was written in 1943, primarily for children. Gupta writes in the forward, "In those days, there was no TV and little cinema to make claims on children's leisure hours, school homework was sensibly limited, and the town was small, with a few trams and only one bus-service." The population of Dehli then was about 700,000; today it is about 13 million. Many of the monuments that were then outside of town are today in heavily populated areas and are thus not as conspicuous.

The descriptions are very clear, often aided by diagrams or maps. In an addition to Spear's text, in "Afterward—Fifty Years On," Sykes, noting how much the city has changed since 1943 (helped by maps of Delhi in 1943 and 1993), has "updated and annotated, illustrated and indexed" the original observations. Through symbols, she has also indicated historical/architectural significance and "charm and atmosphere of the site." Her remarks are helpful and of interest. Indeed, a copy of this slim volume makes sightseeing a much more rewarding experience.

Suraiya, Jug. *Rickshaw Ragtime: Calcutta Remembered*. New Delhi: Penguin, 1993. 120 pages.

In a way this collection of articles by a professional feature writer could stand as a paradigm for such light-hearted, almost nostalgic books in regard to other cities. It has a certain appeal for Westerners, not unlike the type of columns of the late Herb Caen of San Francisco or Mike Royko of Chicago. Calcutta has a strong anglicized element, and the writer's journalism career has been in English—and he is very good. Further, the book puts a focus on everyday people and events, as well as providing reminiscences. It's a fun book.

Thapar, Romila. *Sakuntala: Texts, Readings, Histories*. London: Anthem, 2002. 277 pages.

Kalidasa (mid-fourth to mid-fifth century C.E.) is generally considered India's greatest classical writer. The *Abhijñāna-śakuntalam* (The Recognition of Sakuntala) is his greatest work. Professor Thapar has selected the excellent translation by the late Sanskritist Barbara Stoler Miller. She has surrounded it with a series of articles demonstrating the mixed reaction of Europeans and, first, the epic version of the tale—which, juxtaposed with the play, demonstrates the dramaturgical genius of the playwright. The transformation is astounding. Kalidasa's *Sakuntala* makes an excellent lightning rod for European colonialist attitudes toward India and its culture, which were rather mixed: a grudging respect but a strong sense of ethnocentrism and Orientalist disapproval. The postindependence view of Indians is also included in the text. This book is a bit specialized (in a textbook sense more than as a scholarly tome), but for those with an interest in how this most significant character and literary work have influenced—and been interpreted through the ages in—different cultures, it is an outstanding study and presentation.

Tharoor, Shashi. *India: From Midnight to the Millennium.* New York: HarperCollins, 1997. 392 pages.

An account of India from independence on arranged topically rather than chronologically (e.g., diversity within unity, caste, communalism, nonresident Indians). As a scholar, United Nations official, and novelist, the author brings an interesting combination of attributes to his approach. The book is a collection of personal essays.

Waterstone, Richard. *India: Belief and Ritual, the Gods and Cosmos, Meditation and Yogic Arts.* New York: Thorson, 2002 (Boston: Little, Brown, 1995). 184 pages.

This book has a magazine-style format and presents a wide variety of topics, some rather esoteric. Nevertheless, it is an attractive book, which one might approach by "dipping" into it. It is beautifully illustrated, with the virtue of being a work that would likely raise many questions.

Weightman, Simon, ed. *Traveller's Literary Companion: Indian Subcontinent.* Lincolnwood, IL: Passport Books, 1995. 414 pages.

This book is currently out of print, but because it is rather easily available through http://www.amazon.com and other sources, it is being included here for its potential value to readers of this handbook. The quality lies in the structure and the selections. A concise cultural introduction is followed by eight chapters—one on classical literatures, then seven regional chapters. Each chapter has an introduction (geographical, cultural, and political), bibliography of the selections, biographical details, and short summaries of the major works of the authors presented. The selections are wide-ranging: historical writers, English authors (e.g., E. M.

Forster), and contemporary Indian writers in English and regional languages. The selections are invariably of high literary quality and cultural value, short but of sufficient length to provide contextual insight in terms of the chapter as a whole.

Weller, Anthony. *Days and Nights on the Grand Trunk Road.* New York: Marlowe, 1997. 563 pages.

An account by a U.S. correspondent (and poet) of his journey, adventures, and observations on the 1,525-mile Grand Trunk Road, a centuries-old artery that runs from Calcutta in the eastern part of north India to the Khyber Pass on the western border of Pakistan. The book includes meetings and conversations with contemporary Indians, observations on people and places, and cultural and historical notes and anecdotes. It can be easily appreciated and enjoyed even if one knows next to nothing about India.

Society, Politics, and Economics

Das, Gurcharan. *India Unbound.* New York: Anchor, 2001. 412 pages.

If one were to read only one book on Indian economics and modern economic history, this should be the one. Far from being a dry economic treatise, this book deals with politics and political personalities, contains personal insight and experiences, and provides relevant autobiographical detail. Das recognizes that the economic revolution taking place in India is "a drama of the highest order" (perhaps even more so socially than economically) and treats it as such. With economic insight and business acumen, he yet writes in a fine literary style. He makes an interesting case that those cultural aspects (introspective philosophical thought) that slowed industrial development are actually beneficial for the knowledge of the Information Age. At least twice he observes that far more harmful than the socialist ideology in regard to failures in economic development was, simply, poor management from an overcentralized bureaucracy and the mantra of postindependence economics: no competition. Yet, he recognizes that "it is easy to blame Jawaharlal Nehru. Although he initiated the wrong economic policies, they represented the wisdom of his age." It is his daughter, Indira, who bears the brunt of historical scorn for increasing the rigidity of economic policies, even though by her tenure it was clear that the opposite was needed. He also lambastes the Indian obsession with classifying everything modern as Western, and in a negative way. Finally, he states that India is not going to be an economic "tiger," but an "elephant," as its already established democracy will in the long run result in "a more stable, peaceful, and negotiated transition into the future than, say, China." He expresses great optimism:

> What democracy has done for caste in the twentieth century, capitalism will do in the twenty-first. At the beginning of the twenty-first century, India is one of the fastest growing economies in the world, and there is little to stop it from continuing to grow between 6 and 8 percent a year for the next couple of decades. At this rate there will be unprecedented new jobs, and this will create new opportunities for everyone. (153)

Ganguly, Sumit, and Neil De Votta, eds. *Understanding Contemporary India.* Boulder: Lynne Rienner, 2000. 313 pages.

A note on the last page describes this collection of studies as "an interdisciplinary book designed for use both as a core text . . . and as a supplement in a variety of discipline-oriented curriculums." Twelve experts examine geography, historical context, the nationalist/independence movement, politics, international relations, economy, the role of women, population (including urbanization) and environment, religion (including communalism), caste, the arts, and trends and prospects. This is an informative book, intellectual but far from pedantic. It should have a place as a primary book in any institutional basic library on contemporary India.

Hardgrave, Robert L., Jr., and Stanley A. Kochanek. *India: Government and Politics in a Developing Nation,* 6th ed. New York: Harcourt Brace College, 2000. 536 pages.

The classic textbook for independent India's political history and development, this work is packed with information, analyses, and tables and figures. Its structure is such that the specific topics can be easily located and used. Considering that it is a specialized textbook, it is very readable. Perhaps the most valuable feature for the general reader is that it offers clear, concise references.

Harriss-White, Barbara. *India Working: Essays on Society and Economy.* Cambridge: Cambridge University Press, 2003. 320 pages.

This book is a study that challenges "the prevailing belief that liberalization releases the economy from political interference." Topics include the character of the Indian economy, social issues, and theoretics (e.g., chapter 10: "Postscript: Proto-Fascist Policies and the Economy").

Jaffrelot, Christophe. *The Hindu Nationalist Movement in India.* New York: Columbia University Press. 1996. 592 pages.

This is an intellectual study, an academic tome, but it is far from being dry or dusty. It is a thorough, in-depth study of a dangerous phenomenon unrealized by outside observers, for the most part, until well toward the end of the twentieth century: Hindu (fundamentalist) nationalism. Meticulously and fascinatingly presented, it manages to bring all the roots—religious and pseudoreligious, charismatic and chauvinistic, political, social, and historical—into a coherent study. The author's perceptions can be illustrated by the followingtopics: The RSS (Rashtriya Svayamsevak Sangh—Society of Nationalist Servants), which is treated as a "sect" rather than a party; Nazi racist ideology; allegedly straight political offshoots of the RSS; manipulation of "moderation"; populist appeals; melding of diverse elements in a "Hindu vote"; fusion with "Ram devotionalism"; and stoking of the fires of the "angry Hindu." Part 5 deals with political specifics. For those who wish to obtain some insight into the complicated nature of Hindu politics (sometimes mild, sometimes fascist, sometimes explosive), this is perhaps the outstanding source. The table of contents is so explicatory that readers can easily select among the myriad topics.

Khilnani, Sunil. *The Idea of India.* New York: Farrar, Strauss, Giroux, 1995. 263 pages.

This book offers six insightful essays on modern India: "Ideas of India," "Democracy," "Temples of Fortune," "Cities," "Who Is an Indian?" and "The Garb of Modernity." Khilnani observes in the foreword that "events . . . seem to suggest a broad revision of India's sense of self with disparate views of itself," in spite of chauvinistic attempts to make it otherwise. The approach is literary in style, resulting in a fascinating collection of articles.

Norton, James H. K. *India and South Asia,* 6th ed. Global Studies Series. Guilford, CT: McGraw-Hill/Dushkin, 2004. 224 pages.

Used primarily as a textbook, this anthology makes a good introductory reference and reader, with informative articles, useful maps, illustrations, and statistics. Very useful cultural and historical introductions are followed by thirty-five articles, divided into three sections: articles on the general region (1–7), India articles (8–21), and articles about the other nations in the area (22–35). The India articles include several on the India-Pakistan relationship and on Kashmir; internal communal social, political, and economic problems; computers, cable television, and other technologies; and, of special interest, the invention of zero and the early numerical system.

Schofield, Victoria. *Kashmir in Conflict: India, Pakistan, and the Unending War.* New York: I. B. Tauris, 2003. 304 pages.

An updated edition of earlier academic, investigative study, well-documented, on the seemingly interminable conflict between India and Pakistan over Kashmir. With a fine historical introduction and a broad scope of subjects, this book is a detailed but clearly presented examination of the problem.

Talbot, Ian. *India and Pakistan.* New York: Arnold and Oxford University Press, 2000. 382 pages.

A study of the nationalist movement, including community identities and their politicalization, and the growth of communal nationalism. The problems of nation-building in each country are examined, as are effects of globalization and ethnic pressures. This is a thorough yet concise work, considering how much it covers.

Thapar, Valmik. *Land of the Tiger: A Natural History of the Indian Subcontinent.* Berkeley: University of California Press, 1997. 288 pages.

The dust jacket proclaims that the book "accompanies the PBS television series," but this magnificent book fully stands on its own, with a superb text and beautiful illustrations. Anyone conscious of wildlife ecology is aware of the tiger's downward path toward extinction, with some subspecies already gone. Even where not lost, tigers are endangered—often behind the camouflage of far-too-small reserves in Southeast Asia. The book also fully lives up to its subtitle: it is "a natural history of the Indian subcontinent," with focus on the endangered situation of a whole slew of other species, as is indicated by the captions under a number of the many illustrations. Valmik Thapar is one of the foremost tiger experts in the world and is author of a number of books on tigers and preservation. He is a social anthropologist and an ecologist.

Tully, Mark. *No Full Stops in India.* New Delhi: Viking Penguin, 1991. 336 pages.

The author is a reporter with four decades of experience in India, mostly with the BBC. When he was to be transferred about ten years ago, he resigned and continued to live and work in India. The present book consists of ten articles or essays on Indian popular culture, society, and politics, all written with a sense of detachment and, yet, deep love for the country. He captures something universal within India, so although some of the items might seem historical now, they are not dated except perhaps for detail (e.g., the observation and celebration of the twelve-year Kumbh Mela festival in Allahabad, probably the largest religious festival in the world). The introduction and epilogue are especially insightful.

History

Baron, Archie. *An Indian Affair.* London: Channel Four Books (Macmillan), 2001. 254 pages.

Designed to accompany a British television series, the book stands very well on its own as a remarkably readable account of the British rise to empire in India. More social and cultural in approach than political, the text is accompanied by out-standing illustrations, most especially the contemporary photographs of Monica Eskenazi. The book addresses a number of general misunderstandings (e.g., the nature of the British entry and takeover in India).

Copland, Ian. *India 1885–1947: The Unmaking of an Empire.* London: Longman, 2001. 132 pages.

This is a study designed for seminars. Its value for the general reader lies in its analytical approach, especially in regard to nationalism and Muslim separatism. The collection of thirty-five documents adds depth to the text.

Hiro, Dilip. *The Rough Guide Chronicle: India.* London: Rough Guides, 2002. 378 pages.

This work is basically a chronology, and as such it may well be the best one ever done on India, both in terms of scope and depth. Blocks of cultural information (e.g., Kalidasa, Satyajit

Ray's films) and historical detail (e.g., Mughal emperors, the 1857 "Uprising") are juxtaposed into the text at appropriate places. One might expect such an arrangement to get a bit complicated, but the book is very straightforward in presentation. The chronology is divided into ten chapters. This book is a survey, which contains a useful bibliography and glossary.

James, Laurence. *Raj: The Making and Unmaking of British India*. New York: St. Martin's, 2000. 736 pages.

Despite its length, this is a very manageable book, written in a clear literary style, as absorbing as a novel: the events flow together like a plot, and the major historical figures are described with insightful characterization (e.g., that of General Dyer, responsible for the 1919 massacre at Amritsar).

Keay, John. *India: A History*. New York: Atlantic-Grove, 2001. 608 pages.

Keay is author of a number of books on South Asian and Central Asian history and is a historian but not a academician. This highly readable, comprehensive history treats all eras and areas more or less equally. He devotes as much to the earliest periods as to the most recent. Tables of rulers and dynasties help to clarify otherwise confusing names, years, and regions.

Kulke, Herman, and Dietmar Rothermund. *A History of India*, 3rd ed. New York: Routledge, 1999. 395 pages.

An advanced historical analysis—with analytic maps—well-organized and easy to follow, even though it is thorough, complex, and relatively detailed. Some prior general knowledge of Indian history might be helpful, however.

Ludden, David. *India and South Asia: A Short History*. Oxford: One World, 2002. 306 pages.

The author starts his history (after a brief introduction) by observing, "South Asian history has not one beginning, no one chronology, no single plot or narrative. It is not a single history, but rather many histories." His presentation is, as he subtitles his introduction, "An Approach to Social History." In it he writes, "The vast scale of South Asian history makes it inappropriate for readers to imagine that any one set of peoples or places represents the whole of South Asia's past." It is not so much that this recognition is new in history texts; it is that the centrality of emphasis is. He also states in the concise and pointed introduction that a major difference ("from other surveys") is that "its central subject matter is the historical process of social change, including economic, cultural, and political aspects." And such an approach he does effect, in a long essay constituted of numerous smaller, interrelated essays written in a finely structured, highly readable manner. Compact, the work is yet clear, albeit that it does seem to assume a basic knowledge that most U.S. introductory students probably should have, but do not. In a humanities sense (although not in an anthropological one) it lacks culture—religion, philosophy, literature, arts; but such is not in the declared intentions and would have taken the text far beyond "the short history" that it encompasses for itself. Indeed, it is remarkable that so much has been contained in so few pages.

McIntosh, Jane R. *A Peaceful Realm: The Rise and Fall of the Indus Civilization.* Boulder: Westview, 2002. 224 pages.

The more that we learn about the Indus civilization, the more it becomes apparent that its importance (as well as size) has been vastly underestimated. This wonderful book goes a long way in extending information—discoveries and descriptions—of the civilization beyond the realm of scholars. It advances beyond the archaeological to include crafts, religion, society, trade, and international relations; it examines the script, the origins, the question of peace among the cities, the decline, and the legacy. Such matters are largely speculation—but they are sound (and, one could argue, necessary) speculation. Juxtaposed with the text are items on the modern archaeological exploration and attitudes. One can learn a great deal from the book and enjoy it as well.

Moorhouse, Geoffrey. *India Britannica: A Vivid Introduction to the History of British India.* Chicago: Academy Chicago, 2000 (New York: Harper & Row, 1983). 260 pages.

A cultural and historical narrative that was reviewed in 1983 in *The Times of India* and described as a work of "a mutual sympathy" in regard to both the British and the Indians. Moorhouse, author of a number of works on India, makes the period come alive as well as any other book does on the Raj.

Pandey, Gyanendra. *Remembering Partition: Violence, Nationalism, and History in India.* Cambridge: Cambridge University Press, 2001. 218 pages.

An academic study (and speculation) on the 1947 violence, how it can be historically reconstructed and interpreted, and its impact on localities and the nation. The book's value for the general reader would be in the interviews and reportage, almost anecdotal but still grim and stark.

Robb, Peter. *A History of India.* New York: Palgrave, 2002. 344 pages.

The author states in the preface: "I have tried to keep this book simple. It is directed first at readers who are unfamiliar with the subject. It is meant to be read as a general introduction rather than searched for basic information, as a compendium of 'facts' or comprehensive narrative." To that end, after presentations on historical periods (more topical in nature than chronological), the book focuses on four aspects of modern India: government, politics, society, and economy. A short epilogue speculates on current problems, especially communalism. There is an excellent bibliography for each chapter.

Schmidt, Karl J. *An Atlas and Survey of South Asian History.* Armonk, NY: M. E. Sharpe, 1995. 168 pages.

This is an easily used reference, divided into four large categories: Geography, Climate, and Languages; Political and Military History; Economic, Social, and Cultural History; and Nepal, Sri Lanka, and Bhutan. A glossary and extensive bibliography (as well as an index) are also included. Each map is accompanied by a succinct essay. Comprehensive, but clearly structured and presented, in a sense the book is a survey—just not a narrative one.

Spear, Percival. *A History of India, Volume Two.* Baltimore: Penguin, 1965/1990. 284 pages.

This companion volume to Romila Thapar's Penguin history of India to 1526 (the advent of the Mughals) is now somewhat dated but remains a classic.

Tammita-Douglas, Sinharaja. *A Traveller's History of India.* New York: Interlink, 1995. 270 pages.

This facilely written work is easily read—and is exactly what the title says; it would be a good companion on air or rail journeys. Some of the observations and remarks might be questioned, but likely only by the specialist. It is a fine presentation for the general reader.

Thapar, Romila. *Early India: From Origins to A.D. 1300.* Berkeley: University of California Press, 2002. 556 pages.

An outstanding work of historical interpretation, an updating of "a book of almost forty years ago [that] has brought home to [the author] the substantial changes in the readings of early Indian history." Thapar has also lowered the closing date from 1526 to 1300, which allows for more concentration on the regional nature of Indian politics. This is undoubtedly a major work on ancient Indian history—the latest such, and perhaps the most important ever. It also deals with historiography.

————. *A History of India, Volume One.* Baltimore: Penguin, 1966/1990. 381 pages.

A classic textbook to go with the Spear volume listed above. It is a fairly detailed introduction, with maps and cultural diagrams. Thapar has considerably updated and expanded the work in the item listed immediately above.

Vohra, Ranbir. *The Making of India: A Historical Survey.* Armonk, NY: M. E. Sharpe, 2001. 331 pages.

An advanced history from 1857 (with a brief introduction in regard to earlier history) that is composed of extensive in-depth presentations on British India and independent India. Perhaps a bit heavy for the general reader, it yet contains subjects (and is clearly structured) that could be of interest (e.g., communalism, economics).

Watson, Francis. *India: A Concise History,* rev. and updated ed. London: Thames & Hudson, 2002. 203 pages.

A straightforward and lucid account, compact and illustrated, oriented as a basic introduction to Indian history for the beginner and written by a veteran observer of India. It is a very fine general introduction, assuming no prior knowledge, and has been used in introductory undergraduate and correspondence courses.

Wolpert, Stanley. *A New History of India,* 6th ed. New York: Oxford University Press, 544 pages.

For many years probably the most frequently used textbook in the United States on Indian history. It is a straight college history text, nothing fancy but very solid.

Etiquette, Food, and Cooking

Archarya, K. T. *Indian Food—A Historical Companion,* rev. ed. Delhi: Oxford University Press, 1998. 322 pages.

A history of Indian food from prehistoric times to the present, the study has researched "literature, archaeology, epigraphic records, anthropology, philology and historical and botanical and genetic studies" (http://www.indiaclub.com). Regional cuisines, customs, and classifications of food are all dealt with, as is the importance of food in Indian civilization and history.

Baljekar, Mridula. *Real Fast Indian Food.* London: Metro, 2002. 224 pages paperback.

Great recipes—and ones that can be made fast, which is seemingly impossible regarding Indian foods. The book starts with four key points of organization: a well-stocked cupboard, getting the key ingredients in an easily accessible spot, the same with cooking utensils, and a thorough study of the recipe before starting. Next, "basics" are suggested in regard to tactics (e.g., preparing spices) and standard blends and sauces; this is followed by an exploratory "Guide to Ingredients." The recipes are in categories: soups and snacks, fish, poultry, lamb and pork, vegetarian, salads and vegetables. An innovative chapter is "Microwave Recipes." "Sweet Treats" is followed by "Menu Planner." Perhaps the best feature of this concise and easily understood book is the heading above each recipe that tells how much time it takes to prepare. There are some innovative recipes that one might not easily associate with India—e.g., tuna burgers, bacon omelette—but this feature just adds to the value of this clearly articulated book (e.g., one recipe, and only one recipe, per page). There are also some fascinating titles, to whit: "Spicy Potato Fingers with Whole Eggs" and "Eggs in Curry-Leaf Coconut Milk."

Batra, Neelam. *1,000 Indian Recipes.* Hoboken, NJ: Wiley, 2002. 704 pages.

The author of several books on Indian cooking, as well as a teacher of cooking in the Los Angeles area, Batra at first thought she had produced four books—but decided to make one huge book, "a definitive book encompassing major Indian culinary traditions." Preparation time ranges from twenty minutes to four hours, with recipes adapted "to an American kitchen," yet with "the integrity of a dish . . . maintained," she states (*India Abroad,* April 18, 2003). Her culinary philosophy: "In my family in India and the family I have in America, meals provide much more than sustenance. . . . They strengthen bonds between friends and family members. This book should help [in] creating and strengthening such bonds."

Bharardwaj, Monisha. *Stylish Indian in Minutes.* Delhi: IBH, 2002. 160 pages.

Http://www.indiaclub.com states: "*Stylish Indian in Minutes* will quickly become a well-used kitchen companion." The idea is that "quicker and more efficient methods" have resulted in real Indian cuisine being prepared in minutes. Each recipe is timed for preparation and cooking. A variety of traditional and regional recipes is presented for meats, breads, vegetables, chutneys, desserts, and drinks.

Brennan, Jennifer. *Curries and Bugles: A Memoir and Cookbook of the British Raj.* Boston: Periplus, 2000. 324 pages.

The author (born in 1935) grew up during the Raj and brings a cultural sensitivity—yet balance—to the study of the period. Each recipe is introduced by an anecdote or historical note, and each chapter has a lengthy introduction. Historical photographs and drawings add to the context. The eighteen-page introduction is an excellent, concise essay on the Raj. The recipes are fascinating (e.g., sardine curry puffs, and wild rice and sausage stuffing in red cabbage), presenting a cuisine quite different—albeit with obvious influences—from traditional and regional Indian cultures. These are recipes of the Raj, for its English servants. The recipes are collected into sections depending on the occasion: breakfasts, tiffin (lunch), picnics, travel, tea, buffets and fêtes, celebrations, dinner parties, and at the club. A final chapter contains recipes for items still popular (e.g., chutneys). A glossary, bibliography, directory (i.e., index as to types of food, such as poultry), and a general index are also included. This culturally and historically informative book is highly enjoyable. It provides insights that would be difficult to find elsewhere.

Das Gupta, Minakshie, Bunny Gupta, and Jaya Charka. *The Calcutta Cookbook: A Treasury of over 200 Recipes from Pavement to Palace.* New Delhi/New York: Penguin, 1995. 403 pages.

This 400-page volume is far more than a cookbook. It is a bit of cultural history strung between a myriad of recipes. Following a preface of "Dos and Don'ts," the first chapter provides "A History and Philosophy of Food." There is a certain dryness in humor—perhaps essential for anyone writing a cookbook about Calcutta in the late twentieth century. For instance, "The best compliment paid to a woman who is a good cook is to compare her with Draupadi, wife of the Pandava brothers in the *Mahabharata.* In Bengal, she is the role model for wives and cooks. For, after all, did she not satisfy five husbands and no one was turned away hungry from her kitchen." This well-done book offers respect and allure for both Bengali culture and cooking. It also provides some interesting Calcutta variations on non-Bengali dishes such as Boston baked beans and chili con carne (neither with curry) as well as pizza (no curry, but with other strange ingredients like pickles and sardines).

Davidar, Ruth N. *Indian Food Sense—A Health and Nutrition Guide to Traditional Recipes.* New Delhi: East West, 2001. 293 pages.

A former teacher, the author is a columnist and writer on food for numerous Indian newspapers "who firmly believes that sound nutrition is not about eating poorly prepared tasteless food merely because 'it's good for you'" (http://www.india-club.com). There are six sections in the book: basics of nutrition, an explanation of how to use the book, recipes ("written in easy-to-follow steps so that even a beginner can attempt to cook Indian food"), a bibliography, appendices (including a glossary and some technical information for professionals), and an index.

Hughes, Martin, et al. *World Food: India.* Oakland: Lonely Planet World Food Series, 2001. 254 pages.

Typical of Lonely Planet, this book is sheer quality. It is thorough in breadth and depth, and a delight in format, text, and illustrations. The back cover promotes the book as (among other things) "the essential guide to the culture of eating and drinking in India." Many other features are jammed into this handy book. Yet, there may be a tendency to take itself too seriously, even ideologically (e.g., the section on etiquette admonishes: "If you're hardy and sensitive enough not to clog up Indian sewers with toilet paper you'll eat only with your right hand by instinct"). What is most impressive about this book is the structure and the amount of information it contains. The introductory pages include a clear and useful reference map. A concise section on "The Culture of Indian Cuisine" follows, and includes pages on its history; the relation of food in regard to religion, castes, and cultures; how Indians eat; and etiquette. Then follow sections on various types of foods and drinks, cooking at home, celebrations, regional variations, shopping, "Where to Eat and Drink," street food, health, a glossary, bibliography, and index. Throughout are social and cultural comments and observations, all put together in a highly literary and informative fashion. The book also features an artistic but very practical use of photography.

Kingsland, Venika. *The Simple Guide to Customs and Etiquette in India.* Kent, England: Global Books, 1996. 64 pages.

This handy little jacket-pocket guide, written by a woman born and raised in India but living in England, provides an insight—and concisely so—not easily available elsewhere. The diversities within the culture, with their particular characteristics in regard to custom and etiquette, are succinctly pointed out. What keeps the book (which is almost a booklet) from being merely a manual are the style and organization. The listing of chapter titles best illustrates the advantages and uses of this little book: "Land and People," "Religions," "Custom and Ritual," "The Home" (social relations, greetings, gifts, taboo subjects, sense of humor), "City Life," "Food and Drink" (including tipping and shopping), "Business," "Travel," and "Language."

Merchant, Ismail. *Ismail Merchant's Indian Cuisine.* New York: Penguin, 2000. 246 pages.

The author—famed film collaborator with James Ivory and Ruth Prawer Jhabvala—has upon occasion treated the film crew and cast to his cooking with a meal on the set. Merchant's interpretations of Indian cooking have been described by one reviewer as "sophisticated and remarkably original."

Todiwala, Cyrus. *Café Spice Namaste: Modern Indian Cooking.* San Francisco: Sima, 1998. 144 pages.

The *New York Times Magazine* (April 20, 2003) says of this Parsi cookbook that it "will surprise you not only with the sophistication and subtlety of recipes but also with the ease of preparation." Parsis are descendants of Zoroastrians who fled Persia for the west coast of India in the eleventh century. Todiwala estimates there are no more than 130,000 Parsis worldwide, and Parsi cooking and recipes are likewise rare. They have a special twist with less emphasis than other Indian cuisines on chiles and more on spices, with different combinations for different dishes, rather than relying primarily upon a single basic curry sauce.

Travel

Berlitz. *India: Pocket Guide.* London: Berlitz, 1995. 256 pages.

A considerable amount of information is packed into this pocket-size, handy guide on Where to Go, Eating Out, and Handy Travel Tips. It can be carried in a jacket pocket and is a delight to read, as well as a handy reference with meaningful anecdotes (e.g., Humayun's fatal fall on the stairs of his "pavilion").

Cushman, Anne, and Jerry Jones. *From Here to Nirvana: The Yoga Journal Guide to Spiritual India.* New York: Riverhead (Penguin), 1998. 405 pages.

A guide to contemporary spiritual leaders, places, and institutions (ashrams). For spiritual seekers—or even those just interested or curious—the book is of invaluable practical help. It is thoroughly done and clearly presented. It includes a map of places described in the book, information about what the book portends, practical information like "what to bring" and "staying healthy," and an overview of philosophies and religious tenets. The major part is a descriptive history listing, state by state, spiritual figures and places. These, too, are listed in a practical manner; for example, teachers and teaching, facilities and food, schedules, fees, addresses for contact, how to get there, services available, and books and tapes. Personal experiences are also related.

DK Eyewitness Travel Guides: India. New York: Dorling Kindersley, 2002. 824 pages.

This compendium encapsulates the 5,000-year-old culture of a billion people, and is one of the most impressive guides ever produced on India. It is full and varied in content, yet so well-structured that it goes beyond being merely a travel book: it is a veritable encyclopedia of a nation and its cultures. It is also a beautiful book. The photographs, drawings, and maps—all contextually positioned—are superb and superbly useful. The contents include an introductory section, followed by descriptions of regional divisions: north (including a thirty-page section on Delhi), central, eastern, western, southwestern, and south; then follows a section on "travellers' needs" and a "survival guide," concluding with a bibliography, glossary, and phrase book. It is indexed in detail.

Ellis, Royston. *India by Rail,* 3rd ed. Old Saybrook, CT: Globe Pequot, 1997. 260 pages.

This book is a gold mine for anyone planning on extensive railway travel in India (which is probably the best way to get around in the country). Even if such travel is to be minimal, railways play such a role in India that the book is a fascinating study. Diagrams of the layouts of various classes of railroad cars are provided. Where to go (popular rail destinations), how to get there, what to expect on the way, great trips—it is a very inclusive presentation.

Fodor's 4th Edition India: The Guide for All Budgets, Completely Updated, with Many Maps and Travel Tips, ed. Diane Mehta. New York: Random House, 2002. 472 pages.

The cumbersome title aptly describes this reference, which itself is anything but cumbersome. With its system of "icons and symbols" and "cool tools" (post-it flags, marking of top choices, travel tips, etc.), this volume is an extremely practical reference. It is not strong on cultural aspects (nor is it intended to be)—except for some contemporary observations (e.g., Bombay as "a city of mind-boggling contrasts"). What it does offer is easily accessible practical information and as such is very valuable indeed.

Insight Guide: India. London: Insight Guides and APA, 2002. 433 pages.

Associated with the Discovery Channel, this "visual travel guide" is richly illustrated and rich with all sorts of cultural information, from temples through movies (e.g., the most-watched Hindi-dubbed U.S. film was *Titanic*). There are practical tips as well on shopping, "Traveller's Hindi," travel within the country, etiquette, postal services, money matters, women traveling alone, and gay and lesbian travelers. It is a beautifully done book that offers a great deal of information, including a bibliography of useful and interesting books. The sections on major cities are of particular interest.

Kolanad, Gitanjali. *Culture Shock! India.* Portland, OR: Graphic Arts Center, 2001. 296 pages.

Styling itself "A Guide to Customs and Etiquette," this smart little book is divided into eleven chapters: "India Profile," "Perceptions" (beggars, caste, dharma, stages of life, superstitions, women—all concisely and admirably treated), "Religious Beliefs," "Home and the World" (cultural customs), "Getting the Message" (behavior and no-nos), "Street Smart City Living," "Setting Up House," "Inter City Travel," "Food and Entertaining," "Social Diversions," and "Doing Business in India." There is a section on resources (e.g., hospitals, schools, magazines) and one of hypothetical situations and how to react in them. It is a very useful book for anyone whose plans involve a stay beyond that of being a tourist.

Let's Go: India and Nepal. Cambridge, MA: St. Martin's, annually updated. 827 pages.

This practical guide has much detailed information (e.g., phone rates, travel advisories). The *New York Times* calls it "a sort of streetwise cookbook for traveling alone." Especially valuable are the clearly marked "WARNING" sections (e.g., "*Never* let a cab driver convince you that the hotel you ask for is full or closed"). The descriptions of recommendations and eating places are clear and concise. A lot of smaller cities, which don't often make it into smaller or fancier guides, are included.

Lonely Planet. *India and Bangladesh: Road Atlas.* Oakland: Lonely Planet, 2001. 184 pages.

One should really have a larger map—at least mentally—for reference in using this road atlas. If one plans to travel by road through regions of India, this book is almost a necessity. It is segmented, detailed, and complex. Travel information is provided in five languages: English, French, German, Spanish, and Japanese. Separate editions are available for north India and south India.

Lonely Planet. *India: A Travel Survival Kit,* 10th ed. Oakland: Lonely Planet, 2003. 1,100 pages.

There are many great travel guides on India, but perhaps none as thorough and helpful—especially for use within the country itself—as the Lonely Planet guide. Though bulky, it is easy to use, and focuses on all areas. Its detail (and one assumes accuracy) in delineating places to stay, where to eat, and how to get by, in all areas and cities, is uncanny. It provides cultural context and practical advice. It contains sensitive introductions to the country and its many cultures, meaningful illustrations and maps, useful statistics, and background information. Of the many fine and useful travel guides now available, this is certainly one of the most useful.

Nicholson, Louise. *National Geographic Traveler: India.* Washington, DC: National Geographic, 2002. 400 pages.

In the *National Geographic* tradition of quality, this is a beautiful and impressive guide. It starts with a section on history and culture, followed by a large section on Delhi and the surrounding area, then other regions. It concludes with a section on travel and practical advice and a glossary. The guide is beautifully illustrated and usefully structured and indexed, with maps for each regional section.

The Rough Guide to India, 4th ed. New York: Penguin Putnam, 2001. 1,596 pages.

This publication is much more than a "rough guide"; it is a veritable compendium—a comprehensive summary of the country. It is exemplary of the many fine guides that have become available in recent years. The information provided is so detailed—yet still useful—as to be almost esoteric; for example, "city transport" for Calcutta covers buses, taxis (an "extremely good value"), trams, and rickshaws (useful during the monsoon; "take care not to lean back as your weight will unbalance the driver"). Yet all the detail is easily manageable. The concluding section, "Contexts," provides extensive information on history, religion, women, wildlife, development and "green issues," music, books, language, and a glossary. Each is concisely developed.

Gandhiana

Ackerman, Peter, and Jack Duvall. *A Force More Powerful: A Century of Nonviolent Conflict.* New York: Palgrave, 2000. 544 pages.

Written in conjunction with a three-hour PBS series, this book deals with nonviolence as a method—even a weapon—in numerous countries. Its great interest is in the juxtaposition of India's Salt March and the Nashville, Tennessee, lunch counter sit-in. It is one of the few books to recognize the essential contribution of James Lawson.

Arnold, David. *Gandhi.* London: Longman, 2001. 266 pages.

This book is part of a series entitled "Profiles in Power." The author states that the purpose of his study is to evaluate Gandhi's "place in the history of India and the modern world" and "to examine anew the nature of his often unconventional and controversial 'power.'" It is a first-rate analysis that puts Gandhi into historical forces (more than having him lead them): yet, Gandhi does remain the focus of the study.

Bondurant, Joan. *Conquest of Violence: The Gandhian Philosophy of Conflict,* rev. ed. Princeton: Princeton University Press, 1988. 288 pages.

Still the classic, and probably best, introduction to satyagraha in theory and practice, this study is divided into five chapters (none biographical): introduction, basic precepts, application (including outline analyses of five specific campaigns), satyagraha within traditional contexts, and its relation to political philosophy and dialectic. The first four chapters are particularly valuable as a concise and clear introduction for students. Satyagraha is, of course, the cover term for Gandhi's approach to affecting (and effecting) social and political change through nonviolent means.

Clément, Catherine. *Gandhi: The Power of Pacifism,* trans. Ruth Sharman. New York: Harry Abrams, 1996. 175 pages.

It is arguable that Gandhi was not a pacifist (*War without Violence* is the title of one of the early and best studies on his methodology), but that is a minor point in regard to this beautiful little book, which appears to have been designed for younger students (high school, early college). Points are emphasized through the use of large print and are enriched with photographs and a series of original paintings. The structure is chronological, and the study is supplemented with a selection of outstanding documents and a glossary. The book would be of considerable value as an introduction for the general reader.

Dalton, Dennis. *Mahatma Gandhi: Nonviolent Power in Action,* rev. ed. New York: Columbia University Press, 2000. 304 pages.

An outstanding and popular study that put Gandhi's thoughts and actions in the context of the politics of the Indian independence movement, including critiques from two prominent critics (Rabindranath Tagore and M. N. Roy). The Salt Satyagraha (or Salt March) is treated in detail, as is the fast in Calcutta to curb violence during the Partition. There is also a chapter on Gandhi, Malcolm X, and Martin Luther King Jr.

———, ed. *Mahatma Gandhi: Selected Political Writings.* Indianapolis: Hackett, 1996. 169 pages.

For Gandhi, politics was not a separate category, and this selection of writings reveal that trait. Many anthologies of

Gandhi's writings are overwhelming, but this one is not only manageable but well-chosen and interesting. An enlightening introduction is followed by two divisions of the writings: *Satyagraha:* The Power of Nonviolence; and *Swaraj:* Gandhi's Idea of Freedom. This representative selection of Gandhi's writings avoids the esoteric and clearly presents the nature of Gandhi's views on nonviolence as a method for change and on the nature of what he thought should compose independence.

Hardimanm David. *Gandhi in His Times and Ours: The Global Legacy of His Ideas.* New York: Columbia University Press, 2003. 256 pages.

One scholar has termed this work as "one of the five best books ever written about the Mahatma." It focuses on the idea that "Gandhi's political style was based on a larger vision of an alternative society, one that emphasized mutual respect, resistance to exploitation, nonviolence, and ecological harmony."

Nanda, B. R. *Gandhi and His Critics.* New York: Oxford University Press, 1997. 188 pages.

This concise study traces the development of Gandhi's personality and political thought. The author is an astute student of the Indian independence movement, with a number of books published on the subject.

———. *Mahatma Gandhi: A Biography Complete and Unabridged, 4th ed.* New York: Oxford University Press, 1996. 542 pages.

A thorough and detailed political and personal biography by an Indian political scientist with close ties to the independence movement.

Sofri, Gianni. *Gandhi and India,* trans. Janet Sethre. New York: Interlink, 1999. 190 pages.

The outstanding advantage of this small elementary study is that it provides a context for Gandhi in Indian history. Well-illustrated and easy to read, it is composed of five chapters: culture and early history, South Africa, satyagraha in India, after independence, and Gandhi's legacy.

Wolpert, Stanley. *Gandhi's Passion: The Life and Legacy of Mahatma Gandhi.* New York: Oxford University Press, 2002. 336 pages.

A very touching study of Gandhi during the independence movement, if rather critically loaded in some regards. The first few pages are particularly scathing, painting Gandhi almost as a cult leader. Nevertheless, the book contains much information and insight from one of the greatest U.S. historians on India. One observer dubbed the book as "a five handkerchief read" for its tragic portrayal of Gandhi (or, perhaps more aptly, for its portrayal of the tragedy of Gandhi).

PERIODICALS

Education about Asia

An eighty-page, thrice-yearly magazine published by the Association for Asian Studies, the target readership is kindergarten through twelfth grade, community college, and undergraduate teachers. The articles, which cover the Far East as well as South Asia, are worthwhile for the general public as well: illustrated, uncomplicated, innovative.

Far Eastern Economic Review: Asia 2002 Yearbook
Concise analyses and reviews of economic developments in Asian nations.

India Abroad
An "International Weekly Newspaper" published from Chicago, Dallas, Los Angeles, New York, and Toronto.

Targeted to Indian Americans, the paper has generous coverage of news in regard to India. Of particular interest is the sixteen-page "magazine" insert of cultural and popular news.

India Today

A fortnightly, the most widely read magazine in India, with an international edition available in North America. Similar to *Time* and *Newsweek* in format.

New York Times

Probably the best coverage on India of any U.S. newspaper, with the added advantage of being readily available in most urban areas. The in-depth feature articles are excellent.

WEB SITES

http://www.bawarchi.com

Mostly recipes, "veggie" and "non-veggie" specials, and links to health and nutrition, readers' contributions, festivals, and "healthy recipes."

http://www.Bollywood.com

All sorts of connections in regard to India's fascinating movie world.

http://www.cafonline.org/cafindia.i_search.cfm

A nongovernmental organizations directory for "easy access . . . of 2,350 voluntary organizations in India."

http://www.dinesh.com/india/television/html

This site contains television links.

http://www.fordham.edu/halsall/india/indiasbook.html

Internet Indian History Sourcebook. An outstanding collection of articles balanced between revisionist theories (e.g., the "myth" of the Aryan invasion) and original sources. Not just for scholarly access, it is of use to anyone interested in India.

http//:www.India.org

A "focal point of information on India," including map, sites, "Reading Room" (newspapers and magazines), "Kitchen Corner" (cuisine), and arts. A very useful site.

http://www.indiashop.com

"The best online Indian Grocery Store," with e-mail and telephone orders also accepted.

http://www.indonet.com

This site has links to other sites on: radio and television, business journals, major dailies, weekly news magazines.

http://www.itihaas.com

Itihaas means history, and this Web site presents many differing views on Indian history, some questionable and perhaps more popular than sound. Nevertheless, it is well worth taking a look at.

http://www.redift.com/news

This site is known for news—especially popular news.

http://www.samachar.com or http://www.dhan.org

A most important Web site (one site with two call numbers): major newspapers, with links to full contents of daily editions; BBC and CNN Asian networks; search engines and links; business news; English-language magazines on India; and newspapers and magazines in Indian languages.

http://www.teenstation.com

This site is popular for Indian news and items of interest to teens.

Index

statistical breakdown, 102
Western science and philosophy
  versus, 218
Zoroastrianism, 102, 105
See also Hinduism; Islam;
  specific religions
Reservations, 80, 86
Reserve Bank of India, 240
River systems, 5, 6
Road atlas, 276–277
Roman Catholicism, 102–103
Roy, Ram Mohan, 200, 220
Rudra, 17
Rupee exchange rate, 66
Rural university concept, 96

Sakti, 145–146
Sakuntala, 20, 194, 220, 256–257
Salt tax, 37–38, 54
SAMACHAR, 240
Samata Party, 56
Samsara, 111–112, 118
Samudragupta, 192
Sankara, 200
Sannyasin, 139
Sanskrit, 15–16, 198, 207, 220
  European languages and, 220
  influence outside India, 217
  learning tradition, 89–90
  number of speakers (table), 208
  U.S. academia, 221
Santali, 209
Sardar Sarover dam, 161–162
Sati (suttee), 34, 81, 149, 200
Satyagraha (nonviolent action),
  37–38, 192, 228–229
  influence outside India, 229–232
Savara, 209
Schopenhauer, Arthur, 102
Schumacher, Eric, 55
Science
  ancient Indian thought, 90–92,
    219–220
  length of the year, 219
  print resource, 255
  religion and, 218

Scripts, 207
Secondary education, 94–95
Securities and Exchange Board of
  India, 240
Self-Employed Women's
  Association (SEWA), 67, 152
Sen, Amartya, 65, 76, 165
Separatist movements, 8, 43–44,
  73, 87–88, 124, 132
  Sikh militants, 43, 124, 188
  Tamil Tigers, 44, 198
  See also Communalism;
  Kashmir
Sepoy Mutiny, 34, 82, 196,
  200–201
Shah Jahan, 27, 110, 196, 202
Shankar, Anouska, 201
Shankar, Ravi, 201, 224
Sharma, Nisha, 148
Shekar, Chandra, 44
Shell Oil, 64
Sher Khan, 26
Sher Shah, 52
Shilappadikaram, 146
Shourie, Arun, 57–58, 63
Shridharani, Krishnalal, 230
Shukla, Jagdish, 66
Sibal, Kanwal, 170
Sikh separatists, 43, 124, 188
Sikhism, 102, 107, 123–125, 194,
  197
Sindhi, 154, 207, 208
Singh, Jaswant, 70
Singh, Mohan, 66
Singh, V. P., 43
Singhal, D. P., 219
Sinhalese, 154, 207
Sitala, 113
Siva (Shiva), 17, 113–114
Slave dynasty, 23
Slavery, 150
Slums, 11, 73, 162–163
  public health problems, 165
Soil erosion, 71
South Asia, 3–4
South Asian Association for

About the Author

Fritz Blackwell, with a Ph.D. from the University of Wisconsin and having studied as well at Berkeley and at Delhi University, has spent thirty-five years teaching about India at Washington State University. He was director of the Asia program for thirteen years and has had appointments in the departments of history, foreign languages, and English. He has taught more than thirty-six courses, including history of India, Asian literature, Hindi, Sanskrit, world civilizations, and a comparative course on Gandhi's independence movement and Martin Luther King Jr.'s civil rights movement. His trips to India include guiding a group of world civilization faculty from Washington State University through northern India.